ENCYCLOPAEDIA OF INDIAN GOVERNMENT: PROGRAMMES AND POLICIES

ENCYCLOPAEDIA OF INDIAN GOVERNMENT: PROGRAMMES AND POLICIES

Vol. 11

Cultural Development

Edited by

Satish Tiwari

ANMOL PUBLICATIONS PVT. LTD.
NEW DELHI - 110 002 (INDIA)

ANMOL PUBLICATIONS PVT. LTD.
4374/4B, Ansari Road, Daryaganj
New Delhi - 110 002

Encyclopaedia of Indian Government: Programmes and Policies

First Edition, 2000

ISBN 81-261-0515-1 (Set)

PRINTED IN INDIA

Published by J.L. Kumar for Anmol Publications Pvt. Ltd., New Delhi - 110 002 and Printed at Mehra Offset Press, Delhi.

Contents

Preface

Encyclopaedia of Indian Government: Programmes and Policies contains authoritative information on about fifty departmental policies and their future developmental programmes.

Organised to be completed in 40 volumes, this gigantic work covers Agriculture; Atomic Energy; Chemicals and Fertilizers; Coal; Commerce; Communication, Culture; Defence; Education; Environment and Forests; External Affairs; Finance; Food & Consumer Affairs; Food Processing Industries; Health and Family Welfare; Home Affairs and Internal Security; Human Resources; Industry; Information and Broadcasting; Labour; Law, Justice and Company Affairs; Non-conventional Energy Sources; Ocean Development; Parliamentary Affairs; Personnel, Public Grievances and Pensions; Petroleum and Natural Gas; Planning and Programme Implementation; Planning and Statistics; Posts and Telegraphs; Power; Rural Development; Science and Technology; Social Justice and Empowerment; Space; States Affairs; Steel; Steel and Mines; Sugar and Edible Oils; Surface Transport; Textiles; Tourism; Urban Development; Water Resources; Women and Child development etc.

Based on the information derived from authoritative sources, this work contains authentic facts and figures. I am deeply beholden to all the scholars whose writings are cited or substantially made use of in the present work. I am also thankful to Anmol Publications Pvt. Ltd. for undertaking publication of this encyclopaedia. I am solely responsible for shortcomings in presentation of matter.

Encyclopaedic in nature, this will prove a dependable reference work for scholars and academics besides those appearing for different competitive examinations.

—**Satish Tiwari**

Preface

1

Overview

The last year of the present century presents us with an opportunity to reflect back on our accomplishments in propagating, preserving and conserving the cultural heritage of India. It is also a time to prepare ourselves for the new and emerging challenges. Culture has evolved as a continuum in which different aspects of Indian culture have blended or differentiated at various times. In the course of evolution, Indian culture has developed a distinct identity while at the same time retained the rich diversity.

The Department of Culture primarily deals with the tangible and intangible heritage. However, in a larger perspective, it also addresses the issues relating to history, values and beliefs in conjunction with several other Ministries and Departments like Tourism, Education, Ministry of External Affairs, etc.

The objectives and policies for promotion, preservation and conservation of art and culture are implemented through various schemes operated departmentally, by funding of autonomous organisations and through a well developed infrastructure of attached and subordinate offices. Around 70% of the annual budgetary support is aimed to provide assistance to these organisations and institutions engaged in propagating, preserving and conserving various aspects of tangible and intangible heritage.

The Department of Culture has taken several major initiatives in the last one year to improve the efficiency of these institutions The focus has been to introduce modern management, financial assistance to Museums is being revised so as to cover the State Museums and to help each State set up modern museums.

The Scientific Advisory Committee for the Department o Culture has been set up to ensure that better science and technological inputs are available for conservation of cultural heritage.

The activities of the NRLC are being revitalised to ensure that its research and training activities are made user friendly and application oriented.

To create and apply relevant technical and managerial training inputs for museum functionaries all over the country, the networking of the important institutions has been initiated. This would help the institutions to share their experiences and resources in undertaking in-service training, displays, modernisation, etc.

The distributive network of Museums has been set up wherein the National Museum, Delhi would take up the nodal responsibility for The Northern states; Salar Jung Museum for the Southern States; Indian Museum and Victoria Memorial Hall for Eastern and North-Eastern States; Allahabad Museum for Central India and Prince of Wales Museum and National Gallery of Modern Art, Mumbai for the States in Western India.

The modalities for launching the National Mission for Manuscripts are being finalised. In the first phase we propose to compile a directory of institutions and individuals possessing the manuscripts and collect data on the historical importance and the physical state of these manuscripts.

The scheme for the award of scholarships and fellowships has been reviewed and the number of scholarships and fellowships have been increased substantially. Further, scholarships and fellowships have been introduced for research in new contemporary areas such as Cultural Economics, Management of Cultural Institutions, Scientific Principles of Conservation, studies in epigraphy, indology, numismatics and structural architecture, etc.

The brief overview of the major organisations and activities under the Department of Culture is discussed in the following paragraphs.

Archaeological survey of India

The Archaeological Survey of India (A.S.I.) was established in 1861. It functions as an attached office of the Department of Culture, Ministry of Human Resource Development. Under the Ancient Monuments and Archaeological Sites And Remains Act of 1958, the Archaeological Survey of India has declared 3601 monuments to be of National importance in the country. In the last 136 years of its existence, the A.S.I. has grown from a humble beginning to a large organisation with an organized work force at the base and the Director General at the apex. With the passage of time, its major activities have expanded manifold to include inter-alia:-

- Maintenance, Conservation and Preservation of Centrally protected monuments/sites;
- Conducting archaeological explorations and excavations;
- Chemical preservation of monuments and antiquarian remains;
- Architectural survey of monuments;
- Development of epigraphical researches;
- Setting up and re-organisation of site museums;
- Training in Archaeology and

Creating awareness of the heritage of the country

The A.S.I. takes up nearly 500 monuments annually for special conservation, preservation and environment development apart from executing routine annual maintenance on the monuments under its charge. Besides taking up conservation work on unprotected monuments as deposit work, it also provides assistance for the conservation of the unprotected monuments.

Another important assignment of the A.S.I. is archaeological exploration, surveys and scientific excavations in the country. New sites are being explored and excavations are carried out strictly in accordance with archaeological principles.

The A.S.I. is running a two year graduate diploma course in its Institute of Archaeology where young archaeologists are imparted practical and theoretical training in the multifarious disciplines in the field of archaeology. This is the only institution in the country where extensive training in archaeology is imparted.

Museums

Indian Museums and Art Galleries are the repository of the nation's valuable treasures. The Department of Culture feels that they play a positive and important role in moulding people's tastes and making them aware of the history and creative talent available in India. The emphasis in the Ninth Plan, therefore, is to overcome generally held perceptions that the Museums are only the 'store-house' of curiosities. We are striving to change the Museums into multi-cultural complexes engaged in promoting art, education, research and appreciation.

At present the Department of Culture administers four general museums of national importance. These are: the National Museum, Delhi; The Indian Museum, Calcutta; the Salar Jung Museum, Hyderabad and the

Allahabad Museum. In addition, the Department also administers National Gallery of Modern Art, Delhi with a branch at Mumbai. The National Council of Science Museums, which is a group of 26 Science Centres and science museums also falls under the Department. The Victoria Memorial Hall, Calcutta, which is a period museum, also gets grants from the Department.

National museum

The National Museum was set up in 1960 as a subordinate office under the Department of Culture. It began in 1949 at the Rashtrapati Bhawan when art objects, which returned from an exhibition in London, were put on display for the public. It later moved to an exclusive building. At present there are about 2 lakh works of art objects covering the last 5000 years of our heritage in the National Museum. The main activities of the National Museum are in the fields of Acquisition, Exhibition, Education, Public Relations, Publication and Conservation.

During the year, the National Museum undertook numerous activities in improving the displays and strengthening conservation activities. One of the major exhibitions organised by the Indian Museum was a special exhibition entitled Treasures of Indian Art: Germany's Tribute to India's Cultural Heritage which was inaugurated by the Hon'ble President of India on 14th August, 1998. The exhibition comprising 92 exhibits, was loaned for the first time ever from the collection of the Museum of Indian Art, Berlin, State Museum Prussian Cultural Foundation. Coinciding with the six-week long exhibition a series of ancillary events was also organised at the National Museum in collaboration with the National Museum Institute, the Centre for Cultural Resources and Training and the Max Muller Bhavan.

Allahabad museum

The Allahabad Museum was established in 1931 under the Allahabad Municipal Board. It was taken over by the Government of India. It was declared an Institution of National Importance by the Government of India, Department of Culture, in October 1985. One of the major exhibitions organised by the Allahabad Museum was 'The Himalayan Glory' in December, 1998.

Salarjung museum

The Salar Jung Museum, Hyderabad is one of the most prestigious museums in the country. It has been recognised as an Institution of National Importance. The museum came into existence on 16th December 1951 and is a valuable repository of global art collections. It is named after the erstwhile noble family of the Salar Jungs, the collectors of this treasure trove. A major portion of the Museum's collection was acquired by Mir Yousuf Ali Khan popularly known as Salar Jung-Ill (13th June, 1889 - 2nd March 1949) There are 35 galleries spread over two floors. The ground floor has 19 galleries and the 1st floor has 16 galleries. It also has a wide range of collections of art objects and thousands of rare manuscripts in Persian, Arabic and Urdu.

Indian museum

The Indian Museum, Calcutta is an autonomous organisation of the Department of Culture and is the largest and oldest institution of its kind. The Museum was founded in 1814 under the Indian Museum Act, 1910. It houses unique treasures of Indian and foreign art representing centuries of cultural ethos and traditions. The Museum is a vast repository of paintings, sculptures, bronzes, metals, coins, textiles and decorative arts. Its activities are varied and cover domestic and international exhibitions, seminars, lectures, publications and general awareness programmes.

National gallery of modern art

The National Gallery of Modern Art (NGMA) was established in 1954 by the Government of India with the objective of developing and promoting modem art in India. It has acquired a unique place in the growing landscape of Indian art. It is a repository of contemporary visual art and has been implementing a number of schemes for strengthening its activities and spreading art education amongst the public. NGMA represents the evolution of changing art forms through the passage of time. At present the NGMA owns a permanent collection of more than 14,000 works of art, both Indian as well as Western modem art.

NGMA has a branch at Mumbai at the Sir Cowasji Jehangir Public Hall and is also in the process of acquiring Manikyavelu Mansion from the State Government of Karnataka for opening its branch at Bangalore. NGMA has undertaken a number of exhibitions, lectures, seminars and general awareness programmes during 1998-99.

National council oif science museums (NCSM)

The NCSM which was set up in April, 1978 in Calcutta, is primarily engaged in the task of popularising science and technology through a wide range of programmes, and by establishment of science parks and science museums through out the country. The NCSM is an autonomous organisation under the Department of Culture and has 26 constituent units.

Victoria memorial hall

The Victoria Memorial Hall, Calcutta, a period museum depicting the times under the British Raj is dedicated to the conservation and preservation of the main building, the sprawling garden surrounding it and the artifacts in its collection.The Hall has a rich collection of Company paintings, including several original paintings of the Daniells.

National Research Laboratory for Conservation of Cultural Property (NRLC), Lucknow The National Research Laboratory for Conservation of Cultural Property (NRLC), a subordinate office of the Department of Culture, is a scientific institution. The headquarters of NRLC is at Lucknow. The aims and objectives of NRLC are to build up the conservation capabilities of the country. To meet the objectives, NRLC carries out research in materials and methods of conservation, imparts training in conservation and provides literature on conservation to conservators. NRLC also renders technical advice and assistance to museums, archives, archaeological departments and other similar institutions, in the conservation of cultural property. To render technical advice and conservation services to such institutions in the Southern region of the country, a regional centre of NRLC, the Regional Conservation Laboratory is functioning at Mysore since 1987

Promotion and sissemination of culture

The Department of Culture has been implementing many schemes for promotion, preservation and dissemination of art and culture. It provides grants under various schemes to cultural organisations for this purpose,

The Government of India had set up a High Powered Committee on 19th August,1994, to review the working of the seven Zonal Cultural Centres. This was headed by Prof. U. R. Ananthamoorthy. The Committee was also supposed to suggest how the Centres can serve the purpose of enriching and highlighting the cultural patterns in their respective areas. The Committee submitted its report to the Government in January, 1996. The Committee recommended changes in the structure of ZCCs, reduction in the administrative expenditure and suggestion for better coordination with the noted Akademies. The recommendations of the High Powered Committee were discussed in a meeting of the Chairmen of ZCCs under the chairmanship of the HRM.

There were detailed discussions on the recommendations, in the two day Conference of Directors (ZCCs), the Secretaries of Akademies and Secretaries (Culture) of State Governments under the Chairmanship of Secretary(Culture). Secretary (C) had also addressed the Chief Secretaries/Secretaries (Culture) State Govts/ UTs etc. Most of the recommendations of the Committee are proposed to be implemented during the year 1999-2000 in the programmes of Zonal Cultural Centres.

The Centre for Cultural Resources and Training (CCRT) is an autonomous organisation under the Department of Culture. The broad objectives of the Centre is to revitalise the education system by creating an understanding and awareness among students and teachers about the plurality of regional cultures in India and integrating this knowledge with school education in India.

Orientation courses and workshops are conducted for primary and high school teachers in various activities to provide a practical training in arts and crafts by the CCRT. During the period from April 1998, to November 1998, 1193 teachers and 1055 students were trained in 19 Workshops organized in and outside Delhi.

National akademies and the National school of drama

The three National Akademies, namely the Sangeet Natak Akademi (National Akademi for performing Arts) , the Lalit Kala Akademi (National Akademi for Visual Arts), the Sahitya Akademi (National Akademi for Literary Arts) and the National School of Drama (a National training school for theatre) were brought together by interaction between them so as to create a concerted effort to promote these arts.

Sangeet Natak Akademi

The Sangeet Natak Akademi - the National Akademi of Music, Dance and Drama - an autonomous organisation funded by the Ministry of Human Resource Development, is devoted to the furtherance of the performing arts of India. The Akademi seeks to achieve this by arranging performances by renowned veterans as well as by talented artists of the younger generation, through training programmes, award of scholarships, documentation, etc. The Akademi also bestows honours annually on outstanding artistes in the field of performing arts.

The Akademi runs two teaching institutions - Kathak Kendra (New Delhi) and Jawaharlal Nehru Manipur Dance Akademi (Imphal - for Training in Kathak dance and music and Manipuri dance and allied arts). The Akademi also looks after the management of the Rabindra Rangshala in New Delhi.

Sahitya Akademi

The Sahitya Akademi was founded in March 1954 to promote the cause of Indian Literature and promote national integration through literature by way of publications, translations, seminars, workshops, cultural exchange programmes and literary meets organised all over the country. The Sahitya Akademi recognises eminent writers through Awards in 22 Indian languages for creative writing, 22 translation prizes, fellowships for distinguished contributions to literature, Bhasha Samman meant to promote peripheral languages, the Ananda Coomaraswamy Fellowship for South Asian scholars and Honorary fellowships for foreign scholars who have done significant work in Indian literature. The Akademi publishes books in 22 languages and has three journals - Indian Literature (in English), Samakalena Bharatiya Sahitya (in Hindi) and Samskrita Pratibha (in Sanskrit). Besides, it holds various literary programmes in different parts of the country.

Lalit Kala akademi

The Lalit Kala Akademi (National Akademi of Fine Arts) was established by the Government of India at New Delhi in 1954, to promote and propagate an understanding of Indian Art, both within the country and abroad. The Akademi has regional Centres at Lucknow, Calcutta, Chennai and Bhubaneswar as well as a small office at Mumbai where it has set up Community Artists' Studios with workshop facilities in painting, sculpture, print making and ceramics. There is a similar studio centre at Garhi in New Delhi. Since its inception, the Akademi has been organising National Exhibitions of Contemporary Indian Art during which 10 National Awards, each of Rs.25,000/- are awarded. Special exhibitions are also organized every three years. The Akademi organises Triennale India, an International exhibition of contemporary art at New Delhi. .

To propagate Indian art, the Akademi participates in International Biennales and Triennales abroad and also organizes exhibitions of works of art from other countries. To foster contacts with artists abroad, it sponsors exchange of artists with other countries under the various Cultural Exchange Programmes and Agreements of the Government of India.

The Lalit Kala Akademi extends financial assistance to State Akademies and artists through prizes in exhibitions organized by them. The Akademi also brings out publications of art works and multi-colour reproductions and portfolios for sale.

From the Artists Aid Fund, financial assistance is given to ailing artists.

National School of drama

The National School of Drama, one of the foremost theatre training institutions in the world, and the only one of it's kind in India was set up by the Sangeet Natak Academy in 1959. In 1975, it became an independent entity, fully financed by the Department of Culture, Ministry of Human Resource Development. Over the years, the School has made rapid strides on various fronts including a rapid expansion of its activities in all parts of the country. It has produced a galaxy of talents - actors, directors, script writers, designers, technicians, and educationists who work not only in theatre but also in films and television- winning several awards national and international.

Training in the School is based on a thorough comprehensive, carefully planned syllabus which covers every aspect of theatre in which theory is related to practice, and in which all work is ultimately put to test before the public. The syllabus takes into account the methods of great theatre personalities who have shaped contemporary theatre, in all its facets of expressional forms. The systematic study and practical performing experience in Sanskrit Drama, Modem Indian Drama, Traditional Indian theatre forms, Asian drama and western drama gives the students a solid grounding and a wide perspective in the art of theatre. In order to establish linkages between the traditional theatre forms of India and modem expressions, the School invites experts to train the students in these forms and also sends students to regional centres for training in traditional theatre. The School has also attached to its teaching faculty, some of the finest creative talents from within the country and abroad.

The National School of Drama has a faculty of 14 members. To provide a varied and wide ranging syllabus the school regularly invites professors, theatre personalities and experts from India and abroad to supplement the teaching process. The school admits 20 students per year in the first year of the three-year diploma course. The selection is on an all India basis. All students admitted are awarded a scholarship of Rs. 2,000/- for meeting their academic and other expenses.

The School has a Repertory Company, which is the performing wing. It consists of a group of artists and technicians who are mainly alumni of the school. The Repertory Company staged 58 shows during the period

Archives and libraries

National archives of India

The National Archives of India (NAI), an attached office under the Department of Culture, houses Central Government records of enduring value for permanent preservation and use by administrators and scholars. It has in its custody, private papers of eminent personalities of India and microfilm copies of records acquired from abroad. During 1998-99, regular programmes of the National Archives of India, viz. assisting various Ministries/Departments of the Government of India in their record management programmes, extending research facilities to scholars visiting the Department from all over India and abroad and providing financial assistance to various voluntary organisations for the preservation of manuscripts in their custody as also to State/Union Territory Administration Archives for their development programmes, etc. were carried out. It also continued to tender guidance to various Government Departments, voluntary institutions and individuals regarding technical know-how for preservation of valuable records and papers.

The School of Archival Studies in the NAI imparts training under its One Year Diploma in Archival Studies and various short-term courses to Indian and foreign trainees. As a part of its programme of creating archival awareness amongst the people, an Archival Museum was established and various exhibitions were organized.

The Conservation Research Laboratory conducted investigations for improvement of preservation techniques for better upkeep of records and was actively associated with the dissemination of knowledge of specialised nature in the field of Conservation of documentary heritage. The National Archives of India has one Regional Office at Bhopal, and three Record Centres at Bhubaneswar, Jaipur and Pondicherry.

On the occasion of the 50th year of India's Independence an Archival Museum has been established in the premises of the NAI to make people aware of the documentary heritage which the National Archives of India preserves for the present generation and for posterity. The Museum was formally declared open by Shri K.R. Narayanan, Hon'ble President of India on 6th July, 1998. Several significant exhibitions have been organised in its premises during 1998-99 A total of 247 pages from the files of the Nizam's Government (1951) received from Andhra Pradesh State Archives, Hyderabad were sent to Indian Council of Historical Research, New Delhi for inclusion in the proposed volume Towards Freedom Project.

Khuda Baksh oriental Public library, Patna

Khuda Baksh Khan established a "Public Library" in 1891 out of his family collection of manuscripts. He further added a number of manuscripts through his own resource, and, by a Deed of Trust, donated his entire collection to the public the same year. That Library, now known the world over as the Khuda Baksh Oriental Public Library, has emerged to be one of the richest collections of manuscripts in the sub-continent with over 18,000 manuscripts, 1,80,000 printed books and over 2000 original paintings of the Mughal, Rajput, Iranian and Turkish schools. The Library also possesses a sizeable number of original letters of eminent persons written during their lifetime. It is now managed by a Board headed by the Governor of Bihar. By an Act of Parliament, it was declared the 1969 to be an Institution of National Importance and the Government of India took over its control the same year. The Library provides support to researchers and is a pioneering institute in preservation and conservation of manuscripts.

Rampur Raza Library, Rampur

The Library is renowned all over the world and is considered to be a highly valued treasure house of thousands of rare manuscripts, miniature paintings, illustrated manuscripts, specimens of great calligraphers of the Islamic world, historical documents, letters, printed books, newspapers and periodicals.

The Library was taken over by the Government of India on July 1st 1975. through an act passed by Parliament declaring it an Institution of National Importance. It is managed by an executive board, presided over by the Governor of Uttar Pradesh.

The Library is a centre for Indo Islamic studies as it is a repository of classical and modern source material in Arabic, Persian, Sanskrit, Tamil, Telugu, Hindi, Urdu, Turkish and English.

Raja Ram Mohan Roy library foundation, Calcutta

The Raja Rammohan Roy Library Foundation, a fully financed autonomous organisation under the Department of Culture was set up in May 1972 as a part of the bi-centenary birth celebrations of Raja Rammohan Roy. The main objective of the Foundation is to promote and support the public library movement in the country by providing adequate library services and by popularising reading habits, particularly in rural areas, with the active cooperation of the State Library Authorities, Union Territories and Voluntary Organisations operating in the field of library services.

Nehru Memorial museum and library

The Nehru Memorial Museum and Library maintains a personalia Museum which portrays the life and times of Jawaharlal Nehru against the backdrop of the different phases of the Indian freedom movement; a Library of printed materials, books, periodicals, newspapers and photographs with special focus on the history of modern India and among other things a repository of unpublished records of institutions and private papers of eminent Indians which provide a primary source for historical research.

Anthropology and Ethnology

The Anthropological Survey of India, a scientific research organisation under the Department of Culture, was established in 1945. It is a nodal organisation of the Department for research in the field of anthropology. Anthropological Survey is engaged in activities like collection, preservation, maintenance, documentation and the study of ethnographic materials as well as of ancient human skeletal remains.

During the last 52 years, the activities of the Survey have expanded to a great extent, and to cope up with the demands of research, seven regional centres, one sub-regional centre, one permanent field station and a number of other stations have been established at different parts of the country.

Another organisation engaged in anthropological research and activities is the Indira Gandhi Rashtriya Manav Sangrahalaya. Though the Institution was set up as a small Subordinate Office of the Department of Education and Culture in 1977, in Delhi, the national capital, it started taking the shape of a Museum in 1979 when it was shifted to Bhopal, the capital of Madhya Pradesh, to an open air site.

Gandhi Smriti and Darshan Samiti

"Gandhi Smriti and Darshan Samiti" was formed in September 1984 with the merger of Gandhi Darshan at Rajghat and Gandhi Smriti at 5, Tees January Marg, and is functioning under the constructive advice and financial support from the Department of Culture, Ministry of Human Resource Development. Among the basic aims and objectives for which "Gandhi Smriti and Darshan Samiti" were set up are: Preservation, maintenance and up-keep of Gandhi Smriti and Gandhi Darshan Complex; and

The propagation of the life, mission and thoughts of Mahatma Gandhi by organizing various socio-educational and cultural programmes.

Gandhi peace prize

On the occasion of the 125th Birth Anniversary of Mahatma Gandhi, the Government of India instituted an Annual International Gandhi Peace Prize. The Prize carries a cash award of Rupees one crore, a citation and a plaque. The jury for the Gandhi Peace Prize, under the Chairmanship of the Prime Minister selected Ramakrishna Mission for the award of 1998. The prize was conferred on the Mission by the Honourable President of India at a special ceremony held on 13th February 1999 at the Raj Bhavan, Calcutta.

Centenaries and anniversaries

One of the important activities that the Department of Culture is associated with relates to organization of Centenary Celebrations of important personalities/ events. For this purpose the Department of Culture either constitutes National Committees (which are headed by the Prime Minister/ Minister of Human Resource Development) for rendering advice regarding the programmes for organizing the celebrations at the National level or gives grants to non-governmental organizations, whichever is considered appropriate, for supporting the programmes which the non-governmental organizations propose to organize.

The important committees constituted during the year were for organizing Birth Centenaries of Mirza Ghalib (27.12.1997- 27.12.1998) Gulzari Lal Nanda (4.7.1998 - 4.7.1999); Sant Kabir (June 1998 to June 1999) Birth of Khalsa Panth (13.4.1999 - 13.4.2000); organizing the 125th Birth Anniversary of Sri Aurobindo (15.7.1997-15.7.1998); and observing the 50th Anniversary of the Martyrdom of Mahatma Gandhi(30.1.1998-30.1.1999).

As a part of the Centenary of Enlightenment of Bhagwan Ramana, a commemorative stamp was released by the Hon'ble President of India in a function organized on 14th April 1998. The function was attended among others by Shri R. Venkataraman, former President of India, Minister of Parliamentary Affairs and a number of devotees of Bhagwan Ramana. As a part of the Birth Centenary Celebrations of Dr. Zakir Hussain, a commemorative stamp of Dr. Zakir Hussain was released by the Vice President of India in a function organized on 3rd May, 1998 in the Vice President's House. The function was attended, among others, by Shri SurJit Singh Barnala, Hon'ble Minister of Chemicals and Fertilizers, Shri Khursheed Alam Khan, Governor, Karnataka and Shri Salman Khursheed.

A function to mark the conclusion of the 125th Birth Anniversary Celebrations of Sri Aurobindo was organized on 24th November 1998. Dr. Murli Manohar Joshi, Hon'ble Minister of Human Resource Development released a set of commemorative coins on Sri Aurobindo. The commemorative coins were of the denomination of Rs.100, Rs.50, Rs.10 and Rs.2. This was preceded by a 3-day Seminar, where there was active discussion on Philosophy and Yoga, as propounded by Sri Aurobindo.

A function to release a set of commemorative coins in honour of Deshbandhu Chittaranjan Das on his 128th birth Anniversary was held on December 27, 1998 at Raj Bhavan, Calcutta. His Excellency, the Governor of West Bengal released the commemorative coins.

Buddhist and Tibetan institutes

The Department of Culture supports various institutes engaged in research in Buddhist and Tibetan studies.

Central institute of higher Tibetan studies, Sarnath, Varanasi

The Central Institute of Higher Tibetan Studies was established in 1967 by the efforts of Pt. Jawaharlal Nehru and His Holiness the Dalai Lama. The institution remained associated with the Varanaseya Sanskrit Visvavidyalaya (now Sampurnanand Sanskrit University) till 1975. It was granted autonomy in 1978 under the Department of Culture. In 1988, the Institute was declared a Deemed University, managed with financial support from the Department of Culture.

Sikkim research institute of tibetoilogy, Gangtok

The Sikkim Research Institute of Tibetology, Gangtok is an autonomous organization under the Government of Sikkim with the Governor of Sikkim as the President of its Governing Body. It was set up for research and studies in Tibetology. The Institute has done significant work in promoting research in Tibetology and associated subjects like iconography, medicine, astrology and history. It has special research and publication programmes. The Bulletin of Tibetology is the Institute's regular research journal which is published thrice a year.

Library of Tibetan works and archivess, Dharamshala

The Library of Tibetan Works and Archives, an autonomous registered institution, was established by H.H. the Dalai Lama in 1971, with a view to preserve and promote the rich heritage of Tibetan civilization and Indo-Tibetan learning. Today, this Institution has acquired world stature as a centre for Tibetology and Indo-Tibetan Studies.

Nava Nalanda maha vihara, Nalanda, Bihar

The Nava Nalanda Mahavihara is an Institute for Postgraduate teaching and research in Pali language and literature and Buddhist Studies, functioning under the Department of Culture since 25th February 1994. His Excellency the Governor of Bihar is the Chairman and Secretary, Department of Culture is the Vice-Chairman of the Nava Nalanda Mahavihara Society.

International cultural relations

To boost cultural contacts and cultural relations, India has entered into Cultural Agreements leading to formulation of Cultural Exchange Programmes with a number of countries. Currently we have Cultural Agreements with 107 countries and Cultural Exchange Programmes with 73 countries. While a Cultural Agreement is basically a statement of intent to cooperate in the fields and disciplines specified in the document, a Cultural Exchange Programme incorporates specific provisions for exchanges for a period of 2-3 years relating to a number o activities concerning culture, education, sports, youth affairs, mass-media, etc.

During the current year, Cultural Exchange Programmes were renewed with Bangladesh, Ethopia, Iraq, Italy, Portugal and Russia. A high-level delegation from Pakistan visited India from 12th to 13th Nov., 1998 to discuss friendly exchanges in various cultural fields. The issues were discussed with the Pakistan delegation at the Secretary level. The Indian Delegation to the talks was led by Dr. R.V.Vaidyanatha Ayyar, Secretary (Culture) and the Pakistan Delegation was led by Mr. Syed Roshan Zamir, Secretary (Culture) Government of Pakistan.

A six-member delegation led by Mr. A. Andrew de Silva, Secretary, Ministry of Education and Higher Education, Government of Sri Lanka visited India from 14.12.1998 to participate in the Fourth Session of India-Sri Lanka Sub-Commission on Cultural, Social & Educational Matters. The Meeting of the Sub-Commission provided an opportunity to discuss and negotiate a fresh Cultural Exchange Programme for 1999-2001 with Sri Lanka. In addition to the CEP, the Sub-Commission was expected to report to the Joint Commission

Meeting which was held in New Delhi on 18-19 December, 1998. The Union Minister for Human Resource Development, Dr. Murli Manohar Joshi visited Hungary from 25-10-98 to 28-10-98 and signed the Indo-Hungarian Cultural Exchange Programme for the years 1999-2001. The delegation also participated in the celebrations of the 50th Anniversary of the establishment of diplomatic relations between India and Hungary. During his visit the Honourable Minister also inaugurated a joint symposium.

2

Organisation

The Department of Culture is one of the four departments of the Ministry of Human Resource Development. This Department was set up in 1985 through the 174' amendment of the Government of India (Allocation of Business) Rules, 1961. The Department is under the overall charge of the Minister for Human Resource Development. The Secretariat of this Department is headed by the Secretary, assisted by two joint secretaries. The Festival of India cell, which had been given a separate identity has now been merged with the Department.

The Department of Culture plays a vital role in the promotion and dissemination of art and culture. It directly operates several schemes for the promotion of specific performing, literary and visual arts. It provides assistance for the development of voluntary action in these fields through grants, training programmes, etc. It also endeavours to promote and develop traditional crafts and skills, especially folk art and crafts.

The Department is also concerned with the formulation of the Archival Policy of the Government of India, development and protection of archives both at the Centre and the States, a responsibility which it implements through the National Archives. It is also concerned with the development of public libraries and administers the

National Library at Calcutta and a number of other libraries of national importance.

The Department also looks after the preservation, conservation and protection of the material heritage, namely, archaeology, anthropology, museums, etc. through specialised agencies like the Archaeological Survey of India, Anthropological Survey of India, Rashtriya Manav Sangrahalaya, etc. It administers a number of museums and galleries of National importance. The Department also promotes organizations working in specialized fields such The Department coordinates all matters relating to international cultural relations. It acts as the nodal agency for executing cultural agreements and cultural exchange programmes with different countries, organising incoming and outgoing exhibitions and undertaking programmes envisaged in the programmes of UNESCO in the field of art and culture.

A number of scholarships, fellowships and grants are given by the Department of Culture. Anniversaries and centenaries of important personalities are organized, memorials commemorating certain important persons or a particular period of history are maintained. The Department has two attached offices, six subordinate offices and 26 autonomous organisations as under:

Atttached offices

i. Archaeological Survey of India, New Delhi.
ii. National Archives of India, New Delhi

Subordinate offices

i. Anthropological Survey of India, Calcutta
ii. National Museum, New Delhi.
iii. National Gallery of Modern Art, New Delhi
iv. National Library, Calcutta
v. Central Reference Library, Calcutta

vi. National Research Laboratory for Conservation of Cultural Property, Lucknow.

Autonomous organisations

i. Indira Gandhi Rashtriya Manav Sangrahalaya, Bhopal
ii. National Council of Science Museums, Calcutta
iii. Nehru Memorial Museum & Library, New Delhi
iv. Sangeet Natak Academy, New Delhi
v. Sahitya Academy, New Delhi
vi. Lalit Kala Academy, New Delhi
vii. National School of Drama, New Delhi
viii. Centre for Cultural Resources & Training, New Delhi
ix. Gandhi Smriti and Darshan Samiti, New Delhi.
x. Allahabad Museum, Allahabad
xi. Delhi Public Library, Delhi
xii. Raja Rammohan Roy Library Foundation, Calcutta
xiii. Central Institute of Buddhist Studies, Leh
xiv. Central Institute of Higher Tibetan Studies, Sarnath, Varanasi
xv. Victoria Memorial Hall, Calcutta
xvi. Indian Museum, Calcutta
xvii. Asiatic Society, Calcutta
xviii. Salar Jung Museum, Hyderabad
xix. Khuda Baksh Oriental Public Library, Patna
xx. Rampur Raza Library, Rampur
xxi. Thanjavur Maharaja Serfoji's Saraswathi Mahal Library, Thanjavur.
xxii. Kalakshetra Foundation, Chennai
xxiii. National Museum Institute of History of Art Conservation & Museology, New Delhi.
xxiv. Nav Nalanda Mahavihara, Nalanda, Bihar
xxv. Maulana Abul Kalam Azad Institute of Asian Studies, Calcutta.

xxvi. Indira Gandhi National Centre for the Arts, New Delhi.

Progressive use of Hindi

The work relating to the implementation of Official Language Policy in the Department of Culture and its attached/subordinate offices and autonomous organisations, is looked after by a Deputy Director (Official Language), who is assisted by an Assistant Director and other supporting staff. The Official Language Implementation Committee headed by the joint Secretary (Admn.) is represented by Officers of different Divisions/Sections/Units. Two meetings of the Committee were held during the year.

In accordance with the Annual Official Language Programme for 1998-99 and the orders received from the Department of Official Language, Ministry of Home Affairs, continuous efforts were made towards progressive use of Hindi in the official work of the Department.

During the year under report, 4 employees were nominated for Hindi class, 4 employees were nominated for Hindi stenography class and 6 employees were nominated for Hindi typing class. The Department of Culture organized Hindi Pakhwara from 1st to 15th September, 1998. On the first day of the Hindi Pakhwara, i.e., on 1st September, 1998, a seminar on "Work Culture and Hindi in Government Offices" was organized. Four renowned scholars delivered their lectures at the seminar.

As in the previous years, a "Kavya Gosthi" was organized on 11th September, 1998 where six well known Hindi poets recited their poems. A number of competitions in Hindi Essay, Noting and Drafting Translation, Hindi typing, debates, General Hindi, Handwriting and a Hindi Practice Competition were organized for Hindi knowing/ non-Hindi knowing officers and cash prizes and citations were awarded to the winners

Apart from the Secretariat of the Department, the Official Language Division monitored and guided the attached/subordinate offices of the Department in the progressive use of Hindi. As usual, the Hindi Translation Unit in the Department of Culture undertook translation work of various documents, papers, etc.

3

Archaeology

Archaeological survey of India

The Archaeological Survey of India (A.S.I.) was established in 1861. It functions as an attached office of the Department of Culture, Ministry of Human Resource Development.

Under the Ancient Monuments and Archaeological Sites and Remains Act, of 1958, the Archaeological Survey of India has declared 3598 monuments of National importance in the country. During the last 136 years of its existence, the A.S.I. has grown from a humble beginning to a large organisation with an organized work force at the base and the Director General at the apex. With the passage of time, its major activities have expanded manifold to include inter-alia:

(i) Maintenance, conservation and preservation of centrally protected monuments/sites and remains;

(ii) Conducting archaeological exploration and excavations;

(iii) Chemical preservation of monuments and antiquarian remains;

(iv) Architectural survey of monuments;

(v) Development of epigraphical research;

(vi) Setting up and re-organisation of site museums and

(vii) Training in Archaeology.

The number of centrally protected monuments state-wise are as under:

Sl. No.	*Name of State*	*No. of Monuments*
1.	Andhra Pradesh	134
2.	Arunachal Pradesh	5
3.	Assam	49
4.	Bihar	79
5.	Delhi	166
6.	Daman & Diu	10
7.	Goa	25
8.	Gujarat	199
9.	Haryana	91
10.	Himachal Pradesh	37
11.	Jammu & Kashmir	64
12.	Karnataka	504
13.	Kerala	28
14.	Madhya Pradesh	326
15.	Maharashtra	288
16.	Manipur	1
17.	Meghalaya	6
18.	Nagaland	4
19.	Orissa	72
20.	Pondicherry	8
21.	Punjab	25
22.	Rajasthan	157
23.	Sikkim	3
24.	Tamil Nadu	410
25.	Tripura	5
26.	Uttar Pradesh	785
27.	West Bengal	117

Achievements of Archaeological Survey of India during 1998-99 are highlighted as under :

Conservation and preservation of monuments

The conservation, preservation and maintenance of the

centrally protected monuments and sites is the prime task of A.S.I. At present, there are 3,598 centrally protected monuments declared to be of national importance, which include 16 monuments inscribed on the World Heritage List of UNESCO. The total number of individual structures being maintained by the Archaeological Survey of India is over 5,000.

Circle wise distribution of these monuments are as under:

1.	Agra	323
2.	Aurangabad	284
3	Goa (Mini Circle)	25
4.	Bangalore	203
5.	Bhopal	283
6.	Bhubaneswar	122
7.	Calcutta	117
8.	Chandigarh	153
9.	Chennai	402
10.	Delhi	166
11.	Dharwad	301
12.	Guwahati	72
13.	Hyderabad	134
14.	Jaipur	151
15.	Lucknow	362
16.	Patna	190
17.	Srinagar	64
18.	Thrissur	37
19.	Vadodara	209

During the year more than 500 monuments were programmed for structural repairs, chemical preservation and environmental development. Some of the important activities taken up by the Survey during the 1998-99 are as under:

Agra circle

Taj Mahal, Agra Fort, Akbar's Tomb, Mehtab Bagh,

Mariam's Tomb, Itimadud-Daula, Chini-ka-Rauza, Rambagh Gate, Fatehpur Sikri in Agra; Ashokan Rock Edict, Kalsi, District Dehradun; Baijnath Temple, Jageshwar Temple, Dandeshwar Temple, Balapir Tomb and Mosque of Makhdum Jahanian, District Kannauj; Excavated site at Jagatgram, District Dehradun; Tomb of Nawab Rashid Khan, Rashidabad, District Farrukhabad.

Aurangabad circle

Pateleshwar Caves, Baja Caves, Lenandri Caves, Karla Caves, Shaniwarwada, Junnar, Pune; Panhala Fort, Kolhapur; Vijaydurg Fort, Sindhudurg; Raigad Fort, Pachad, Elephanta Caves, Raigad; Mandepeshwar Caves, Borivali; Kanheri Caves, Kondivate Caves, Jogeshwari Cave Temple, Majaswar, Mumbai; Kolaba Fort, Alibag, Raigad; Pandav Lena Caves, Nasik; Daulatabad Fort, Ghrishneshwar Temple, Ellora, Tomb of Rabia Durani, Bibi Ka Maqbara, Chand Minar (Fort), Daulatabad; Aurangabad Caves, Aurangabad; Ancient sites, Mansar, Nagpur; Gate & Fort at Pauni, Bhandara; Khopeshwar Temple, Khidrapur; Sindhudurg, Malvan; Sholapur Fort, Sholapur; Farahbagh Palace, Ahmednagar; Shiv Temple, Ambarnath, Distt. Thana; Mahadeva Temple Kuda Caves, Kuda;janjira Fort, Murud, Alibag, Distt. Kolaba; Fort Wall, Chandrapur; Badi Dhar & Daitasudan Temple, Lonar, Distt. Bulthana; Gond Raja Tomb, Fort of Ballarsha, Chanda; Lalpeth Monoliths, Distt. Chandrapur.

Bangalore circle

Someswara Temple, Distt.Kolar; Tippu Sultan Palace, Bangalore; Kedareswara Temple, Nagalapur, Distt. Tumkur; Hill Fort & Palace, Uchangidurga, Ashokan inscription, Nittur, Katti Basaveswara Shrine, Hirehadagali, Ananthasayana Temple, Achutaraya Temple, Mahanavami Dibba, Kamalapura, Zenana Enclosure, Krishna Temple, Hemakute, Hampi in Distt. Bellary; Fort Chitradurga, Gopalkrishna Temple in Distt.

Chitradurga; Amritesvara Temple, Fort & Dungeon, Manjarabad, Veeranarayana Temple, Belavadi, Distt. Chickmagalur, Jaina Temple complex, Halebid, Distt. Hassan; Ananthapadmanabha Temple, Karkala, South Kanara; Fort & Large Masonary Elephant, Mercara, Coorg; Sri Kanteswara Temple, Nanjangud, Vijayanarayana Temple, Gundlupet, Keerthi Narayana Temple, Talkad, Gowreeswara Temple, Yelandur, Distt. Mysore; Fort at Kavaledurga, Rameswara Temple, Keladi, Renukamba Temple, Chandragutti, Aghoreswara Temple, Ikkeri, Tripuranteswara Temple, Belligavi, Shimoga; Mallikarjuna Temple, Basaralu, Narayana Swamy Temple, Melkote, Gumbaz Complex, Dariya Daulat Bagh, Jumma Masjid, Srirangapatna, in Distt. Mandya; Vittal Temple, Venkatapura, Chandrasekhara Temple, Karnalapuram in Distt. Bellary.

Bhubaneswar circle

Lord Jaganath Temple, Puri; Sun Temple, Konark; Dakshya Prajapati Temple, Banpur; Kedareswar Temple Choudwar, Barabati Fort in Distt. Cuttack; Rameswar Temple, Dist. Khurda; Yameswar Temple, Bakreswar Temple, Lord Lingaraj Temple; Kandagiri, Udaigiri Caves in Distt. Bhubaneswar.

Bhopal circle

Palace Complex Fort, Ater, Bhind; Chaunsath Yogini Temple, Duladeo Temple, Jagati of Laxshmana Temple, Vamana Temple, Khajuraho, Chhatarpur; Rang Mahal Palace, Hatta, Damoh; Siva Temple, Nohta in Distt. Damoh; Beer Singh Palace, Distt. Datia; Cave no. 1 to 3 & 7, Bagh, Bhojshala, Asharfi Mahal, Monuments at Mandu, Distt - Dhar; Baz Bahadur Palace, Gadashah Palace, Jahaz Mahal, Jal Mahal, Jali Mahal, Kapoor Tank, Nahar Jharoka, Sat Kothari, Sopi Tank & Ujali Baodi at Mandu, Distt. Dhar; Jama Masjid, Koshak Mahal, Nankhanda Palace, Singhpur Palace and Shahzadi ka Rauza at

Chanderi in Distt. Guna; Fort monuments, Hullaras in Moh'd Ghaus and Tansen's Samadhi Complex, Jain Colossi, Ek Pathari ki Baoli, Man Singh Palace Complex, Sas Bahu Temple & Teli-Ke-Mandir, Fort Gwalior, in Distt. Gwalior; Chaunsath Yogini Temple, Bheraghat, Madan Mahal, Vishnu Varah Temple, Karitalai, Gauri Shanker Temple, Bheraghat at Jabalpur; Fort & Idgah at Asirgarh, Bilri ki Masjid, Bhushanpur in Khandwa; Begum Palace, Ramnagar, Distt. Mandla; Rock Cut Buddhist Cave and Rock Cut Brahmanical Temple, Dhamnar, Mandsaur; Nav Toran Temple, Khor; Yasodharman Victory Pillar Distt. Mandsaur; North Group of Temples, Bateshwar, Ekotarso Mahadeo Temple, Mitauli, Group of Temples, Naresar, Gadhi; Padavali, Kankanmath Temple, Suhania in Distt. Morena; Rangmahal No 3 & 4, Ajaigarh, Chaumukhnath Temple, Nachna, Panna; Fort at Raisen, Group of Monuments, at Sanchi in Distt. Raisen; Siva Temple, Bamora, Sagar; Group of Stupas, Panguraria, Sehore; Gadarmal Temple & Saptamatrika Caves, Badohpathari, Caves at Udaigiri, Bijamandal, Vidisha; Koteshwar Mahadeo Temple, Kashitola, Fort at Lanji in Distt. Balaghat; Mahadeo Temple, Amrol, Somnath Temple, Badgaon.

Calcutta circle

Shyam Sunder Temple, Madanpur, Gokul Chand Temple, Natmandapa, Gokulnagar, Ramancha, Shyam Rai Temple, Jor Mandir, Kalachand Temple in Distt. Bankura; Patpur Temple, Murali Mohan Temple, Radha Madhab Temple, in District Bishnupur; Hazarduari Palace; Imambara, Khosbag, Katra Mosque, Babulabona Cemetery in District Murshidabad; Adina Mosque, Eklakhi Tomb, Tantipara Masjid and Loton Mosque in District Malda; Brindaban Chandra's Math, Guptipara, Jatar Deul, LaIji Temple, Dutch Cemetery, in District Kalna; Cooch Behar Palace, District Cooch Behar; Metcalfe Hall, Calcutta; Dubdi Monastery, Sikkim.

Chandigarh circle

Bhatinda Fort, Bhatinda; Ancient site Ropar, Distt. Rupnagar; Mughal Bridge Jahangir, Distt.Jalandhar; Dakhni Sarai, Shamsher Khan's Tomb, Batala, Takhet-e-Akbari, Kalanaur, in Distt. Gurdaspur; Shahjhan ki Baoli, Meham, Distt. Rohtak; Ferozshah Palace, Prithviraj Fort, Hansi, Distt. Hissar; Sheikh Chilli's Tomb, Thanesar, Dist. Kurukshetra; Suraj Kund, Distt. Faridabad; Narbadeshwar Temple, Sujanpur Tira, Distt. Hamırpur; Rock Cut Temple, Masroor; Hari Rai Temple, Lakshmi Narain Temple, Distt. Chamba; Kangra Fort, Distt. Kangra; Laxmi Narain Temple, Naggar, Distt. Kullu; Panchvaktra Temple, Distt. Mandi; Mirkula Devi Temple, Udaipur, Phoo Gumpha, Buddhist Monasteries; Tabo in Distt. Lahaul & Spiti.

Chennai circle

Block No. XXXVI/2, Clive Building, Fort St. George, Distt. Chennai; Muruganathasvami Temple, Tirumuruganpoondi, Distt. Coimbatore; Dhenupurisvara Temple, Madambakkam, Dolotsvava Mandapa, Shore Temple, Mamallapuram, Dutch Cemetary, Sadras, Tirupulisvara Temple, Vayalur, Distt. Kanchipuram; Narasimhasvami Temple, Distt. Namakkal; Brihadesvara Temple, Distt. Perambalur; Minakshisundaresvara Temple, Amman Kurichi, Siva Temple, Ariyur, Uttamanathasvami Temple, Kiranur, Sikhanathasvami Temple, Kudumiyanmalai, Valarmadisvara Temple, Nirpalani, Siva and Vishnu Temples, Tirumayam, Agastisvara Temple, Vellanur, Distt. Pudukkottai; Airavatesvara Temple, Darasuram, Brihadesvara Temple, Thanjavur, Distt. Thanjavur; Group of monuments, Arcot, Distt. Vellore; Brahmapurisvara Temple, Brahmadesam, Alghiya Narasimhaperumal Temple, Ennayiram, Distt. Villupuram; Moolanathasvami Temple, Bahur, UT Pondicherry.

Delhi circle

Humayun's Tomb, Rajan ki Baoli, Safdarjung Tomb, Ashokan Rock Edict, Srinivaspuri, Vijay Mandal, Begumpur, Hauz Khas monuments, Rang Mahal, Red Fort, Kotla Firoz Shah, Qutab Minar, Zauq ki Mazar, Delhi Gate, Tughluqabad Fort Sheesh Mahal, Shalimar Bagh, Wazirabad Mosque, Sher Shah Gate, Khairul Manzil Mosque, Purana Qila, Badli ki Sarai in New Delhi/Delhi.

Dharwad circle

Jothirlinga Temple, Durga Temple complex, Tarabasappa Temple, Veniyar Gudi Aihole, Mallikarujuna Temple, Pattadakal, Caves at Badami, Group of Temples, Badami, in Distt. Bagalkot; Old Jain Temple, Panchalingeswara Temple, Kamala Narayan Temple, Deogaon, Hooli in Distt. Belgaum; Madhukeswara Temple, Banavasi, Chandranatha Basadi, Hadavalli, Chaturmukha Basti, Gersoppa, Fort at Mirjan in Distt. North Kanara; Solakambh Mosque, Group of Monuments at Bidar, Distt. Bidar; Ain-ul-Mulk's Tomb & Mosque, Ainapur, Gol-Gumbaz, Asar Mahal, Badi Kaman, Arquilla, Group of Monuments in Distt. Bijapur; Tarakeswara Temple, Hanaga, Siddeswara Temple in Distt. Haveri; Doddabasappa Temple, Dambal, Amitesware Temple, Annigere in Distt. Gadag; Haft Gumbaz, Fort in Distt. Gulbarga.

Guwahati circle

Karenghar Palace, Ranghar Ghanashyam's House, Joysagar, Gaurisagar Tank, Group of four maidam's, Charaideo in Distt. Sibsagar; Idgah, Rangmati Mosque, Distt. Dhubri; Shri Suryapahar, Bahtipara, Distt. Goalpara, David Scott's Memorial, Cherapunjee, Ekhasi Hill, Nagaland; Chaturdas Devata Temple, Udaipur, Thakurane Tilla, Pillak, Rock-cut-Sculpture, Unakoti in

Tripura; Shiv Temple, Negheritting, Golaghat, Cachari Ruins, Cachari; Panbari Mosque, Dhubri in Assam; Gunavati Group of Temples, Udaipur, Tripura.

Hyderabad circle

Sri Chintalarayaswami Temple, Tadpatri, Virabhadra Temple, Lepakshi, Hill Fort Gooty, in Distt. Anantapur, Gandikota Fort, Fort Siddhout, Distt. Cuddapah; Sri Kodandarama Swamy Temple, Vontimitta; Golkonda, Charminar, Ibrahim Mosque, in Distt. Hyderabad; Konda Reddy Burz,, Uma Maheswara Swamy Temple, Yaganti, Group of Temples, Alampur, Mehboobnagar; Nandavararn Temples, in Distt. Kurnool; Maha Stupa, Sankaram, Distt. Vizag; Sri Bhimeshwara Swamy Temple, Draksharama, Bhimeshwara Temple, Bhimavaram, E. Godavari; Group of Temples, Mukhalingam, Distt. Srikakulam; Buddhist Stupa, Bhattiprolu, Stupa, Amaravati, Distt. Guntur; Ramalingeswara Swamy Temple, Satyavolu, Distt. Prakashan; Bandar Fort, Machilipatnam, Distt. Krishna; Fort at Warangal, Temple at Hanumakonda, Distt. Warangal; Group of monuments Udayagiri, Ancient mound Badipathi Dibba, Ramathirtham, in Distt. Nellore.

Jaipur circle

Deeg Palaces, Kaccha Bagh, Usha Mandir, Bayana, Fort Bayana in Distt. Bharatpur; Fort Mandaur Distt. Jodhpur, Fort Jaisalmer; Ancient site, Bhangarh, Shiva Temple, Neelkhanth in Distt. Alwar; Fort Ranthambhor, Distt. Sawai Madhopur; Fort Bhatner, Distt. Hanumangarh; Wall Paintings of Haroti School in the Palace, Bundi; Gateway of Taragarh Hill, Saheli Bazaar Building, Ajmer Distt. Ajmer; Somnath Temple, Deo Somnath, Distt. Dungarpur.

Lucknow circle

Asaf-ud-daula's Imambara, Amjad Ali Shah's

Mausoleum, Begurn Kothi, Residency, Banquetting Hall, Residency, Dilkusha Palace, Dianut-ud-daula's Karbala, Residency Complex, Sikander Bagh Gate in Distt. Lucknow; Bahu Begum's Tomb, Beni Khanam's Tomb, Distt. Faizabad; Panch Mahal, Jhansi Fort, Distt.Jhansi; Neelkantha Temple, Kalinjar Fort, Distt. Banda; Shiva Temple, Urvara, Mohari Temple, Distt. Mahoba; Katcheri Cemetery, Distt. Kanpur; Vishnu Temple, Garhwa Fort, Allabhabad.

Mini circle Goa

Church of St. Francis of Assisi, Basilica of Bom Jesus, Se Cathedral Church, Church of Lady Rosary, St. Cajetan Church in Old Goa; Aguada Fort, Candolim; Safa Masjid, Ponda; Mahadevi Temple, Tamdi Surla Temple; Rock cut Caves, Arvalim; Mahadevi Temple, Kurdi.

Patna circle

Excavated remains, Kumrahar, Makhdum Shah Maneri's Tomb, Maner, Graham's House, Distt. Patna; Excavated remains at Nalanda, Distt. Nalanda; Excavated site, Stupa, remains of Hindu Temple Complex, Jain Temple, Votive Stupa Complex, Antichak in Distt. Bhagalpur; Stupa & Ashoka Pillar complex, Kolhua, Muzaffarpur; Dr. Rajendra Prasad's House, Jiradei, Distt. Siwan; Rohtas Fort, Rohtas; Shiv Temple, Konch, Distt. Gaya; Sher Shah Suri's Tomb, Hassan Shah Suri's Tomb, in Distt. Sasaram; Old Fort, Jaunpur, Nirwan Temple, Ramabhar Stupa, Kushinagar, Distt. Padrauna; Ancient Stupa, Nandangarh, West Champaram;Jama Masjid, Hadaf, Distt. Sahibganj; Mundeshwari Devi Temple, Distt. Bhabhua; Excavated remains, Sarnath, Distt. Varanasi.

Srinagar circle

Mughal Arcade, Verinag, Distt. Anantnag; Siva Temple, Fategarh, Dist. Baramulla; Fort at Akhnoor, Distt. Jammu;

Ancient Palace, Leh, Ancient Palace & Shrine, Shey, Ancient Gompa, Phyang, Buddhist Monastaries, Alchi, Ancient Gompa, Thiksey, Hemis Gompa, Buddhist Monastery, Lamayuru in Distt. Leh; Ancient Temple,Loduv, Avantisvara Temple, Distt. Pulwama; Tomb of Zain-ul-Abdin's mother, Group of arched terraces/structural complex Parimahal in Distt. Srinagar; Ancient palaces of Raja Suchet Singh, Ramnagar, Group of temples, Kiramchi, Dist. Udhampur.

Thrissur circle

Tenkailasanatha (Vadakkunnatha) Temple, Thrissur; Siva Temple, Peruvanam; Siva Temple, Chemmanthitta; Siva Temple Thrivanchikulam; Siva Temple, Netrimangalam Pattambi; Mattancherry Palace, St. Francis Church, Cochin; Siva Temple, Pallimanah; Fort at Palghat; Fort St. Anjelo, Kannur; Bekal Fort, Pallikere; Jain Temple, Wynad; Tellicherry Fort, Tellicherry; Fort at Anjengo, Anjengo, Sri Parthasarathy & Krishna Temples, Parthivapuram; Sri Parasurama Temple, Thiruvallem; Sri Bhakthavatasala Temple, Cheramadvi; Remains of Fort, Thangassery; Fort at Vattakottai; Sri Valiswara Temple, Thiruvaliswaram; Sri Bhagawathy Temple, Chitral; Rock-cut-Cave, Thirunandikkare; Ancient Site, Kunnathur; Megalithic site, Kothagiri; Siva Temple, Pallimanah; Vishnu Temple, Kadavallur, Siva Temple, Thiruvanchikulam.

Vadodara circle

Veni Mahdev Temple in Dwarkadhish Temple Complex, Dwarka, Distt.jamnagar; Church of Lady Remedies, Fort, Bastion, Daman (U.T.), Premabhai Gate, Vadigam, Astodia Gate, Distt. Ahmedabad; Old Dutch & Armenian Tombs, Surat, Distt. Surat; Fresco/rooms in Tambekarwada, Jami Masjid, Distt. Goghra; Ancient sites, Kayavarohan Distt. Vadodara; Budhiya Gate, Shaikh Farid Tomb, Gateway of Khan Sarovar, in Distt. Patan;

Siva Temple, Kotai, Excavated site, Dholavira, Distt. Bhuj; Vithalbhai Haveli, Vaso, Distt. Khedia; Buddhist Caves, Distt. Junagarh.

Science branch

Chemical treatment and preservation

The Science Branch of the Survey has carried out chemical treatment and preservation of the following major monuments:

Andhra Pradesh

Sri Mukhalingeswara Swamy Temple, Srimukhalingam, Distt. Srikakulam; Charminar, Hyderabad; Sri Bheemeswarswamy Temple, Samalkota, East Godavari.

Delhi

Hamam and Moti Masjid of Red Fort, Gateway of Arab Ki Sarai, Nizamuddin, Isakhan Tomb, Nizamuddin, Rampart wall of Red Fort, Humayun Tomb, Bara Gumbad Mosque, Lodhi Garden.

Goa

St. Francis of Assisi's Church, Se Cathedral, Born Jesus Church, Velha Goa;

Gujarat

Malik Alam's Mosque, Ahmedabad; Jami Masjid, Pavagadh; Three cells & Custom House, Pavgadh; Armenian Cemeteries and remains of Dutch Cemeteries, Surat;

Jammu & Kashmir

Mural Paintings, Shey Palace, Shey, Distt. Leh.

Karnataka

Paintings, Tipu Sultan Mausoleum, Gumbaz, Paintings, Daria Daulat Bagh, Hazara Ramchandra Temple, Hampi; Ranganathaswamy Temple, Srirangapatna, Mandya;

Horticulture branch

The major activities for development of Monuments and augmentation of irrigation facilities have been carried out at the following monuments. Hampi, Cooch Behar Palace; Kalachand Temple, Rash Manch, Bishnupur; Katara Mosque Murshidabad; Adina Mosque, Maldia, etc. Relaying of Mughal Gardens opposite to Taj Mahal at Mehtab Bagh.

Development of gardens have been taken up at the following palaces:

Fort at Ramnagar (J&K); Raja Sucheet Singh Palace, Madan Mohan Temple, Jore Bangla, Buhaliman Garden, Humayun's Tomb, Khane Khana Garden, Purana Qila, Khairul Manzil, Safdarjung Tomb, Taj Mahal, Archeological site at Kalsi, Distt. Dehradun; Chini-ka-Rauza, Agra; Shahi Fort Garden, Jaunpur; Alambagh Cemetery Lucknow; Mariam's Tomb Sikandra, Agra; Sun Temple, Konark; Zormander Temple, Bishnupur; Nand Lal Temple Bishnupur; Radhey Govind Temple, Bishnupur; Roshani Bagh, Murshidabad; Begum Azimunisah Tomb, Murshidabad; Shamraj Temple, Bishnupur; Zorbungla Temple, Bishnupur; Rameswar Temple Garden, Bhubaneswar; Lal Gumbaz, New Delhi; Red Fort, Delhi, Isa Khan Tomb inside Humayun's Tomb Complex, Delhi; Gopal Bhawan Deeg Palace, Deeg; Ansagar Baradari, Ajmer; Qutab Minar, Delhi; Firoz Shah Kotla, Delhi; Padmini Palace, Chittorgarh; Salim Garh Fort, Khajuraho; Sas Bahu Temple, Gwalior; Shah Shuja Tomb, Burhanpur; Rani Ki Vav, Patan; Bom Jesus Church at Goa; Amrutheswara, Karnataka; Hampi, Kumatagai Bijapur; Mallikarjuna Temple Complex, Pattadakal; Ellora, Aurangabad; Shanidwara Fort Pune; Golkonda, Hyderabad.

Financial assistance to monuments less than 100 years old

Archaeological Survey of India is providing Financial

Assistance for Preservation of Monuments which are less than 100 years old.

Publication Section

The Archaeological Publications brought out during the year under review highlight activities of the Archaeological Survey of India in conservation, archaeological excavation and epigraphy. Guide books and folders published : -

i. Indian Archaeology - A Review: the issue for the year 1993-94 is in the final stage of printing and the issue for the year 1994-95 is being made ready for the press.
ii. Memories of the Archaeological Survey of India: No. 75 (Vol.II) Nagarjunakonda is in advanced stage of printing and twenty-four issues of Memories were reprinted.
iii. New Imperial Series "Revised List of Antiquarian Remains in the Bombay Province", was reprinted.
iv. Three guide books viz. Hampi, Konark, Fatehpur Sikri (English) were reprinted and two issues Nagarjunakonda (English) and Fatehpur Sikri (Hindi) are in advanced stage of printing.
v. Kalachuri Chedi Era, Vol.4 (Part 2) was reprinted.
vi. One issue of inventory of monuments and sites of National Importance, Vol.I Part I was brought out and Part II is ready for being sent to the press. The Story of Indian Archaeology (Hindi) is in press. 50 years of Excavations at Harappan Sites in India; Buddhist Sites in India, and the World Heritage Monuments (English) was published and World Heritage Monuments (Hindi) is being made press-ready.

Excavation and exploration

A number of sites and ancient remains ranging from Prehistoric to medieval times have been discovered in different parts of the country under the various programmes of problem oriented investigation and village to village survey. Major salvage operations were conducted in the Submerged area of Sardar Sarovar Project covering parts of Gujarat, Madhya Pradesh and Maharashtra; of Upper Bhadra Project covering Gulbarga District 'Karnataka. Village to Village Survey was undertaken in the Districts of Bellary, Dharwad, Bijapur, Chitradurga, Coorg and Raichur in Karnataka State and problem oriented Survey in Trans Ghaggar Plains (District Siddhartanagar and Basti UP) were carried out bringing a large number of fresh sites to light.

Excavation

Twenty small and large scale excavation were undertaken. Major portions of the Pradkshinapath of Stupa No. 1, Satdhara, District Raisen, (MP) were exposed and apsidal Temple was brought to light. The excavations at Kanganhalli (Karnataka) has yielded several images of Buddha belonging to 2nd - 3rd century A.D. Sites like Mohammad Nagar and Harnol in Haryana revealed occupational evidence of painted Greyware culture and Northern Black Polished ware culture. Two collaborative works one at Mahet (District Sravasti, UP) in association with Kansai University, Japan and another at Paithan (District Aurangabad, Maharashtra) in association with the Society for South Asian Studies of Britain, London (UK) and ASI were conducted.

Temple and building survey projects

Chola Temples in Karnataka were studied and a report has been finalized. Six new Chola Temples in Mysore district have been explored and detailed analysis of the inscriptional dates and stylistic idioms of these Temples are in progress.

The Building Survey Project located at Delhi is documenting the colonial buildings of India. In Calcutta, listing of 32 buildings has been done. Photo documentation of St. Xavier's College, St. Andrews Church, Bishop House, Portuguese Church and St. Pauls Cathedral has been completed. Preliminary survey of the building of old Fort William, Government House, Horticultural and Botanical Garden will be taken-up.

Epigraphy branch

More than a hundred Perso- Arabic inscriptions in various districts of Andhra Pradesh, Maharashtra, Uttar Pradesh and Delhi pertaining to the medieval period have been explored and translated for further study.

Site Museums

Archaeological Survey of India is maintaining 33 site museums located all over the country. The organization work of the galleries at Archaeology Site museums at Ratnagiri (Orissa), Roop Nagar (Punjab), and Chanderi (MP) have been completed. The reorganization work of the galleries in the Archaeological Museums at Murshidabad (West Bengal), Velha Goa (Goa), Red Fort (Delhi), Indian War Memorial Museums (Delhi), Sanchi (MP) Gwalior (MP), Sarnath (UP) are in progress. A proposal to organize site museums at Jageshwar, Almora (UP) is in the pipeline. Proposals have been initiated to set up Site Museums at Burzahon (J&K), Pillalk and Banavari (Karnataka).

Exhibitions

On the eve of 501h Year of India's Independence all Circle/Branch Offices of the Survey arranged photo exhibitions throughout the length and breadth of the country to highlight the achievements of the Archaeological Survey of India during the last 5 decades in conservation, preservation and exploration. Special exhibitions were arranged at Chandigarh and Vadodara to highlight the Archaeological excavations carried out during the last 5 decades and the importance of these excavations.

Projects with International/Private collaboration

The conservation of Ajanta - Ellora Caves have been taken up for funding by OECF Japan, through a project of the Maharashtra Tourism Development Corp. Indo-British 50th Anniversary Trust, Oberoi Hotels & the Aga Khan Trust are funding a project of revitalizing the ancient water supply system, gardens of the Humayun's Tomb, Delhi and its illumination. UNESCO has already agreed to fund for investigations of the Jagmohana of Sun Temple, Konark under Emergency Assistance of UNESCO.

4.20 The proposal for monitoring Air Pollution at Agra and stone conservation has been started with TaJ Mahal, funds from Rhone Poulenc Foundation through UNESCO. The conservation work of the Buddhist Monuments at Sanchi and Satdhara under a UNESCO Project are in progress. The first phase of mausoleum of St. Francis Xavier Goa, has been taken up jointly by the Italian After conservation team of Restorers and A.S.I. and the work is in progress.

World Heritage monuments

World Heritage Day was celebrated at 16 monuments listed under the World Heritage List on 181h April, 1998. Photo-Exhibitions on monuments heritage were organised at various places in India. World Heritage Week from 19'h to 25", November, 1998 was also celebrated at selected monuments with the active involvement of students and the general public.

Unprotected monuments

The Archaeological Survey of India has taken up

conservation work on the following unprotected Monuments, in addition to its normal functions as deposit works viz.

1. Victoria Memorial Museum, Calcutta
2. Rampur Raza Library, Rampur, U.P.
3. Dupleix Palace Chandernagar
4. Temples at Patra, West Bengal.
5. Council Hall, University of Delhi.
6. Temples at Bora, West Bengal.
7. Transplantation of monuments being submerged under Narmada Valley Development Authority.

Institute of Archaeology

The Post-Graduate Diploma in Archaeology is of two year's duration. During the year 1998-99 the Diploma Course for the batch 1996-98 has been concluded. The batches 1997-99 and 1998-2000 are undergoing training.

Training in excavation

Students of 1996-98 and 1997-99 batch participated in the archaeological excavations at Rakhigarhi, Distt. Hissar, Haryana. Twenty-nine students participated in field excavations from December 97 to February 98. Besides PGDA students, students of the Jawaharlal Nehru University, New Delhi; Rajasthan Vishwavidyalaya, Jaipur; Ruhelkhand University, Bareilly also visited the site and were imparted field training.

Chemical preservation

.26 Students have participated in the chemical conservation training camp organized at Science Branch, Dehradun from 3rd August to 12th August '98. During the training course students were given practical training in the chemical conservation of archaeological objects.

Special demonstration lectures on Satellite Remote

Sensing in Indian Institute of Remote Sensing, Dehradun, were organized in the sequel of chemical conservation training.

Structural conservation

Students and officials of the Archaeological Survey of India and state archaeology department participated in the structural conservation training camp organized at Mandu from 17th August to 7th September '98. Participants were given lectures on the conservation problems in India and abroad and also practical training on various types of structural conservation and chemical conservation of ancient monuments by the field staff of the Archaeological Survey of India.

Authenticity of antiquity and art objects

A workshop was organized for the first time from 2nd November '98 to 12th November '98. The aim of the workshop was to explain / expose officers of the Archaeological Survey of India, Customs, DRI, students etc. to differentiate genuine antiquities from fake handicrafts. The workshop was attended by archaeologists from all parts of the country including inservice archaeologists of ASI, Departments of Archaeology, CBI, DRI and students of the Institute etc.

Awards

The Archaeological Survey of India was given tourism award for best maintenance of Khajuraho Monuments and the award was presented on 24.1.1998 by the Honourable Prime Minister to the Director General A.S.I.

4

Museums

National museum

The National Museum was set up in 1960 as a subordinate office under the Department of Culture. At present there are about 2 lakh works of art objects in the National Museum. The main activities of the National Museum are in the fields of Acquisition, Exhibition, Education, Public Relations, Publication and Conservation.

Exhibitions

Exhibitions organized by the Department of Culture through National Museum as a part of the Golden Jubilee Celebrations of India's Independence.

(i) Karuna (7th, February '98 to 28th February '98).

(ii) Columbia: World Heritage Sites (10th March '98 to 19th April '98).

(iii) Art Treasures from Kotah (25th March '98 to 19th April '98).

(iv) An exhibition of Ceramics by Raphael Bordallo Pinheiro (7th April '98 to 14th April '98).

(v) Gods, Kings and Tigers: Art of Kotah (April to June '97). This exhibition had also travelled to Harvard Museum as well as to Zurich.

(vi) Treasures of Indian Art: Germany's contribution to India's cultural heritage (14th August '98 to 30th

September '98). This is the concluding event of the Golden Jubilee Celebrations.

(vii) Exhibition material was also despatched to Mexico for setting up an Indian Hall at the National Museum of Culture at Mexico City.

As a part of the programme for Celebrating the Golden Jubilee of India's Independence, the National Museum, New Delhi in collaboration with the Indian Council for Cultural Relations and the Embassy of the Federal Republic of Germany, organized a special exhibition entitled "Treasures of Indian Art: Germany's Tribute to India's Cultural Heritage" which was inaugurated by the Hon'ble President of India on 14th August, 1998. The exhibition comprising 92 exhibits, were loaned for the first time from the collections of the Museum of Indian Art, Berlin State Museum, Prussian Cultural Foundation. The exposition remained open to the public up to 30th September, 1998. Coinciding with the six-week long exhibition a series of ancillary events was also organised at the National Museum in collaboration with the National Museum Institute, the Centre for Cultural Resources and Training and the Max Mueller Bhavan.

This exhibition also travelled to the Indian Museum, Calcutta and was on display from 6.10.98 to 15.11.98 and in the National Gallery of Modern Art, Mumbai from 4.12.98 to 4.1.99. The National Museum being the nodal agency for the exhibition, extended infrastructural support at both places.

The National Museum was also designated the nodal agency for organizing the Exhibition entitled 'Use and Significance of Coral in Indian Jewellery and Handicrafts' at the Banca Di Credito Popolare Toera Del Greco, Naples, Italy from 22.12.98 to 31.1.99. The exposition comprised of 37 art objects, out of which 3 exhibits were loaned from the Indian Museum, Calcutta.

The National Museum also acted as the nodal agency and entered into an agreement with the Tobu Museum of Art, Tokyo Japan for an exhibition entitled St. Francis Xavier: His Life and Times from, 15.1.99 to 5.12.99. The exhibition was inaugurated by H.R.H. Emperor of Japan at Kawasaki City Museum, where it will be on view from 15.1.99 to 14.3.99. The other venues In Japan are: (a) The Yamaguchi Prefectural Museum of Art (from 6.4.99 to 30.5.99), (b) Tobu Museum of Art, Tokyo (from 10.6.99 to 20.7.99), (c) Kagoshima Prefectural Museum (from 31.7.99 to 29.8.99), (d) Okazaki Mindscape Museum (from 11.9.99 to 24.10.99) and (e) the Nagasaki Prefectural Museum (from 12.11.99 to 5.12.99).

Seminars, special lectures and cultural events

A number of seminars, lectures and workshops were organized on conservation of art objects, museology and display to coincide with the Berlin Exhibition.

Seminars

On 11.9.98 a whole day seminar was organized on the following topic: Relationship of Stone Sculptures to Temple Architecture in which the following speakers participated: Dr. R. Nagaswamy, Dr. Gerd Revissen, Prof. R Champakalakshmi, Mr. Krishna Deva, Prof. S. Sethar, Mr. M.M. Deshpande.

Workshops

Museum Education and Communication by Peter Roester.

Lectures

(i) A series of lectures were organized every Tuesday. The inaugural one was delivered by Dr.B.N. Goswamy on Indian Art-Its Form, Essence and Revelation.

(ii) Ways of Seeing: Artist, Patron and Vision in Indian Miniature Painting by Ms. Monica Joneja.

(iii) Indian Traditions and our links with Central Asia by Ms. Jasleen Dhamija.
(iv) The Glory of Ajanta by Dr. Walter Spink.
(v) Stones that Tell Tales by Dr. Saryu Doshi.
(vi) Images of India in Germany by Dr. Rainer Lotz.

Dance performances

Dance Performances were given by:

(i) Ms. Veronique Azan
(ii) Madhavi Mudgal &
(iii) Sonal Mansingh during the six week span of the exhibition

Musical Performances

(i) Mr. Lalgudi Jayaraman gave violin recital and
(ii) Pt. Ajay Chakravarti gave a Hindusthani musical performance.

Play and poetry

The museum was also the venue for the following three events:

(i) Heart String by The Action Players, a hearing impaired group from Calcutta.
(ii) Tumhari Amrita by Ms. Shabana Azmi and Mr. Farooque Sheikh.
(iii) a Poetry reading by Mr. Javed Akhtar.

Educational activities

Several lectures by eminent scholars have been organized in the museum as part of its academic activities. Educational services were extended to students of schools, colleges and universities for the preparation of their project reports/dissertations.

(i) A summer holiday programme for school children entitled The Toy Box was organized from 10.6.98 to 25.6.98.

(ii) Practical training in Museology was organized for the post- graduate students of museology from Prachiniketan, Bhopal.

Public relations

The following facilities were also provided for the benefit of visitors:

(i) Conducted tours through the galleries for sponsored groups, Indian and foreign delegations and VIPs.

(ii) Sale of plaster casts/fibre glass replicas and publications belonging to the National Museum.

(iii) Supply of photographs and colour slides.

(iv) Photography and filming of art objects, access to the reserve collections and library, identification of art objects owned by individuals and reproduction of works of art in publications, calendars, diaries, etc.

Visitors

Till 31st December, 1998, 95,229 visitors, including VIP's visited the National Museum. Some of the VIP's who visited the Museum were: H.E. President, of India, Hon'ble Vice President of India, Vice Admiral, Chief of South African Navy, H.E. Mr. Ivan Antoomovich, Minister of Foreign Affairs, H.E. EUM, Yong Ky, Belarus Foreign Minister, Seoul, Korea, H.E. President of Bulgaria, a Finnish parliamentary delegation, Sardar S.S. Barnala, Cabinet Minister, Govt. of India, etc.

Photo unit

During the period under report, 3061 black and white photographs were made; 1200 negatives prepared in colour; 8414 black and white prints were prepared; 1527 colour prints and 260 colour slides were prepared.

During the period, the conservation laboratory prepared, 350 black and white negatives and 630 photo prints. In addition to this, 200 colour photo prints were also prepared.

Library

47,402 books were added to the collection of the Museum Library. About 4055 readers visited and availed of the research and reference facilities. 143 books were acquired.

Modelling unit

1461 raw plaster casts were prepared, 1796 casts were coloured and finished, 67 raw fibre glass casts prepared and 63 fibre glass casts coloured.

Hindi unit

The National Museum celebrated Hindi week during 14th to 21st September 1998. During this period, competitions in Hindi Nibandh, Shrutlekhan, Vad-vivad and Hindi Typing were conducted for the officers and employees of the National Museum and the National Museum Institute. Successful participants were rewarded with cash prizes.

All sorts of labels, such as individual labels, general labels, introductory labels, leaflets etc. were prepared both in Hindi and English. Hindi versions of the booklets, folders, invitation cards, press releases, write-ups of exhibitions and other official communication were prepared for effective implementation of the Official Language Policy of the Government.

Publication unit

The following publications were brought out: -

i. Brochures and a catalogue of the exhibition entitled Treasures of Indian Art: Germany's Tribute to India's Cultural Heritage.
ii. A Guide to the National Museum
iii. Pre-Columbian Art Catalogue.
iv. NOC's are being obtained for printing the following publications.

a. Arms and Armour Catalogue
b. A Portfolio on Indian Miniature Painting
c. A Portfolio on Rajasthani Miniatures
d. Two hand lists on Indus Valley Collection
e. Gallery Sheet on Arms and Armour
f. Gallery Sheet on Indus Valley
g. Invitation Cards, labels, digital posters and banners for various exhibitions.

Conservation laboratory

During the period under report, the Conservation Laboratory of the National Museum, attended to the following projects :

i. The laboratory examined about 1240 art objects to either fix priority for conservation or preparation of condition reports and checking of condition reports.
ii. The laboratory checked and preserved 212 objects out of 368 objects received, for conservation treatment in the laboratory. Work on 156 objects is in progress.
iii. The laboratory cleaned and preserved 592 objects displayed in the rotunda, foyer, courtyard and galleries prior to the visit of VIPs, for the inauguration of exhibitions in the National Museum.
iv. The laboratory successfully completed conservation of the mural paintings in the domes of the South Block.
v. Fumigation of 44 almirahs and 500 museum objects were carried out to prevent attack by insects and fungi, in the reserve collection of the Museum.
vi. The laboratory conserved panel paintings in the Parliament House.
vii. Mural Paintings in the Prime Minister's Office were also chemically cleaned and preserved.

viii. Cleaning and restoration work was also completed on the oil paintings of the Pondicherry Municipal Corporation.

ix. Conservation treatment to the flag of Rashtriya Rifles, Delhi Cantonment..

x. Conserved one stone sculpture displayed in the Prime Ministers Office.

Teaching activities

i. The staff of the laboratory delivered lectures to the students of M.A. Conservation, M.A. History and M.A. Museology and also conducted their practical classes.

ii The laboratory staff also assisted students in their dissertation work.

iii. The staff also evaluated answer sheets of students and conducted the viva-voce examination.

Technical studies

Analysis of about 170 objects of APC 1997-98 is in hand for checking their authenticity. So far, work has been completed on 24 objects.

Radiology of 40 objects was carried out either to preserve their finger prints or to locate the internal matrix of the object in question.

Miscellaneous work

- The laboratory is also monitoring temperature, relative humidity and light level in the galleries of the museum so as to maintain the optimum micro climate.
- The laboratory also identified and classified 97 slides on conservation.
- The staff members participated in a National seminar on conservation at Guwahati and presented papers on different topics.

- From time to time staff was also deputed either for escorting the exhibits from National Museum to other Museums or to take exhibits/ showcases back to National Museum.
- Laboratory staff also visited various institutions such as the CBI Museum, Lodhi Complex and rendered necessary advice for shifting of artefacts to Noida (UP)
- Survey of collection of Vidyamandir Trust, Varanasi was also carried out by the laboratory.
- Attended by students and visitors from various Museums/Institutions.

National gallery of modern art

The National Gallery of Modem Art (NGMA) has established a unique place in the growing landscape of Indian art. NGMA, founded in 1954, is the only institution of it's kind in the country, which is run and administered by the Department of Culture. It is a repository of contemporary visual art and has been implementing a number of schemes for strengthening its activities and spreading art education amongst the public. NGMA represents the evolution of changing art forms through the passage of time.

NGMA has a branch in Mumbai at the Sir Cowasji Jehangir Public Hall and is also in the process of acquiring Manikyavelu Mansion from the State Government of Karnataka for opening its branch in Bangalore.

NGMA has undertaken a number of activities in the year 1998-99 towards implementing various plan schemes.

Special exhibitions

A number of exhibitions were organised during 1998-99.

1. An exhibition of limited edition prints of American artist Robert Rauchenberg-a pivotal figure of the 20' century entitled Tribute 21 was held from 21st

August to 12th September, 1998. This exhibition is a series of 21 limited edition paper prints dedicated to the 211t century. It celebrates 21 humanitarian themes like world culture, peace, human struggle, social justice, ecology, arts, etc. Tribute 21 series was donated by Robert Rauschenberg and Felissimo and is now part of the collection of the NGMA. Another notable gift was a high-tech ceramic sculpture by the Swiss artist Max Bell.

2. A retrospective exhibition of paintings, drawings, prints and films of renowned artist Viswanadhan was organised.
3. An exhibition from the collection of the Municipal Gallery of Athens entitled "Greek Contemporary Art" was held from 10th April, 1998 to 10th May, 1998. This exhibition provides an overview of Neo-Hellenic painting from the mid 191 century to the present times.
4. To commemorate the 50th Anniversary of India's Independence, an exhibition of Contemporary Croatian Graphic Art was organized in collaboration with the Embassy of Croatia from 14th May, 1998. Dashrath Patel is a pioneer in disciplines like industrial design, industrial ceramics, multi-screen projections and stadium scale exhibitions.

In conjunction with the exhibition, four workshops on Vegetable Dyes, Tensile Structures, Black Terracotta and Screen Printing and Poster Making were held with participants from different walks of life as an educational and outreach programme. Colloquiums on issues of Crafts and Art, on Design and Architecture, on Ceramics and on Photography were also organized involving students and participants from different and diverse disciplines.

An Indo-Austrian contemporary art exhibition entitled, The Search Within comprising a selection of works by 10 contemporary Austrian and 10 Indian artists was inaugurated by Shri Krishan Kant Vice President of India on 23rd October, 1998. A seminar was organized in conjunction with the exhibition in which the participating artists shared their experiences.

6. A major exhibition of contemporary Japanese Art entitled Tastes and Pursuits :Japanese Art in the 1990s was organized at NGMA from December 26, 1998 to January 20, 1999, in collaboration with the Japan Foundation.
7. A Retrospective exhibition of Photographs of eminent photographer Raghubir Singh, River of Colours - The India of Raghubir Singh was held in the month of February 1999.
8. The largest ever exhibition of Contemporary Art from Korea was held in February 1999 to coincide with the Indian Engineering Trade Fair in which Korea was the partner country with India. The exhibition was inaugurated by H.E. Mr. Kim Jongpil, the Prime Minister of the Republic of Korea on 11th February, 1999.

Activities of Ngma, Mumbai

During the year 1998-99, the NGMA, Mumbai was able to create its own niche in the world of art in the commercial capital of India through two international exhibitions i.e. The Enduring Image and Treasures of Indian Art. The Enduring Image, which started on 10.2.98, continued upto 31.5.98 and was able to reach out through various programmes to a vast public.

Treasures of Indian Art from the Berlin Museum which was held from December' 98 to January '99, as one of the concluding events of the 50th Anniversary celebrations, with a number of support events including seminars, workshops and performing art events of music and dance, was also well received by the public.

The NGMA also held the following exhibitions:

i. Indo-Austrian contemporary art exhibition entitled The Search Within.

ii. Exhibition of Indian contemporary art entitled Collectors Eye: from the Jehangir and Nicholson Collection.

iii. An exhibition entitled Shantiniketan - the Making of Contextual Modernism featuring the works of Rabindranath Tagore, Nandalal Bose, Binode Behari Mukherjee, Ram Kinker Vaij. This was part of the Kala Ghoda Festival which made NGMA a focal centre for all art activities during this festival.

iv. An exhibition of Indian Contemporary Art from the collection of NGMA was organized at the prestigious Centro Cultural Borges, Buenos Aires, Argentina, as one of the events to celebrate 50 years of India's Independence.

v. An exhibition of Indian Contemporary art comprising 40 works was organized at the National Gallery, Colombo, Sri Lanka.

Opening of branch at Bangalore

The Government of Karnataka has agreed to provide a building, Manikyavelu Mansion, at a prime location for setting up a branch of NGMA at Bangalore. Formalities are being worked out for opening the Bangalore branch after carrying out necessary renovations.

Educational programmes

1. One of the major concerns of NGMA is to disseminate modern art through non formal art education. NGMA has an Art Reference Library and conducts Art appreciation Courses, Art Sketch Club meets and organizes Painting, Modelling, Quiz Competitions and summer vacation programmes to inculcate interest in the field of art by bringing students to the Gallery and exposing them to

different techniques, styles and mediums adopted by the great masters of India. Films on art are regularly screened at the Gallery.

2. NGMA conducted a summer workshop for children from 16 May 1998 to 25 May 1998 in which 150 students participated.
3. A basic Art Appreciation Course with 60 students for a period of 4 months was conducted to popularise and create awareness about Indian Contemporary Art.
4. NGMA organized a series of lectures by eminent artists and art historians on different aspects of Contemporary Art. Dr. Geeti Sen, a well-known art critic and art historian delivered a lecture, on The Body as a Subversive Site on 11th September '98. Dr. Parabha Sahasrabudhe, Professor of Art and Art Education, Teachers College, Columbia University, New York gave a talk entitled Tradition and Modern Sensibility on 13th August 1998; Kavita Singh, an art historian on Chinese Avant Garde Art and Vivan Sundaram, a well-known artist gave an illustrated talk on Structures of Memory: Modern Bengal based on his site specific installation at the Victoria Memorial Hall, Calcutta.

Development of slide library and art reference library

NGMA organizes art appreciation courses as a part of its educational programme. In order to support the educational programmes and to provide information to researchers and scholars the slide library was further developed. The computerization of the library and bar coding of books has been undertaken in the art reference library.

Photo documentation

NGMA has a collection of more than 14,000 art objects comprising paintings, drawings, graphics and sculptures, etc. of contemporary Indian artists including national art treasures. Proper documentation, access and availability of information on these art works is of permanent concern and importance to NGMA. With the rapid strides made in technology it is now possible to improve the management of data and images, making them accessible through faster and more reliable methods. A complete solution for archival and retrieval of images which is both quick, simple and reliable and which enables the gallery to make its collection accessible to scholars, students and researchers in high resolution images without constant handling and damage of the original art works is now possible through the photo CD disc technology and is in the process of being developed.

Film production

NGMA received an award from the President of India at the 45th National Film Festival Awards function at Vigyan Bhavan for a film produced by it, entitled "The Official Art Form" which won an award for the best. non feature film on art and culture.

Restoration

During the period under review, status reports for 125 works of art for incoming exhibitions were prepared. Necessary cleaning was done for 60 works of art and 7 paintings were restored.

Publications

Coloured catalogues were published to complement the exhibitions held at the Gallery. NGMA has a comprehensive programme of bringing out portfolios of eminent artists. The memoires of B.C.Sanyal, the doyen of Indian Art entitled, Vertical Woman Reminiscences of B.C.Sanyal : 1902-1947 published by NGMA was presented to the Vice-President of India on 19.5.1998 by the Honourable Minister for Human Resource Development. Volume II is under publication.

National council of science museums (NCSM)

The National Council of Science Museums (NCSM), an autonomous organ in under the Department of Culture, is primarily engaged in popularising Science and Technology amongst students in particular and the masses in general, through a wide range of activities and interactive programmes.

Main objectives of NCSM

1. To popularize Science and Technology in cities, urban and rural areas for the benefit of students and the common man by organizing exhibitions, seminars, popular lectures, science camps and various other programmes.
2. To inculcate a scientific temper and to create scientific awareness among students and the common people.
3. To supplement science education imparted in schools and colleges by organizing various out of school educational activities to foster a spirit of scientific enquiry and activity among students.
4. To organize training programmes for science teachers, young entrepreneurs and technicians on specific subjects of science, technology and industry.
5. To render assistance to universities, technical institutions, museums, schools, colleges and other bodies in planning and organizing science museums and also in training of museum professionals.
6. To design, develop and fabricate science museum exhibits, demonstration equipment and! scientific teaching aids for science education and popularization of science.
7. To collect, restore and preserve important historical objects, which represent landmarks in the development of science, technology and industry.

8. To conduct research into the history of science and technology with special reference to India.
9. To enter into agreements with foreign scientific agencies, science and technology museums/ centres and like institutions for exchange of museum professionals, study tours, training in specialized areas in the fields of museology and museography, providing technical assistance in the establishment of science and technology museums/ centres and for other matters consistent with the aims and objectives of society.

Constituents of NCSM

Science Museums/Centres administered and managed by NCSM throughout the country

1. Birla Industrial & Technological Museum (BITM), Calcutta.
2. Visvesvaraya Industrial & Technological Museum (VITM), Bangalore.
3. Nehru Science Centre (NSCM), Mumbai.
4. National Science Centre (NSCD), Delhi.
5. Central Research & Training Laboratory (CRTL), Calcutta.
6. Science City, Calcutta.
7. Shri Krishna Science Centre, Patna.
8. Regional Science Centre, Lucknow.
9. Regional Science Centre, Bhubaneswar.
10. Raman Science Centre & Planetarium, Nagpur.
11. Regional Science Centre, Guwahati.
12. Regional Science Centre, Bhopal.
13. Regional Science Centre, Tirupati.
14. Regional Science Centre & Planetarium, Calicut.
15. District Science Centre, Purulia.
16. District Science Centre, Gulbarga

17. District Science Centre, Dharampur.
18. District Science Centre, Tirunelveli.
19. Bardhaman Science Centre, Bardhaman.
20. Dhenkanal Science Centre, Dhenkanal
21. Digha Science Centre & National Science Camp, Digha.
22. North Bengal Science Centre, Siliguri
23. Kapilas Science Park, Kapilas
24. Science Activity Centre, Gwalior.
25. Science Activity Centre, Sirsa.
26. Panorama Museum, Kurukshetra.

BITM, VITM, NSCM, NSCD and CRTL are national level museums /centres while the others function as their satellite units.

Planning, conceptual development of exhibits and activities and major achievements

NCSM laid particular stress on the planning and development of new exhibits for the permanent galleries of the Museums/Centres, commissioning of new galleries, setting up of new centres, planetaria, science parks and in organizing travelling exhibitions at national and international levels.

The major activities and achievements of NCSM during the year under review are:

New centres

a. Developmental work for setting up Panorama Museum at Kurukshetra (Haryana) is in progress. The Museum will be opened in two phases. The first phase contains an exhibition on Indian Heritage in Science & Technology and Fun Science and is ready for inauguration. Exhibits for this section have been fabricated at CRTL, Calcutta, NSC, Delhi and RSC, Lucknow. Another exhibition tided 'Viswaroopa' depicting the unity in diversity and diversity in unity in nature is also on display. Work for the other facilities in the Museum e.g. auditorium, activity corner, Taramandal, Science Park, etc. are also complete. The second phase will contain large scale panoramic scenes on Kurukshetra War, work of which is going on in full swing.

b. A New Science Centre at Goa is in an advanced stage of planning. Conceptual development of the exhibits have started. The Centre will emphasize the science of the oceans and their impact on human life.

Exhibits

Altogether 250 exhibits have been fabricated during this period in NCSM units. CRTL, Calcutta fabricated the exhibits for "India-a Tradition in Science, Technology and Culture" - for exhibition at Bangladesh and for Panorama Museum, Kurukshetra. CRTL also fabricated twenty geodesic domes and Taramandal (inflatable dome planetarium) units for different centres. CRTL is also developing exhibits for the Energy Education Park at Calcutta. BITM, Calcutta is developing a Solar Energy Corner. At RSC, Guwahati a chemistry gallery is being set up during this year. Work for setting up a Jurassic Park at Digha Science Centre and installation of two Dinosaur models at North Bengal Science Centre, Siliguri are continuing. At VITM, Bangalore, developmental work for the "Space" gallery is nearly complete. RSC, Tirupati is developing an exhibition on "Science Behind Beliefs."

A "Dinosaur Enclave" has been set up at NSC, Delhi. The enclave displays robotic dinosaurs. NSC, Delhi also fabricated 10 outdoor exhibits for Bal Vigyan Udyan at Delhi. Fun Science exhibits for Panorama Museum, Kurukshetra have been fabricated at NSC, Delhi and RSC, Lucknow.

At NSC, Mumbai the development of a Life Science corner and a Discovery Hall is going on in full swing. The centre is also developing an exhibition on Atom for Peace. A new planetarium show "Visitors from Outer Space" has been introduced at RSC, Calicut.

Different national level centres have fabricated a large number of giant robotic insects for the national exhibition 'Giants from the Backyard'. The exhibition was inaugurated on 25th September 1998 at NSC, Mumbai, the first site. Other units of NCSM have developed a large numbers of kits and teaching aids. Interesting demonstration lectures and science shows have also been developed.

As part of its catalytic support programme, NCSM has developed science park exhibits for IUCCS, Pune. Park exhibits meant for the Weizmann Institute of Science, Israel Two Space Theatre shows have been introduced at Science City, Calcutta.

Two National Science Camps on Geology and Bio-technology were organized at Digha Science Centre.

Travelling exhibitions

A unique exhibition developed by NCSM, India - a Tradition in Science, Technology and Culture was opened at Dhaka on 16th June 1998 as a part of the golden jubilee celebrations of Indian Independence. The exhibition portrayed the 4500-year history of development of science and technology in India and has attracted a large number of visitors. The exhibition continued for one and half months. A mobile science exhibition We are One also travelled throughout Bangladesh during this period.

A national exhibition on robotic insects and arthropods titled Giants from the Backyard was inaugurated at Nehru Science Centre, Mumbai in September 1998. The exhibition displayed a large number of pneumatically controlled robotic insects enlarged 200-300 times their actual size. This was supplemented by another interactive exhibition illustrating the different aspects of insect life. This exhibition will also take place at Bangalore, Nagpur and Bhopal.

International collaborations

NCSM has signed a Memorandum of Understanding (MOU) with the Government of Mauritius to set up a Science Centre at Port Louis for which work will start shortly. NCSM will develop exhibits for the Centre and train their personnel. Conceptual development of exhibits has already started. Catalytic support proposals by way of supplying exhibits to Israel and South Africa have been received.

School science centres

The Council has set up more than 300 School Science Centres in rural schools throughout the nation and is providing them with teaching aids, kits books and training facilities. 4 School Science Centres have been established in Rajasthan during the period. 12 more such centres will be established in Punjab shortly. More proposals for setting up school, science centres in different states like Haryana, Orissa, Gujarat etc. are under consideration.

Major activities undertaken during this period by the units of NCSM

a. The countrywide students' science seminar on the topic 50 Years of Science and Technology in Independent India -Aspirations and Achievements culminated in a National Science Seminar. The participants were selected on the basis of Block, District and State level seminars held throughout the country. Master Brajesh Ranjan of Ramakrishna Mission Vidyapith, Deoghar, Bihar was adjudged the best participant.

b. Science Fairs were organized in many NCSM units. Successful participants went on to participate in the zonal fairs like Eastern India Science Fair, Western India Science Fair, Northern India Science Fair, etc.

c. Twenty-two Mobile Science Exhibition (MSE) buses crisscrossed the country and visited rural schools with relevant exhibitions and activities. More than 1.6 million people visited these exhibitions.
d. In different museums and centres under NCSM, large numbers of Science Demonstration Lectures, Science Quizzes, Popular Lectures, Creative Ability Programmes, Computer Training Programmes and Computer Fairs, Science Film Shows, Taramandal Programmes, Teachers' Training Programmes, Community Training Programmes, Anti-superstition demonstrations, etc. were held.
e. Special events for public awareness like World Environmental Day, World Health Day, Wild Life Week, Space Week, World Aids Day, National Science Day, etc. were conducted in all centres.
f. Science camps and Nature Study programmes were held in many centres.

Victoria memorial hall Calcutta

The Victoria Memorial Hall, Calcutta, a period museum depicting the times under the British Raj is dedicated to the conservation and preservation of the main building, the sprawling garden surrounding it and the artifacts in its collection. Repairs to the main building and remodelling and renovation of the five galleries has been entrusted to the supervision of the Archaeological Survey of India.

The Victoria Memorial organized two major exhibitions under the national calendar of events namely an exhibition on the Sepoy Mutiny of 1857 and another on the Contemporary Art of Bengal. Another exhibition based on the Great Movements in Indian National Life was organized in collaboration with the Philadelphia Museum of Arts. A live demonstration on the folk music of Bengal was held to provide city dwellers with a glimpse of the rich musical tradition of Bengal. Son et Lumiere, a programme of light and sound depicting the history of Calcutta also continued, much to the appreciation of the general public.

Salarjung mesum, Hyderabad

The Salarjung Museum, Hyderabad, an Institution of national importance which came into existence on 16th December 1951, is a valuable repository of Global Art collections. It is named after the erstwhile noble family of the Salarjungs, the collectors of this treasure trove. A major portion of the Museum's collection was acquired by Mir Yousuf Ali Khan popularly known as Salarjung-III (13th June, 1889 - 2nd March 1949) There are 35 galleries spread over two floors. The ground floor has 19 galleries and the 1st floor has 16 galleries.

Collections

The collections of the Museum consists of Indian Art, Middle Eastern Art, Far Eastern and European Art. Apart from this, there is a gallery devoted to the illustrious Salarjung Family, a Children's Section, a rich reference Library, a reading room and a rare manuscripts section with Arabic, Urdu and Persian Manuscripts, that makes the museum a place of education and enjoyment for people from all walks of life.

Major attractions on display In various galleries of the salar jung museum

- Indian Collection: A Bharhut rail slab (1st or 2nd century BC; standing Buddha image of lime- stone from Nelakondapally (2nd or 3rd century AD); Mukhalinga from Kausambi (4th or 5th century AD) Ananthasayi Vishnu, ten incarnations carved on top, (12th century, Kakatiya, Warangal); Jain, Buddhist and Hindu bronzes going back to later Pallava, Chola and Vijayanagara periods (Gallery No.'s 3/3A)

- Ivory chairs presented to Tipu Sultan by Louis XV (France); a handsome beer mug, early 20th century German circus figures (Gallery No.14)
- Veiled Rebecca: A poem in pure marble by the Italian Sculptor G.B.Benzoni (Gallery No.16). Mephistopheles & Margaretta: A 19th century French sycamore wood carving portraying a double statue in the Neo-classical style (Gallery No. 16)
- Arms of Mughal Emperor Aurangazeb, Tipu Sultan, Mohammed Shah and Bahadur Shah; sword of the Qutub Shahi Period with Dasavatara engraving (Gallery No. 16A)
- 19th Century Musical Clock: Acquired from Britain (Near Gallery No. 16)
- Oil Paintings: 'Soap Bubbles' by Francesco Hayez 1791-1882, Italy; 'Piazza of San Marco' by Antonio Canaletto (1697-1768); 'Venice' by Marc Aldine - 19th Century, Italy (Gallery No.20).
- Pottery from Dresden (Germany) Sevres (France) CapodiMonte (Italy) Wedgewood and English Porcelain (Gallery No.21).
- Glassware from Venice, Ireland, England, France, Belgium, Czechoslovakia, Istanbul (Gallery No.24)
- Celadon of Sung (960-70); Yuan (1279-1365) Ming and Ching periods (Gallery No.31)
- Jade : Inscribed Jade book, (Quran); stand of Altamash (1209-10 AD); fruit knife of Mughal Empress Noor Jahan - 17th Century; hunting knife of Mughal Emperor Jehangir; 17th Century dark green jade inscribed archery ring of Mughal Emperor Shah Jahan (Gallery No.25).

Manuscripts

Arabic Al-Quran in Naskh, Calligrapher -Yaqut-al-Must'sami in 1288 AD, bearing autographs of Mughal

Emperors Jehangir, Shah Jahan, and Aurangazeb; Persian Bukhara MSS; 'Raudat-ul-Muhibbin by Amir Hussaini Saadat (1329AD), Salman Savji (1377) and Ibn-e-Imad (1397). Urdu poetic composition 'Diwan-e-Mohd QuIi Qutub Shah 1595 AD by Sultan Mohd. Quli Qutub Shah from the Royal Library of Golconda (Gallery No.29)

Major activities of the museum during 1998-99

Educational activities of the museum:

(i) An exhibition was organized by the Indian Museum in collaboration with the Salarjung Museum at Hyderabad under the Inter-State Museum exhibition programme which aimed at highlighting the interlinking of Museum activities and arriving at a better understanding and cooperation among people of various states in India. It was inaugurated by Prof. A.K. Bhatnagar, Vice-Chancellor, University of Hyderabad on 16th August 1998.

(ii) On the occasion of the closure of the Golden Jubilee celebrations of Indian Independence, the Salar Jung Museum organised a two-day National Seminar on 'Concepts of New Museology & Challenges of 21st Century on 16th and 17th August, 98.

In order to deliberate on vital issues like development of infrastructural facilities and functional roles being faced by personnel engaged in the museum profession, 20 eminent scholars from leading National Institutions participated in the Seminar. The deliberations were a source of inspiration for the museum personnel in their functioning.

(iii) The Salarjung Museum organized a summer art camp to tap the inherent talent in children, college students and professionals. There was an overwhelming response to the press note and 100 students from various schools and colleges and professionals displayed keen enthusiasm in taking part in the Summer Art Camp. The children exhibited the paintings drawn by them. Prof. Kavita Deuskar, Head, Department of Paintings, Jawaharlal Nehru Technological University, Hyderabad and grand daughter of late R.W Deuskar, personal painter of late Salarjung III delivered a lecture on "Art in Education" and also drew a figure to inspire the students of the Summer Art Camp.

During the Summer Art Camp, the children were trained to draw in different mediums like crayons, oil pastels, water colours and oils. Some of the selected art works by the children were exhibited in the Salarjung Museum.

Training courses

i. The Salarjung Museum organized a short term orientation course covering the various aspects of upkeep and maintenance of the Museum for in service personnel from 20th to 31st July 1998.

ii. Officers were deputed to the IGNCA (Indira Gandhi National Centre for the Arts), New Delhi, from 5th to 7th October 1998 to attend a workshop on Interactive Computer Multi media Applications for Art and Cultural Heritage.

iii. A workshop on New Media Orientation was jointly organized by Orient Foundation of USA and INTACH (Conservation) at Sarnath from 5th to 7th October 1998.

iv. Monthly Gallery Talks were delivered on Indian sculptures; bronzes & painted textiles; Indian Textiles and Mughal Glass; Ivory Room; Arms Gallery; Metalware Gallery and European Glass by the officials of the Educational wing of the Museum.

Under planned school visits, 12,359 students accompanied by 1591 teachers from various education institutions visited the Museum and availed themselves of the facilities of the Museum. Fifty eight video films shows on art, archaeology, National Monuments, Important National personalities, freedom struggle and children's films were screened for the benefit of visitors.

The following publications were released during the period under report.

1. Memories of Great Personalities
2. A brochure on special exhibitions

Activities of the manuscripts section

S.No.	Activities	Number
(i)	Physically verified (Arabic, Persian and Urdu) Manuscripts	4606
(ii)	Number of scholars who visited the Section and consulted Arabic, Persian and Turkish Manuscripts	190
(iii)	Number of manuscripts fumigated and preserved	302
(iv)	Number of index cards xeroxed and xerox copies checked	700
(v)	Entries of Master ledgers of Persian, Arabic and Urdu MSS checked	2887
(vi)	Entries f Persian Manuscripts checked	602

Library

S.No.	Activities	Number
1.	Books acquisitioned and accessioned	132
2.	Catalogue Cards prepared	1560
3.	Books fumigated	505
4.	Books dusted, cleaned and preserved	25421
5.	Books bound	83
6.	Readers visited	393
7.	Books consulted	1111

Chemical conservation laboratory

Seven hundred and seventy four (774) objects including 7 oil paintings were chemically treated in the laboratory. The Section has also attended to the deacidification, lamination, repair and binding of manuscripts, books and records of office.

National museum institute of history of art, conservation and museology, New Delhi

The National Museum Institute of History of Art, Conservation and Museology New Delhi, is a Society registered under the Societies Registration Act XXI of 1860. It started functioning from January 1989. On the recommendation of the Universities Grant Commission the Institute was declared to be a 'Deemed University' on 28th, April, 1989 by the Department of Education, Ministry of Human Resource Development, New Delhi. The main thrust of its activities are focused on acquisition of teaching aids and soft ware (ii) setting up of a slide studio (iii) preparation of syllabus oriented video films (iv) awarding Fellowships/Scholarships and (v) conducting seminars and symposia.

The Institute conducts M.A. & Ph.D. Courses in three disciplines namely, (1) History of Art, (2) Conservation & Restoration of works of Art and (3) Museology. Three certificate courses on (a) Indian Art & Culture, (b) Art Appreciation and (c) Bhartiya Kala Nidhi are also conducted by the Institute. The Institute conducts Diploma/Certificate courses of one year and less than one year duration in areas like Museum Administration and Art Appreciation.

Teaching in the Institute is conducted through a semester system. Each semester is of four months duration, and there are two semesters in a year. (i) January to April (ii) July to October. The months in-between the two semesters, i.e. May-June and November-December are utilised for conducting written examinations, practicals, and paying visits to other museums.

Indian Museum, Calcutta

The Indian Museum, Calcutta, which was founded in 1814 is the oldest and largest institution of its kind in the country. It houses unique treasures of Indian and foreign art representing centuries of cultural ethos and traditions. The Museum has a vast repository of paintings, sculptures, bronzes, metals, coins, textiles and decorative art.

The Museum implements the following schemes:

a. Acquisition of antiquities, art objects, and ethnographic artifacts, through purchase field collection.
b. Reorganisation of Galleries and reserve collections of Art, Archaeology and Anthropology sections.
c. Strengthening of security arrangements.
d. Conservation of cultural property.

Exhibition

i. Terracottas of Bengal' on the occasion of the 84th anniversary of the Indian Museum (2nd February, 1998). Sri K.V. Raghunatha Reddy, Governor of West Bengal inaugurated the exhibition which included two hundred specimens of Terracotta art, both from Bangladesh and West Bengal.
ii. Kalighat Paintings from Gurusaday Museum, 1st - 7th April, 1998 was inaugurated by Dr. G. Gugielmino, Consul General of Italy in Calcutta.
iii. Structures of Indian Heritage, 18th May, 1998 from the collection of National Science Centre, New Delhi under interlinking of museum activities programme.
iv. Golden Books of Olden days, 9-26th June, inaugurated by Dr. A.R. Kidwai, the Governor of West Bengal.

v. Music and Musicians in India in the 17th, century, 27th-30th November, 1998, inaugurated by Dr. G. Gugielmino, Consul General of Italy in Calcutta.

vi. The Indus flows On from the collection of Archaeological Survey of India and Indian Museum is scheduled to be inaugurated by Dr. A.R. Kidwai, the Governor of West Bengal on 2nd February, 1999. This will continue till 15th February 1999.

Inter-state exhibitions

i. Panorama of Bengal Art at Salarjung Museum, Hyderabad, 14th-30th August, 1998, inaugurated by Prof. A.K. Bhatnagar, Vice-Chancellor, University of Hyderabad.

ii. Bengal Paintings from Bharat Kala Bhawan, Varanasi, 7th-21st August, 1998, inaugurated by Sri Chintamoni Kar.

International exhibition

i. Yogi & Buddha: Glimpses of Indus Valley Civilisation and the Life of Buddha at Kyongia in South Korea, 1st September - 10th November, 1998, inaugurated by Mr. Kim Dae Jung, President of the Republic of Korea.

ii. Treasures of Indian Art from Germany, 16th October - 15th November, 1998, inaugurated by Dr. A.R. Kidwai, Governor of West Bengal.

Participation in national and international exhibitions

i. Indian Museum sent three specimens of decorative jewellery to the National Museum, New Delhi, in connection with an exhibition in Italy in December, 1998.

ii. Indian Museum participated in an exhibition sending twenty replicas of Gandhara sculptures to Chandigarh Museum and Art Gallery in March, 1998.

Mobile exhibition

The Museum on Wheels displaying the theme of Man's creation and manifestation of Nature, visited educational and cultural organisations as well as village fairs in the districts of 24 Paraganas (both South & North), Howrah, Midnapore, Malda, Dinapur, Jalpaiguri, Bankura, and Burdwan in West Bengal, Varanasi and Sarnath in U.P.; Patna and Nalanda in Bihar, covering 5,318 kms. About two million students and the general public witnessed the mobile exhibition throughout the year.

The Mobile Conservation Laboratory is scheduled to be commissioned on road on 2nd February, 1999. During the first spell of the journey, it will cover Purulia, Bankura and Midnapore districts, of West Bengal, catering to the needs of conservation of the cultural heritage in the rural areas.

Seminars

i. International seminar on Art of Baked Clay from 2nd - 6th February, 1998.
ii. Treasures of Indian Monuments, on 18th May, 1998.
iii. Ustad Allauddin Khan - His life and works, on 6th September, 1998.
iv. Brazen Images on 13th November, 1998.

Annual lecture series:

v. Dr. Nathanial Wallich Memorial Lecture on Natyashastra, and the Karanas by Dr. Padma Subrahmanyam on 7th February, 1998.

Special lectures

i The Paintings from Lahore during the reign of Raja Ranjit Singh by Dr. Barbara Schmitz, U.S.A., on 1st April, 1998.
ii. Kalighat Paintings in U.S.A. collection by Dr. Jyotindra Jain, New Delhi on 1st April, 1998.

iii. Harikela Coins: Some New interpretations by Sri Vasant Chowdhury on 18th June, 1998.

iv. The concept and Iconography of Mahisamardni by Dr. B.N.Mukherjee on 23rd October, 1998.

Exhibitions

i. Central Asian Antiquities in January, 1998.

ii. People of North-East States in February -March, 1998.

iii. The Epic Heroes in May 1998 inaugurated by Dr. M.M. Joshi, Hon'ble Minister of Human Resource Development, Government of India.

iv. 'Gems of Bengal Art' inaugurated by Mr. Gaziul Haque, eminent freedom-fighter from Bangladesh, on 26th May, 1998.

v. The Meteorites in November-December, 1998.

Workshops

i. Conservation of Documentary Heritage: 5th-9th January, 1998 in collaboration with National Science Centre, New Delhi.

ii. A face to face with eminent citizens of Calcutta on Sponsorship for museums on 10th August, 1998.

iii. A two-day workshop on Techniques for preparing and re-evaluation of the visit of the museum conducted by Dr. Peter Rossler from Germany on 18-19th September, 1998 in collaboration with Max Mueller Bhavan, Calcutta.

iv. Mime by Indian Mime Theatre on 22nd October, 1998.

v. Classical music by Pt. V.G. Jog on 25th October, 1998.

vi. Manipuri Dance by Smt Kalavati Devi on 27th October, 1998.

vii. Terracotta pithwork by Ananta Malakar on 31st October, 1998.

viii. Scroll paintings by the Patuas of Midnapore on 1st November, 1998.

ix. Dinosaur Alive on 2nd November, 1998.

x. Puppet making by Dr. Sanat Kumar Mitra on 12th November, 1998.

xi. Conservation conducted by Mr. W. Porzezeinski. from Berlin on 15th November 1998.

Mass Communication Programmes

i. Gaudiya-Nritya organised in February, 1998.

ii. Basant Utsav on the occasion of Holi in collaboration with the Tourism Department, Government of India in March, 1998.

iii. A cultural programme of music and recital of poetry by artists from Bangladesh and India in May, 1998.

iv. Children's Day on 14th November, 1998: Documentary film on Museum of the Ghosts and Puppet show.

v. A concert of Italian Baroque Music by the Ensemble Stramantale Italino on 27th November, 1998.

vi. Korean Folk Dance Drama scheduled to be organised on 2nd February, 1999.

vii. Nautanki Dance performance by a cultural troupe from Varanasi on 3rd February 1999.

Special events

The Indian Museum hosted a month-long exhibition on Treasures of Indian Art from the collection of the Museum of Indian Art in Berlin, Germany in October - November 1998. A colourful cultural event and educational programme was arranged during the period which included dance, music, poetry - reading, workshop, lectures, seminars, film-shows and video-presentation.

The Museum celebrated its 185th anniversary. Programmes scheduled as a part of the celebrations included seminars, folk-festivals, lectures, etc. for a week beginning from 2nd February 1999. During the year, important publications will be released and some new projects will be undertaken.

The Corridor gallery on the first floor has be set up on the following themes (a) Animal motifs in Indian Art, (b) Plant motifs in Indian Art and (c) Tridhara-cult images of Hindu, Buddhist and Jain religions.

Allahabad museum, Allahabad

It was Pt. Jawaharlal Nehru who envisaged need to establish a museum in Allahabad as far back as 1923-24 when he was the vice-president of the Allahabad Municipal Board. The museum, however came into being in 1931, under the aegis of the Allahabad Municipal Board. It started taking shape since then, and in 1938 Jawaharlal Nehru donated most of his family assets, and the mementos of the freedom struggle to enrich the museum. Recognising its utility and service to the community Jawaharlal Nehru laid the foundation stone of its new building in Alfred Park (now renamed the Chandrashekhar Azad Park), after independence on 14th December 1947, and the museum moved into its new building in 1953.

However, the growth of the Museum came to a standstill due to paucity of funds, under the Allahabad Municipal Board. The elite of Allahabad approached the then Prime Minister, Smt. Indira Gandhi, and on her initiative and inspiration, the Government of India, recognising its status and invaluable art collection of national and international importance, agreed to take it into its fold to nurture for further development. Accordingly, it was declared an Institution of National Importance by the Government of India, Department of Culture, in October

1985. A 'Society' came into being under the Registration of Societies Act, 1860, in May 1986 to administer the activities of the Museum. It is full funded by the Government of India and a token grant of Rs. 5.36 lakhs is also given by the State Government.

Acquisition

The Art Purchase Committee of the Allahabad Museum Society met on 29th and 30th October 1998 and recommended purchase of various objects to fill up gaps in the collections of the Allahabad Museum.

Seminars/Colloquiums

i. A National Seminar on Vigyan Aur Sanskriti was organised under the Project Literary and Cultural History of Allahabad of the Allahabad Museum as a tribute to the explosion at Pokhran (Rajasthan). The seminar was inaugurated by Dr. Murli Manohar Joshi, the Hon'ble Minister of Human Resource Development and Science and Technology, Government of India and was presided over by Prof. Devendra Sharma.

ii. A two-day colloquium on Allahabad Mein Chitrakala was organised on September 9th - 10th, 1998. Shri Lakshmi Kant Verma, a noted litterateur, read his paper on the history of 'Various Facets of Paintings in Allahadad'

iii. On 2nd and 3rd December 1998, a National Seminar on Swatantra and Mulya Vimarsh was organised. The seminar was inaugurated by Prof. G.C. Pande, Chairman, Allahabad Museum Society. The proceedings of the seminar have been sent to the press to be published in the form of a monograph.

iv. A National Seminar on The Himalayan Glory was organised by the Museum on December 12th - 14th, 1998 which was inaugurated by Prof. G.C. Pande, Chairman, Allahabad Museum Society.

It was for the first time that a national seminar organised by the Allahabad Museum, invited views from various streams of study for a multifaceted approach to understand the Himalayan Glory.

Exhibitions

On the occasion of the National seminar on 'The Himalayan Glory' held on 12th-14th December, 1998, three exhibitions were organised.

i. An exhibition of photographs of glimpses of 53 Himalayan peaks by Shri Ashok Dilwali, New Delhi, a photographer of great repute, was organised in the Museum.

ii. Another exhibition of photographs of Himalayan mountain peaks and Buddhist Shrines was organised courtesy the Institute of Comparative Research Oslo, Norway. The photographs were taken by Dr. A.K. Singh, Reader of the Department of Fine Arts, BHU, Varanasi.

iii. Glimpses from the Himalayas consisting of 17 paintings of Prof. Manjula Chaturvedi, Head, Department of Fine Arts, M.G. Kashi Vidyapeeth, Varanasi was organised. This exhibition was kept on view for one month on public demand at the request of art students and art lovers.

Lectures

i. Prof. Manoj Das, an exponent of the Philosophy of Shri Aurobindo and a great litterateur in his own right, delivered a couple of lectures on 12th and 13th October 1998.

ii. Prof. Nand Kishore Devaraj spoke on 31st October 1998 on the world of Srijan-Parives.

iii. On 19th December 1998, Ms. Diana Dimitrova of Bulgaria spoke on Upendra Nath Ashq Ke Natak.

iv. Prof. G.C. Pande, Chairman, Allahabad Museum Society spoke on History as a dialogue between past and present on 9th January 1999.

v. On 24th January 1999, Prof. Ram Swarup Chaturvedi gave a talk on Sanskritik Upniveshvad aur Uske Pradooshan Ki Samasya.

Documentation

Numerous documents were collected shedding light on the literary and cultural history of Allahabad from Modem review, Journal of U.P. Political Society, Deshdoot, Stridarpan, Maryada, Khilona, Chand, Hans, Spabh, Harish Chandra, Abhyudaya and Saraswati to name a few. The scheme is continuing.

Transcription

Lectures delivered by Shri Srilal Shukla, Dr. Murli Manohar Joshi, the Hon'ble Minister of Human Resource Development and Science and Technology, Govt. of India, Shri Lakshmi Kant Verma, Shri Giriraj Kishore, Shri Nemi Chand Jain and Smt. Rekha Jain were transcribed for publication.

Workshops

A one-month workshop on Care and Maintenance of Museum, Library and Archival Material was organised by the Allahabad Museum from 7th October to 6th November 1998. Eminent scientists from the National Research Laboratory for Conservation of National Property, Lucknow and th National Museum Institute, New Delhi, took part in the workshop and gave demonstrations to participants. Local conservators also took keen interest in the event.

Children's week

The Museum celebrated Children's Week from 14" to 1911, November 1998. Important events of the week included Collage Competition, Painting Competition,

Elocution contest, Debate, Folk dance and Classical Dance Competition. Over 3,000 students from Allahabad and neighbouring areas participated in various programmes.

Special course

The classes, in P.G. Diploma in History of Indian Art, Culture and Tourism which commenced in the month of February 1998, concluded in January 1999. It is a one year P.G. Diploma Course in which over 150 lectures have been delivered covering various aspects of Indian art, culture and tourism. The course has been designed to facilitate students get suitable placements in Museums, other cultural organisations and in the tourism industry.

National research laboratory for conservation of cultural property, Lucknow

The National Research Laboratory for Conservation of Cultural Property (NRLC), a subordinate office of the Department of Culture, is scientific institution. The headquarters of NRLC is at Lucknow. The aims and objectives of NRLC are, to build up the conservation capabilities of the country. To meet the objectives, NRLC carries out research in materials and methods of conservation, imparts training in conservation and provides literature on conservation to conservators. NRLC also renders technical advice and assistance to museums, archives, archaeological departments an other similar institutions, in the conservation of cultural property. To render technical advice and conservation services to such institutions in the Southern region of the country, a regional centre c NRLC, the Regional Conservation Laboratory is functioning at Mysore since 1987.

NRLC maintains close collaboration with the International Centre for the study of the Preservation and Restoration of Cultural Property (ICCROM), Rome, and is represented at its Council for 1996-99.

The activities of the laboratory for 1998-99 are given in the following paragraphs:

Research

1. Development of a method for the Conservation of bronzes.
2. Development of a method to remove harmful salts from corroded iron objects.
3. Removal of stains on paper objects by using chelating agents.
4. Control of growth of algae and higher plants on monuments and historic buildings.
5. Use of homeopathic drugs in the control of fungal growth on paper and textiles.

Conservation

Following conservation works were completed.

Consolidation and cleaning of wall paintings (Approx. 200 sq. ft) of the Rang Mahal, Quila Androon, Patiala; 10 masterpiece bronzes of Tanjore Art Gallery; 8 stone sculptures, 6 thankas, 16 miniature paintings, 2 oil paintings and 1 pichhwai of the State Museum, Lucknow; 16 miniature paintings and 1 manuscript of the Ram Katha Sangrahalaya; preservative treatment of one Mandapa and cleaning of 1 big size ratha of the folklore museum of Mysore University.

Library and documenttation service

In addition to procurement of literature on conservation and their classification, cataloguing and accessioning, the following publications were brought out: for distribution to different conservation laboratories of the country.

1. Annotated Bibliography on Textile Conservation.
2. Annual Holdings of Journals on conservation (1997).
3. Abstracts of papers on conservation (1998).

Training

Under training activities of NRLC, the following 4 programmes were conducted:

Workshop on care and preservation of textiles

Handloom centres of the Ministry of Textiles, Government of India have exquisite collections of old textiles and textile designs on paper done by master weavers/artists of the past. These collections represent the designs and techniques of textile making in different parts of the country; many of which have now become rare. Thus these objects form a very important part of our cultural heritage. At the request of the NHDC, a one-week workshop on care and preservation of textiles was conducted at NRLC in November 1998 for the Zonal Directors and Directors of different centres. In all, 16 participants from different centres of the country, participated in the workshop.

Workshop on care and maintenance of Museum objects

A two week orientation workshop on care and maintenance of museum objects was organized at the NRLC in the first fortnight of August 1998 for curators and custodians of collections in museums, archives, archaeology departments, libraries etc. The workshop dealt with all aspects of preventive conservation and practical demonstrations were also given in relevant areas.

Six-month consrvation course

A six month training course in conservation of art/ archaeological objects and archival material was conducted at NRLC from September 1998 to February 1999, The course aims at training candidates on conservation of different types of art/ archaeological objects viz. metals, stone ceramics, paintings, archival material, textiles, wood, bone and ivory. The course was attended by participants from Bhutan, Bangladesh, Malaysia and 2 in-service Indian conservators.

Conservation of archaeological objeccts

A one week course was organized In June 1998 at the request of the Department of Ancient Indian History for the students of Diploma in Archaeology, wherein different aspects of conservation of archaeological objects and the precautions to be taken during excavations, were discussed.

Publications

The following research papers were published during the current year.

1. Efficacy of homeopathic drugs for the control of fungal growth on cellulose materials, fungi. Proc. ICBCP-4, Teheran (1998).
2. Influence of temperature and pH on the celluloytic activity of Ajanta, wall paintings fungi. Proc. ICBCP-4, Teheran (1998).
3. Fungal fouling of historical wall paintings, fungi. Proc. ICBCP-4, Teheran (1998).
4. Deterioration of cultural property by algae and fungi. Proc. ICBCP-4, Teheran (1998).
5. Effect of Zn-chelation on biocidal properties of benzohydroxamic acid. fungi. Proc. ICBCP-4, Teheran (1998).
6. Microbial deterioration of colour slides. Fungi. Proc. ICBCP-4, Teheran (1998).
7. Problems in the conservation of copper-lead coins. Conservation of Cultural Property in India (Communicated).

The Department of Culture operates a scheme for rendering financial assistance for Promotion and Strengthening of Regional and Local Museums. Details of the scheme are in below.

Scheme	Promotion & strengthening of Regional and Local Museums
Objective	To strengthen local and regional museums.
Applicable to	Voluntary organizations for setting up and strengthening regional and local museums for promotion of arts, textiles, crafts, antiques, numismatic, personal memorials, paintings and photographs, which are managed by voluntary institutions, Societies, Trusts, Colleges, Universities, Municipalities etc., excepting those directly managed by the Central or State Government.
Financial Assistance Provided/ period	Financial Assistance is given to the Institutions for construction of building minor extension, repairs to building and other allied requirement for maintaining and depicting the local culture including mini theatre auditorium as per requests and merit of each case. The grant for construction is given in the ratio of 3:2 i.e. 60% of estimated expenditure will be met by the Central Government and 40% by the Institution or the respective State Government. The grants for purchase of art objects / rare manuscripts is given in exceptional cases, in the ratio fixed in the case of building grant. ii) The Government has the discretion to consider a proposal / request from a regional or local museum whether the financial assistance can be provided on the lines of financial assistance to the

	voluntary institutions for setting up or creation of endowment funds for regional and local museums.
Number of beneficiaries during 1998-99	Financial assistance was granted to 19 museums located in different parts of the country.

5

Institutions of Anthropology and Ethnology

Anthropological survey of India

The Anthropological Survey of India, a scientific research organisation under the Department of Culture, was established in 1945 and from a very modest beginning, it has now earned a name as a premier organisation of anthropological research in the country. Over the last 52 years of glorious existence, the Survey has continued its commitment for research activities on the human population from bio-cultural perspectives with special attention to the weaker sections of the population. It has also engaged in activities like collection, preservation, maintenance, documentation and the study of ethnographic materials as well as of ancient human skeletal remains.

During the last 52 years, the activities of the Survey have expanded to a great extent, and to cope with the demands of research, seven regional centres, one sub-regional centre, one permanent field station and a number of other stations have been established in different parts of the country.

During the year 1998-99 the Survey has taken up four new research schemes and continued with the five old schemes of the 8th Plan period. Considering the scope and magnitude of the study, it was decided to continue the project Nutritional Status of Indian Population during the 9th Plan period. The findings of this study, made during the 8th Plan, was well appreciated by eminent nutrition scientists. During 1998-99, under this project, another four locations were studied, while studies continued in two other locations. The projects Study of Scheduled Castes : Structure and Transformation and Study of Health and Health Care Issues, initiated during the 8th Plan period could not be effectively implemented due to non-availability of adequate manpower. Another 8th Plan project, Urban Anthropology, initiated at the field station level was later on taken up for implementation with wider coverage and with the deployment of more scholars.

Nine workshops, including one field based workshop, were organized with the participation of all deployed scholars and the coordinators of each project, along with other senior scholars of the Survey to finalise the research formats, guidelines, schedules and work plans of the 9th Plan projects. Since then, all the necessary academic exercise and administrative work has been completed for launching the projects and a number of scholars have taken up their field investigations at different places.

The Survey during the 9th Plan, proposes to further develop laboratory facilities in order to facilitate advanced research on DNA Polymorphism. In its attempt to develop infrastructure, such as laboratory facilities and technical expertise the Survey negotiated with BARC (Bhabha Atomic Research Centre), Mumbai and an MOU was signed between the two organisations to strengthen academic collaboration.

The Survey continued its collaborative activities with the National Institute of Science, Technology and

Development, New Delhi, for preparation of reports on 'Boat typology and Fishing Communities : A contextual study, Bengal and Andaman'.

The Survey continued its programme of dissemination of information on the bio-cultural heritage of our people, through organization of exhibitions. The Survey took part in the Island Festival at Port Blair and Dassera festival at Jagdalpur and also organized a number of exhibitions at various places. It also collected several ethnographic specimens for enriching its Zonal Museums.

Publication of 'People of India' volumes remained an important programme. Two more State volumes one each on Rajasthan and Chandigarh were published. To commemorate the Golden Jubilee of Indian Independence the Survey, along with the nation, celebrated the event in an elegant and befitting manner. Two programmes of the Survey were approved by the Government of India for this occasion. An exhibition entitled 'Continuity of knowledge: Traditional Wisdom, Crafts and Craftsmanship' was organized at all the Regional/ Sub-regional Centres and at the Camp Offices of the Survey. The exhibition organized at Port Blair (A & N Islands) was visited by the Hon'ble President of India Shri K.R. Narayanan. The Survey has decided to bring out a special publication on the 'People of India'. A few scholars of the Survey have been engaged to finalize the same. The other publication, namely 'Social Institutions and Cultural Values of Indian Artisans', will be a collection of essays contributed by eminent scholars while the volume on 'Bio-cultural linkages among the populations of SAARC countries' will be prepared by the Survey's researchers on the basis of secondary source material. Work on all these publications continued and is expected to be completed soon.

The second Birsa Munda Award which was conferred on Mother Teresa, was handed over to the Missionaries of Charity in a solemn and graceful function specially arranged at the Mother House, Calcutta on 27th June, 1998. His Excellency, Governor of West Bengal Dr. A.R. Kidwai handed over the statue, a cheque of Rs. One lakh and a citation to Sister Nirmala. Dr. R.V.V. Ayyar , Secretary to the Government of India, Department of Culture, presided over the function.

Indira Gandhi Rashtriya Manav Sangrahalaya, Bhopal

The Indira Gandhi Rashtriya Manav Sangrahalaya which translates as the National Museum of Man (in the generic sense of all Mankind) was born as a public purpose institution in response to a resolution and request from the Anthropology section of the Indian Science Congress, Calcutta session in 1972, to the Prime Minister of the country, Mrs. Indira Gandhi. Though the Institution was set up as a small subordinate office of the Department of Education and Culture in 1977, in Delhi, the national capital, it started taking the shape of a Museum in 1979 when it was shifted to an open air site in Bhopal, the capital of Madhya Pradesh. However, it was only in 1985 when the Museum was converted from a subordinate office of the Department of Culture, Ministry of Human Resource Development, Government of India, into a Registered Autonomous Society, that it could formally get the allotment of the land earmarked, and start functioning with a clearly defined project plan for outdoor and indoor display and land use by 1987.

The Museum of Man was set up with a charter of objectives, which moved away from the traditional charter of Museums by defining its role in national integration, salvage and revitalisation of vanishing but valuable traditions, in promoting research and development, and, what was most important, in promoting a new Museum movement in the country. The charter did not exclude the conventional objective of the Museum, that is, of collection, storage and display of objects, but gave this objective a new dimension by insisting on the survey, documentation, preservation and presentation of the living patterns of culture in the background of the bio-cultural evolution of mankind, and by asserting a new notion of display with interpenetration of indoor and outdoor exhibitions. It has been designed to reverse the process of separation of man from nature, life from art, society from artist, form from function, to make art living and life artistic, to reunite shape with its meaning, to provide synoptic concepts, about the 'common area of resonances' among all men rather than mere taxonomic categories of knowledge, relevant to the needs of particular groups; to describe what we are, what is wrong with us now, and what new directions are necessary and possible.

With this novel charter, the Museum began primarily as an open air Museum in 197 acres (797 thousand square metres) of land, on undulating hills, on the seven mile long lake-front of Bhopal, Madhya Pradesh. The choice of the site itself was deliberate, intended to establish a hermeneutic circular dialogue through the Museum between the past, present and the future. After the site was chosen, the Museum immediately launched programmes and activities for building up a new kind of Museum with the direct participation of communities. The Museum staff fanned out all over the country, established direct contacts with about fifty communities, both folk and tribal, in different eco-climatic zones of coasts, deserts, hills, and river valleys, identified housing types and settlements, items of visual and performing arts, household appliances and subsistence technologies, which such communities wanted to be represented in the Museum, and invited them to the Museum to build and present the segment of the Museum, dedicated to the display of their cultures. Simultaneously the folklore, the rituals, the mythology, the songs, the dances and the chants, which were connected with such presentations in the living context among the communities were also enacted or performed in the Museum from time to time, to give sanction and meaning to display as a genuine activity, which fulfilled the norms set by the communities.

What distinguishes the Museum of Man at Bhopal from other open air Museums of the world is the fact that this museum considers itself as a dynamic instrument for preserving communities, their habitats, their bio-cultural diversities, their location specific bio-conservation strategies, their life enhancing knowledge and skills. It considers ex situ conservation through display or storage, collection and documentation as an unavoidable and evil necessity, and as a very insignificant contribution to its primary objective of in situ salvage and revitalisation. The Museum has been trying, therefore, through pilot projects on ethno-medicine, ethno-architecture, ethno-archaeology, ethno-biology, ethno-zoology, ethno-musiology and navigation, on water management systems, on sacred groves and precincts, on rich cultural and physical landscapes, to identify and highlight those elements of community lifeways in rural hinter lands, which can be adopted with advantage by urban communities, that have been cut off by the engulfing tide of homogenisation, technification. and industrialization. from the variety, complexity and flexibility of such life ways.

The Museum does not consider the past alone as its preserve, the Indian tribal or prehistoric man as its only concern, or the indigenous traditional knowledge systems as the only areas of its investigation. It has concerned itself seriously with issues of scientific research and investigation, hearing on community well-being, in ethno-sciences, interface between contemporary and traditional architecture, urban and country planning, in and ex situ preservation of germ-plasm in minor forest timber produce, including bamboo and rattan, viable patterns of water and physical resource sharing and their impact on cultural patterns in the Himalayan system, and measures to deal with ecological degradation. It has looked beyond the Indian frontiers and organized programmes to explore the identity and difference of Indian communities in the context of other communities of the globe, in South, South-East, Far-East and Central Asia, and even in Europe, among the Roma communities, which have migrated there carrying many facets of nomadic culture and language from India. It has participated in World Congresses on Archaeology, Ethno-biology, Musicology, Rock Art, Museography, Eco-tourism, Bio-diversity, Indigenous Knowledge systems and Cultural Diversity, Conservation, Globalisation and Translation, in order to establish common platforms for intra and intercommunity dialogue, technology transfer, and collaboration for community - regarding action, combining Ecology, Equity, Economics and Employment.

The museum has so far organized about 45 periodical exhibitions, 55 'do and learn' educational programmes, 100 craft demonstrations by tribal and folk master craftsmen, and organized around 140 presentations of folk, tribal and classical, visual and performing arts, about 65 museum popular lectures, 28 national and international seminars, symposiums, and about 25 field camps of artists as part of its Education Outreach and Salvage programmes. It has built up a collection of more than 11 thousand ethnographic specimens, 215 thousand slides, colour and black and white prints and negatives, 3 thousand hours of audio video recording, nearly 16 thousand books and journals, and made five 16 mm films through field documentation and collections. It has also developed open air exhibitions based on the tribal habitat, coastal, desert and Himalayan cultures and the rock art heritage. It has created infrastructure without any investment in buildings or staff, through inter institutional networking and contacts, for taking the museum to the doors of communities.

Programmes and activities carried out by the museum, during the year

Exhibitions

i) Tribal Habitat: The maintenance of exhibits situated in this open air exhibition continued. Programme were chalked out for massive upkeep of these exhibits by the respective tribal artisans related to the exhibition complex.

ii) Rock Art: Upkeep and maintenance of the rock shelter and improvisation of the house was carried out.

iii) Coastal Village and Desert Village: Besides the continuation of regular maintenance of the Coastal Village and Desert Village, repair of the traditional Rabari house was undertaken by calling artisans of the respective tribes from Kutch, Gujarat.

iv) Himalayan Village: Construction of a house type from Himachal Pradesh as an exhibit continued. The work is at its final stage and the exhibit is likely to be ready very soon.

v) Mythological Trail: Work for the development of this open air Delhi exhibition was continued during the year. Several objects and installations were made, and work for the identification of artisans in the remaining parts of the country continued.

Programmes for Celebration of the The 50th Year of Independence

The Museum of Mankind has organized a series of events for the preservation of local knowledge systems and deepening awareness about and strengthening the vitality of community traditions and knowledge systems in Kerala and Tamil Nadu, by organising a national workshop and exhibition on tribal medicine, in collaboration with the Kerala Institute for Research Training and Development Studies of Scheduled Castes and Scheduled Tribes (KIRTADS) at Calicut, with the participation of nearly 100 tribal medicine men from all over India. The workshop was attended by representatives from the Ministry of Welfare and from the Department of Indian System of Medicine, Government of India. The workshop was intensely participatory with tribal medicine men directly offering suggestions for documentation, popularisation, development, preservation and compensation of the tribal medicinal system. The participating tribal medicine men got together with legal experts, tribal rights spokesmen and representatives of different departments, looking after tribal interests, to evolve suggestions on research and training in tribal medicine, and for protecting the Intellectual Property Rights (IPR) of tribal communities. On the basis of the resolutions passed by the workshop, a committee was set up to compile the available regional, national and international legislation on IPR for medicine, based on organic forms, extracted by folk and tribal people.

The Museum also organized freedom celebrations in the North East in collaboration with the State Government of Tripura with programmes in three remote centres of Tripura among different tribal groups with workshops, cultural events and exhibitions focusing on the local literary traditions, scripted as well as unscripted, on visual and performing arts and crafts and skills and technologies specially in the area of water management.

6.17.04 In Tamil Nadu, the celebrations began with a three-day programme at Devakottal with the participation of about 1000 members of the Chettiar Community from remote villages of what is known as Nagrathar Nadu. A three day seminar on banking, trading, educational, cultural, spiritual, and the art & craft traditions of the Nagarathars (Chettiars) was accompanied by a workshop on Ethnic Cuisine and Kolam with the participation of 250 Nagrathar women. Through this programme, an attempt was made to look into the possibility of revitalisation of the monastic modes of education based on Sastras, Agamas, Kala and Sahitya, structured in ten disciplines. This was followed by a Tamil cultural festival entitled Mannin Maraboo. The programme began with a seminar on the performing art traditions, literary, ritualistic as well as oral traditions in Tamil Nadu. One more workshop was organized on indigenous metallurgy and metal casting traditions in Tamil Nadu, designated Ulogavival, in an attempt to explore the possibility of rediscovering the ancient manufacturing process of wootz steel for studying measures for technology upgradation of surviving iron smelters and for protecting their livelihood and intellectual property right.

Three other workshops were organized with performance, presentation, interpretation and documentation, entitled Adavu on drums and dramatic and ritualistic dance forms, Bombalatam on string and shadow puppets and Thottil on the prayer, invocation, music and ritual, accompanying the various Tamil rites of passage from birth to death. Along with this, an exhibition-cum-workshop called Izhaigal was organized on the best Kolam selected from workshops at Devakottai and Chennai as well as on the costumes and accessories used in performing arts.

The Freedom 50 celebrations culminated with a synoptic exhibition titled Sankshep on the various exhibitions, workshops, expeditions and cultural events organized by the museum at Bhopal and in different parts of the country in celebration of the autonomy and variety of community knowledge systems and traditions.

The final celebrations were dedicated to the very strong but neglected element of folk contributions to freedom lore. Two groups of freedom fighters, balladeers, reciters, musicians and scroll painters were invited from Bengal and Andhra Pradesh, to render Swaraj Geet, culled from the repertoire of songs about folk heroes and about burning contemporary issues, created by itinerant musicians, actively engaged in the freedom struggle through direct narrations by participants. This was performed in different venues in Bhopal city, among children as well as among citizens and was accompanied by documentation of rare archival material about the extremist movement from the Calcutta Police Archives.

Outreach and salvage programmes

As a part of the museum's Operation Salvage programme, regional workshops of resource persons were held in the districts of Burdwan, Bankura and Midnapur in West Bengal by the Centre for Social Research, Calcutta with museum assistance to launch documentation and collection of the evidence of the tangible and intangible culture of the village communities in these districts. Another workshop was organized by the Gobardanga Renaissance Institute at Gobardanga in North 24 Parganas in West Bengal to assess the socio-economic problems of the tribal inhabitants of Habrah and Gaighata blocks, and to work out an action plan for the alleviation of such problems. The programme was attended by West Bengal Government Officials.

As a part of the combined programme of Salvage and Museum Education and Outreach, a Sitar recital and lecture demonstration by the renowned maestro Ustad Usman Khan of Pune, was organized on two successive days under Poonam-18, to enrich the ethno-musicological archives of the Museum.

Collections of ethnographic specimens were made from the Oraons of Bihar, Saunas of Rajasthan, Muchis of A.P. and from Bundelkhand. Megaliths were surveyed and identified for collection and display in the museum by the Anthropology Department of Vishakhapatnarn University with museum assistance. The Curator of the Museum visited Tripura for meeting with the Chief Secretary and other officials to plan district wise programmes with local tribal communities under the aegis of the museum.

During the year, 659 objects have been collected from Andhra Pradesh, Gujarat, Himachal Pradesh, Orissa, Tamil Nadu, Madhya Pradesh, West Bengal, Rajasthan, Kashmir, Nagaland and Uttar Pradesh. These objects belong to different folk and tribal communities of the states. These objects were received and accessioned and categorised typo logically. Nearly 600 objects in the reserve collection were photographed, 8500 objects were digitally entered and 45 objects have been digitally documented during the year.

In fulfilment of the objectives of Salvage and Conservation of Community Knowledge Systems, the

(i) IGRMS collaborated with Eco-net, Pune to convene a meeting of about 80 traditional water managers from the local community at Bhandara (near Nagpur in Maharashtra), to discuss and compile the Traditional Water Management practices for the revitalization and recycling of a local water harvesting structure, as a pilot project, to be taken up by the community and the local administration.

(ii) The Museum also initiated a project on the IGRMS premises, in collaboration with the Regional Research Laboratory, Bhopal, on the analysis and upgradation of the Asur Iron Smelting Technology, by inviting the tribal Asur group from Bihar, and by working with them on the modification of their kiln building and smelting practices. Within a month, a considerably higher output had been achieved within the framework of the same technology. Simultaneously, a global search into the iron smelting patents, if any, is being conducted, to protect and patent the intellectual property of the smelter in any process improvement that may finally occur.

(iii) Work on the installation of a Himalayan hut, using 200 year old material, collected from an abandoned princely palace in Himachal Pradesh, was completed. Simultaneously, about 130 specimens of Himalayan culture were received and taken into the specimen store.

The Museum organized a Salvage field programme at Baripada in Mayurbhanj district of Orissa with the participation of five tribal groups of Orissa, with a demonstration of their life ways, rituals, arts and knowledge systems. This was accompanied by local workshops, organized with the help of the Department of Anthropology, Utkal University, and the District Administration, Mayurbhanj. The key-note address in this workshop was delivered by Dr. L.L. Mahapatra, the eminent anthropologist, and the workshop was steered by Dr. D.P. Pattanayak, the eminent linguist and member of the IGRMS Samiti.

As part of its Outreach Programme, the Museum organized a performance by the Mamta Shankar Ballet troupe and staged by Ms. Mamta Shankar, the daughter of Pt. Udaya Shankar, on the theme of enhancing awareness about the need of upgradation of the mental and physical environment in India. As part of the same programme, the Museum hosted three folk theatrical presentations on traditional and contemporary social issues, in the Chhatisgarh dialect directed by the renowned theatre artist Shri Habib Tanvir in its open air theatre.

Under its 'Do and Learn' museum education programme, the museum organized (i) a 2-week long demonstration-curn-training programme on the traditional Phulkari embroidery of Punjab and (ii) a 15-day long craft demonstration-curn-training workshop on the traditional textile jewellery of Kutch, Gujarat, attended by about 45 persons (iii) and another 15-day demonstration-cum-training programme on traditional pottery and terracotta art of Molela, Rajasthan.

The education programme for school children was carried out, in which children from various schools of Bhopal participated. These children visited the museum exhibitions in batches of 50 to 100 and were given exposure to the theme of man, habitat and environment. They were also given an opportunity for creative work on this theme through the media of clay modelling, drawing, etc.

Museum popular lectures

The museum organized popular lectures on themes relating to its aims and objectives. The lectures were designed for the dissemination of knowledge on various aspects relating to man-nature relationships, and on the survival of planet earth and its organic and inorganic community, of which the human community is an integral part. This year, some of the speakers who delivered lectures and the topics of their lectures.

S.No.	*Topic of the Name*	*lecture*
1.	Quaternary climatic change and Stone Age Cultures of India	Dr. S.N. Gupta
2.	Bio-diversity of the Past	Dr. K.N. Prasad
3.	Bio-Cultural Practices Relating to the Conservation of Bio-diversity and Bio-Resources	Dr. A.B. Balasubramaniyarn
4.	Glimpses of Material Culture of Tamil Nadu	Dr. L.Kannan

Computer Section

ISP-Dialup Internet service has been established, Library information is being computerised through the package LIBSYS and 12,000 records have been keyed. Abstracts, special booklets and other related publications were brought out on the various occasions and events taking place in the museum at Bhopal and other places. Compilation and Printing of Bibliographies on Water Management, River Valley Cultures and on the Himalayas was undertaken by the Computer Section of the museum. The unit was also engaged in preparing 12 publications which are in the final stage now and colour publications on Gypsies, Narmada Paleontology and Veena are ready for printing.

Photography section

Besides the photo documentation of the events organized by the museum in its premises at Bhopal and other places, the photography unit also contributed to mounting thematic periodical exhibitions by exposing and making enlargements of colour and black & white photographs on relevant themes. 1181 enlargements, 1140 transparencies, 1709 black & white photographs, 5495 colour prints of postcard size were developed by the unit during the year.

Artist camps

The museum organized 4 artists camps-cum-workshops

in its premises at Bhopal and other places like Devakottai and Chennai during the year entitled 'Dwipantari'. The museum also organized a supportive artist's camp in collaboration with SPIC-MACAY on the occasion of the 13th Annual convention of SPIC-MACAY. 6.22.02 Two camps were organized during the programme series at Tamil Nadu, one on traditional floor drawing and the other was on indigenous metallurgy and metal working tradition in Tamil Nadu.

Workkshop

A National workshop on Tribal Medicine was organized in collaboration with the Kerala Institute for Research Training and Development Studies of Scheduled Castes and Scheduled Tribes (KIRTADS) at Calicut with the participation of about 100 tribal medicine men from all over India. Workshops on Ethno-cuisine at Devakottai, Tamil Nadu; for exploring the geophysical and cultural aspects of the River Valley Cultures of India and the Physical & Cultural Ecology in North East India was organised in collaboration with the North East Hill University.

Graphic unit

The unit prepared designs for museum publications. The screen printing facility attached to this unit produced posters, greeting cards, invitation cards, banners and other materials for use during various programmes and activities.

Cultural programmes

1. Sitar recital and lecture demonstration of the renowned maestro, Ustad Usman Khan of Pune under Poonam 18.
2. Ritu Chakra: Classical Instrumental recital by Shivendra Kumar Dasgupta, Arun Morone, Praveen Shivlikar and Yedunandan Goswami.

3. Kamdeo Ka Apna Basant Ritu Ka Sapna: Shakespeare's "A Midsummer Night's Dream" in Chhattisgarhi - Hindi by the artists of Naya Theatre under the direction of renowned drama director Habib Tanveer.
4. Lok Raag-1, Lok Raag-2 :Cultural presentations from their culture/region by artists from India and South East Asian countries participating in the workshop, Dwipantari
5. Samanvaya: Hindustani classical vocal recital by Sajjan Lal Bhat, Ustad Abdul Latif Khan and Ramswarup Ratonia.
6. Swaraj Geet by two groups of folk performers from Bengal and Andhra Pradesh who rendered songs about folk heroes and their contribution to freedom lore by showing scroll painting, etc.
7. Nadu Utsav: The festival of rivers was performed by about 60 folk artists from Tamil Nadu, Himachal Pradesh and Orissa.
8. Milap: The museum organized a performance by the Mamta Shankar Ballet troupe and staged by Ms. Mamta Shankar, the daughter of Pt. Udaya Shankar, on the theme of enhancing awareness about the need for upgradation of the mental and physical environment in India.
9. The Museum also hosted 3 folk theatrical presentations on traditional and contemporary social issues, in Chhattisgarhi dialect, directed by Shri Habib Tanvir in its open air theatre.
10. On the occasion of the International Seminar on Shared Social Ecology of seven Himalayan areas, a programme of folk and tribal performances by artists from Himachal Pradesh, Nagaland, Manipur, Tripura, Uttar Pradesh and China were organized.

Dwipantari

An International exhibition-cum-workshop called Dwipantari was organised, with UNESCO help with the participation folk and tribal artists from South-East Asian countries like Brunei, Thailand, Malaysia, Indonesia, Myanmar, Vietnam, Philippines, Laos and Papua New Guinea in different arts and crafts including puppetry, pina-fibre and silk embroidery along with the approximately 140 folk and tribal artists from all over India in a variety of crafts including metal craft, lacquer, terracotta, puppetry, etc. This programme had been designed to explore the 'Realm of Mind and Tradition in the changing world' of India and South East Asia. It was accompanied by a series of cultural events with the participation of performing artists from India and abroad and of eminent dramatists and classical musicians from India. The programme received wide coverage and was extremely well attended. It helped in building up interaction among the artists involving an inter-regional transfer of knowledge and skills, and in assessing the problems coming in the way of preservation of many of these artistic forms in their pristine integrity. The folk and tribal artists have directly benefited from large scale sale of their products. This has partially helped the Museum to fulfill its objective of presenting Indian culture in the global perspective, specially in terms of the shared South and South East Asian heritage, and to plan its future cultural exchange, revitalisation and protection strategies.

Salila: Nadi Utsav

A multi pronged exercise was undertaken to explore the geophysical and cultural aspects of the river valley cultures of India, by organising an inter-disciplinary workshop, a field expedition, an exhibition and a festival on rivers. About 100 scholars, drawn from Geology,

Archaeology, Ecological Science, Hydrology, Folklore, Anthropology, History and Art History came together in a three day long workshop to look at the state of hydraulic civilisations that have developed on the banks of Indian rivers, to understand the cultural patterns, bio-cultural wealth, and risks shared by these civilisations, to assess the environmental impact of anthropogenic interventions in the course of rivers, and to take stock of the equity and efficiency in the management of rivers. A GSI data base was developed by the IGRMS with the help of ISRO on this occasion to offer a three dimensional cartographic mosaic, based on satellite images of the entire length of the Narmada River basin. A demonstration was also mounted on this occasion with the help of Deccan College, Pune, for survey and documentation of deltaic plains and cultures through low altitude, aerial reconnaissance photography, using unmanned remote controlled aero models. Techniques for analysis of geochronology, stratigraphy, palaeo climatic history and flood history for river valley cultures were discussed and demonstrated. The three day workshop was followed by an inter disciplinary field visit in the Betwa source region, with a scientific field guide. The workshop was accompanied by an exhibition, designated Salila, on the river valley cultures of India, using photographs and specimens from the subsistence technologies, cultural practices and folk ways of human communities, living on the banks of rivers. A further component was a festival of rivers, performed by about 60 artists, drawn from Tamil Nadu, Himachal Pradesh and Orissa.

Himalaya bandhav

An international event, designated Himalaya Bandhav, on the Shared Social Ecology of the seven Himalayan countries, namely, Bangladesh, Bhutan, China, Myanmar,

Nepal, Pakistan and India, was held in the Museum. The event comprised a three day seminar, attended by nearly 125 delegates from India and abroad. It was accompanied by cultural performances on all the three days with the participation of about 125 performing artists, including Tripuris from Tripura, Konyak Nagas from Nagaland, Jagoi Marup tribal troupes from Manipur, Lamas from Tabo Monastery in Himachal Pradesh, Jaunsari tribals from Garhwal Hills in U.P., and artists and students from China. Simultaneously, an exhibition titled "Sanjhi Virasat" was mounted on the Shared Himalayan Heritage in three segments, namely, (i) the Shared Environment, (ii) Human Adaptation, and (iii) Creative Bounty. The exhibition included contributions of photographs and other audio-video material from the RRSC, Nagpur, Officers of the GSI, international delegates, field photographers in the Himalayas and the archives and collections of the IGRMS. The event was followed by a field visit of the delegates to Sanchi and surrounding areas.

The conclusions that emerged out of the cross disciplinary deliberations was the need for transborder collaboration among these countries for regulating the unequal, proto colonial flow of knowledge, resources and skills, from the hills to the plains, looking into the interests of local state holders, as custodians of eco specific land races, herbal, medicinal and food plants, water management systems, subsistence technologies, settlement patterns and conservation approaches. The Himalayas was perceived as one of the last surviving islands of geophysical and bio-cultural diversity, which had to be protected by inter community and international collaboration, in the interest of human survival.

Attention was drawn to the Alpine convention signed in 1992 among seven European countries on tourism, traffic, nature protection, mountain farming and forestry as a possible model. The need to recognise the collective IPR for the mountain communities in terms of the UN Economic and Social Council Convention and the 1989 ILO Convention 169 was stressed as against the accent on individual IPR in the GATT-TRIPS regime. The need was emphasised to move away from centralised approaches of planning, for decentralised management and banking practices, in harmony with the location specific needs and skills of the remote communities of the Himalayas.

Apart from these material considerations, there was a common recollection of the incessant movement of traders, pilgrims, artists, craftsmen, itinerant story tellers and balladeers across the Himalayas as also of the corpus of motifs, patterns, ideas and nuances, shared by the monastic and housing architecture, rituals, languages and scripts of art and creative expression in all these countries. The common idea was stressed, of the Himalayan mountains as the body and house of God, inspiring the architecture of the imperial palace at Beijing, the Pagodas, Stupas, Chhortens, Gompas in Burma, Tibet, Bhutan, China and India. The need was felt, to work together for unravelling the layering of Chinese, Tibetan, Newari, Gupta and Karkota, styles in Himalayan arts, and to differentiate the influence of pre Buddhistic, Shamanistic, Bonpo, Shaivite faith from the impact of the Hinayana, Mahayana, and Vajrayana varieties of Buddhism, and from the influence of the devotional Bhakti cults or Daoism, Taoism and Confucianism.

The event culminated in a discussion of the Director with the international delegates for setting up a platform for introducing transactional R&D initiatives, in the Himalayas using IGRMS as a resource base, in view of the fact that the movements of water, soil, weather, life and strategies for dealing with shared risks and conserving the shared heritage, transcending national boundaries. The valedictory session was a business session, involving both Indian and international youth and scholars drawn from various disciplines.

Infrastructure development

The museum has gone out this year to remote hill and forest based communities of India to celebrate the idea of freedom expressed in the autonomy, variety and complexity of their identity in their own habitats.

It has brought together, on one platform, traditional artists and practitioners of knowledge systems, including medicine men, to ensure an intra and inter-regional transfer of knowledge and technology. It has worked for the upgradation of such knowledge and technology, within their own eco-specific parameters, and for raising awareness about the collective nature of IPR in these areas. It has presented India in the global perspective, by introducing a dialogue between Indian communities of artists and scholars from India and other countries in the Himalayas and South-East Asia.

Finally, it has tried to use the museum to decolonise the museum movement, taking the museum out of itself to the doors of the people, who curate the living museum of the bio-cultural variety in our country.

6

Archives & Archival Libraries

National archives of India

The National Archives of India (NAI), an attached office under the Department of Culture, houses Central Government records of enduring value for permanent preservation and use by administrators and scholars. It has in its custody, private papers of eminent personalities of India and microfilm copies of records acquired from abroad. During 1998-99, regular programmes of the National Archives of India, viz. assisting various Ministries/ Departments of the Government of India in their record management programmes, extending research facilities to scholars visiting the archives from all over India and abroad and providing financial assistance to various voluntary organisations for the preservation of manuscripts in their custody as also to State/Union Territory Administration Archives for their development programmes, etc. were carried out. It also continued to tender guidance to various Government Departments, voluntary institutions and individuals regarding technical know-how for preservation of valuable records and papers.

The School of Archival Studies imparted training under its One Year Diploma in Archival Studies and various short-term courses to Indian and foreign trainees. As a part of its programme of creating archival awareness amongst the people, an Archival Museum was established and various exhibitions were organized. The Conservation Research Laboratory conducted investigations for improvement of preservation techniques for better upkeep of records and was actively associated with the dissemination of knowledge of specialised nature in the field of conservation of documentary heritage. The National Archives of India has one Regional Office at Bhopal, and three Record Centres at Bhubaneswar jaipur and Pondicherry.

Accession

The holdings of the Department were further enriched by the acquisition of the following public/ private records.

Public records

4,348 files (1920-1963) of the Ministry of Communications, Department Posts, and Kashmir.

75 files (1922-1945) of the Controller of Defence Accounts, Pune.

2928 files (1916-1965) of the Office of the Commissioner of Central Excise, Chennai.

Private papers

Two volumes containing the transcripts of the trial of Udham Singh, who was tried and convicted of the murder of Michael Francis O' Dwyer in London.

15 letters written by Sri Yashpal Kapoor, ex-Member of Parliament, to his wife during his tour of Allahabad, Bangalore, Shillong, etc. (1956-64).

22 printed photographs of Viceroy Lord Willingdon and Lord Linlithgow and the Raja of Saurashtra in the form of a booklet (1871-1948).

25 items and 48 photographs received from Chaudhury Ranbir Singh relating to the freedom movement, Constituent Assembly etc. (18981990).

One L.P. record and cassetee entitled 'vocie of Rajaji' on the subjects 'World Government' and 'God-fearing Life'.

4 microfilm rolls (premier series 2, 3, 11 (1928-56) relating to Chinese troops for Burma and India, a record of the conversation between Lord Swinton and Jawaharlal Nehru and Krishna Menon's visit to U.K. have been purchased from the Public Record Office, London.

2 microfilm rolls 'Defence - 5' relating to the American proposal to accelerate evacuation of the united Nations Security Force and Australian liaison with British Defence Committee in south East Asia have been purchased from the public Record Office, London.

1 microfilm roll (dominion Office-35) relating to the discussions in the United Nations on the treatment of the Indian Community in South Africa was purchased from the Public Record Office, London.

302 files of Late shri Phool Chand Jain's Papers (1900-1947) and (1985-1992), relating to jails, Indian States, Quit India Movement, Bio data of Freedom Fighters, etc.

Research and reference

Three thousand two hundred & nine (3,209) visits were made by scholars to the Research Room of the Department. 267 scholars were newly enrolled of which 33 were foreign scholars. 16,927 requisitions for records, maps and books received from scholars were attended to.

Records management

24,360 files have been appraised pertaining to various Departments/Offices located in New Delhi and Hyderabad which include Ministry of External Affairs (1966-1973), Archaeological Survey of India (1909-1974) and Office of the Commissioner, Central Excise (1958-1972). Out of these, 12,615 files were recommended for permanent retention.

The Departmental Record Rooms of 5 Ministries/ Departments have been inspected which include President's Secretariat, Ministries of Industry, Steel and Coal, Departments of Food and Expenditure and the National Archives of India.

327 Ministries/Departments/Attached and Subordinate Offices/Public Sector Undertakings of the Government of India have so far nominated DRO's (Departmental Record Officers) in their organisations.

Twenty one (21) Departmental Record Officers from various Ministries/Departments/Offices and Public Sector Undertakings of the Government of India participated in the five day orientation course on Records Management (7th September to 11 th September, 1998) and 18 Departmental Record Officers participated in the second five-day orientation course (26th October to 30th October, 1998).

Study Reports along with the vetted Record Retention Schedules were prepared and forwarded to the following Departments for implementation:

1) Department of Post

II) Coaching cum Guidance Centre for SC'ss/ST'ss.

III) Indian Government Mint, Mumbai and NOIDA, UP.

On the spot study for vetting the Records Retention Schedules of the following Directorates of the Quarter Master General Branch (QMG) of the Army Headquarters, New Delhi was completed and their reports are under preparation.

i) Directorate of Coordination of Quarter Master

General Branch

ii) Directorate of Operations and Logistics of Quarter Master General Branch

iii) Directorate of Land Works and Environment of Quarter Master General Branch

iv) Directorate of Supply of Transport of Quarter Master General Branch.

v) Directorate of Movements of Quarter Master General Branch

vi) Directorate of Technical Examinations of Quarter Master General Branch.

vii) Directorate of Military Farms of Quarter Master General Branch

viii) Directorate of Pioneers of Quarter Master General Branch

ix) Directorate of Army Postal Services of Quarter Master General Branch.

x) Directorate of Canteen Services of Quarter Master General Branch

xi) Directorate of Remount and Veterinary of Quarter Master General Branch.

School of archival studies

The School of Archival Studies continued to conduct the One year Diploma Course in Archival Studies as also various short-term courses of eight and four weeks duration for the benefit of professionals and sub-professionals. Details of the courses are as follows:

(a) 10 trainees successfully completed the One Year Diploma Course in Archival Studies (1997-1998) while the 1998-1999 session of the Diploma Course in Archival Studies commenced on lst September, 1998.

(b) 5 short term courses, viz. Reprography

(2 courses), one from Ist April-26th May, 1998, second from 7th September-29th October 1998, Records Management (Ist May-29th May, 1998), Servicing and Repair of Records (2 courses, 4th May-26th june 1998) and (7th September - 30th October, 1998), Care and Conservation of Books, Manuscripts and Archives (6thjuly-28th August 1998 and 2nd Nov. 199824th Dec. 1998).

Workshop

A two-day workshop on'Towards a new era of Archival Studies'was organised on 17th and 18th November, 1998. The workshop was attended by 25 delegates from various State Archives/Universities and individual scholars. The workshop was inaugurated by Dr. R.VVaidyanatha Ayyar, Secretary, Department of Culture.

Exhibitions/Museum

On the occasion of the 50th year of India's Independence, an Archival Museum has been established in the premises of the archives to make people aware of the documentary heritage which the National Archives of India preserves for the present generation and for posterity. The Museum was formally declared open by Shri K.R. Narayanan, Hon'ble President of India on 6thjuly, 1998 in the presence of eminent personalities like Shri R. Venkataraman, former President of India, Dr. Karan Singh, Shri G.V.G. Krishnamoorthy, Election Commissioner, and representatives from diplomatic missions and freedom fighters.

An exhibition on 'Shri Chakravarti Rajagopalachari: First Indian Governor General' was inaugurated by Shri K.R. Narayanan, Hon'ble President of India on 6thjuly 1998. This coincided with the 50 years of the assumption of the office of the Governor General by Rajaji. The inaugural function was attended by Shri Raj Mohan Gandhi, grandson of Rajaji, Smt. Sukanya Bharatram, great grand daughter of Rajaji, Shri S.K.Singh, former Foreign Secretary, Shri M.K.Rasgotra, former Foreign Secretary and many freedom fighters.

A visual display entitled In Their Memory' highlighting the role of unknown and unsung freedom fighters was organized and opened to the public from 17th August, 1998. It also portrayed the popular literature and poems which were banned by the British Raj. This display was organized to mark the completion of 50 years of India's Independence. Photographs collected from old Intelligence records, the sacred soil from the cremation site of martyrs Bhagat Singh, Rajguru, and Sukhdev, collected by the mother of martur Sukhdev; Golden Scroll of the speech "'Ilryst with Destiny" and memorabilia relating to our freedom movement were some of the significant items of the display.

An exhibition on Andhra Kesari Tanguturi Prakasam was mounted in the premises from 2nd November, 1998 to 14th November, 1998. The exhibition, comprising of numerous original records, rare and contemporary photographs of Andhra Kesari Tangutqd Prakasam both as freedom fighter and First Chief Minister of Andhra Pradesh, was formally declared open by Shri Bandaru Dattatreya, Hon'ble Union Minister of State for Urban Development and Employment, in the presence of Shri G.V.G. Krishnamoorthy, Election commissioner and Dr. R.VVaidyanatha Ayyar, Secretary, Department of Culture, Government of India.

Towards freedom project

A total of 247 pages from the files of the Nizam's Government (1951) received from Andhra Pradesh State Archives, Hyderabad were sent to Indian Council of

Historical Research, New Delhi for inclusion in the proposed volume Towards Freedom Project.

Publications

The following volumes were published by the National Archives of India during the year 1998:

1. The Indian Archives, Volume XLIV, XXLV, Nos. 1-3, Jan.-Dec. 1995-1996. Nos. 1-2 January-December 1995)
2. Bulletin of Research Thesis and Dissertations, Volume 17
3. Azadi Ki Goonj (Gurmukhi).
4. Netaji Samsamaik Sakshi (Hindi)
5. Lahuluhan Vaisakhi (Hindi version)

Technical Services

Apart from providing technical information on conservation and reprography to government/ private institutions and individuals, a total number of 75,971 sheets were repaired and 4242 volumes/ books/ miscellaneous items were bound. Leather preservative mixture was also applied to 4132 volumes. Besides 1,00,493 xerox/photocopies of documents and 14,537 metres of positive printing were also prepared.

Security microfilming

Under the ongoing programme of security microfilming, the Department is engaged in microfilming important series of records housed in its repository with a view to providing security to the original records. In this connection 3,60,000 exposures were prepared.

Meetings (national)

The first meeting of the Group constituted by the Government of India for identification of rare manuscripts of national and international value was held under the chairmanship of Dr. S. Sarkar, Director General of Archives on 24th April 1998 at National Archives of India.

Dr. S. Sarkar, Director General of Archives participated in a meeting of the National Mission on Manuscripts on 29th August 1998 held under the Chairmanship of Secretary (Culture) in National Archives of India, Annexe Building. The meeting was also attended by Shri H.D. Singh, Dr. T.V. Haranatha Babu, Shri Shitla Prasad, Shri Raghunath Meena, Deputy Directors of Archives and Dr. S. Sengupta, Officer on Special Duty.

A meeting of Committee of Secretaries was held on l7th June 1998 in the Cabinet Secretariat to discuss declassification, computerisation and proper storage of records. The meeting was attended by the Secretary, Department of Culture, besides the Director General, National Archives of India.

Dr. R.P. Malik, Assistant Director of Archives was deputed to attend a meeting at the Central Council for Research in Ayurveda and Siddha, New Delhi on 20-8-1998 to offer advice on preparation of project for preservation of manuscripts.

Sri A. R. Singh, Assistant Library and Information Officer was deputed to attend a 5-week short term training course on Computer applications to Library and Information Activities, organised by Indian National Scientific Documentation Centre, INSDOC, New Delhi w.e.f. 24th August 1998.

International relations

Director General of Archives was deputed to Singapore to attend the 30' Anniversary Celebrations of Singapore Archives and delivered a keynote lecture at a seminar on 'Role of the Archives in the 21st Century' at the National

Archives of Singapore from 29th April to 4th May 1998.

Deputations

(I) On the invitation of the International Records Management Trust, London, the Deputy Director of Archives was deputed to attend an International Seminar on "The 'Transition to Electronic Records as a Strategic Resource" and "Accountability in Government in an Electronic Age" at Kuala Lumpur (Malaysia) from 22nd-26th June, 1998 along with the Director (Library), Department of Culture and the Curator of Bhandarkar Oriental Research Institute, Pune.

(II) The Officer on Special Duty was deputed to attend the I st Regional Committee Meeting for the Memory of the World Programme, in Asia Pacific held in Beijing, China from 17th-21st November, 1998.

Visitors

A number of visitors came to the Archives for discussions with the Director General of Archives.

i. Mr. Hong King Young, High Commissioner of Singapore in India on 20.4. 1998.

ii. Mrs. Narissa Ramdhani, Director, African National Congress Archives, South Africa on 10.6.1998.

iii. Former Home Secretary, Government of India on 22.7. 1998.

iv. Prof. Takoshi Fujii of Tokyo University of Foreign Studies and Mr. Shusaku Matsumoto from Institute of Developing Economics, Tokyo on 78.1998.

v. Representative of Konrad Adenauer Foundation (Germany) in India on 8.9.1998.

vi. Head of Cultural affairs, Press and Information Royal Netherlands Embassy, New Delhi visited this

Department on 8 November, 1998 for discussions with Director General of Archives.

Khuda Baksh oriental public library, Panta

An illustrious son of Bihar, an advocate by profession and a bibliophile by taste, Khuda Baksh Khan, established a "Public Library" in 1891 out of his family collection of manuscripts. He further added a number of manuscripts through his own resource, and, by a Deed of Trust~ donated his entire collection to the public in the same year. That Library, now known the world over as the Khuda Baksh Oriental Public library, has emerged to be one of the richest collections of manuscripts in the sub-continent with over 18,000 manuscripts, 1,80,000 printed books and over 2000 original paintings of the Mughal, Rajput, Iranian and Turkish schools. The Library also possesses a sizeable number of original letters of eminent persons written during their lifetime. It is now managed by a Board headed by the Governor of Bihar. By an Act of Parliament, it was declared in 1969 to be an Institution of National Importance and the Government of India took over its control the same year.

Acquisition

Acquisition of manuscripts and books through purchase, exchange, gifts is a continuing feature of the Library. Concerted efforts to acquire manuscripts have been paying dividends. During the period April - September 1998, the Library has acquired 2520 books and manuscripts by purchase/gift/exchange. However, by the end of the financial year it will be able to add more than 5000 books to its collection.

The Library has a scheme of acquiring copies of rare manuscripts available in other collections. So far collections of Aligarh, Rampur, Bhagalpur, Maher,

Phulwari sharif, Asafiya (Hyderabad) and Asiatic Society (Calcutta) have been covered. The British collection of India Office and Cambridge have also been covered by acquiring microfilms of the choicest manuscripts. The Library had acquired 26 manuscripts by November, 1998. It is expected that 50 manuscripts will be acquired by the end of the financial year.

Presentation of living eminent persons

A separate collection of audio and video tapes is being built up to record and preserve literary celebrities and eminent persons of the composite culture of India. More than 932 audio and 615 video tapes of eminent persons have been acquired which - along with preservation and dissemination of the written word - would be one of the finest gifts to posterity in the form of -original records of persons of eminence while they were actually alive. During the period April - November 1998, the Library added to its collection, 62 Audio and Video Cassettes.

It is hoped that through its non-conventional and multidimensional devices, the Library would serve as a model in the preservation and dissemination of knowledge.

Preservation of manuscripts & rare material

The Library is engaged in the preservation and dissemination of knowledge along with the acquisition of valuable national heritage in the form of manuscripts in particular and books in general. With the help of trained hands and binding, the manuscripts and rare books are being given a new and lasting life through chemical treatment, lamination, necessary repairs and binding. This is done in our preservation laboratory, which is being developed on modem lines.

Restoration activities of the library

Manuscripts / Books fumigated	1384
Folios of manuscripts deacidified	1132

Palm Leaves deacidified	490
Folios of Books deacidified	3173
Folios of Books laminated and	3457
manuscripts repaired and bound	1462

In respect of preservation, the Library is also extending its cooperation to other collections as well so that the precious heritage of manuscripts and rarities is saved from decay.

Indexing and documentation

The entire periodical collection of the Library, old and new, is being indexed to provide microinformation to scholars.

Lectures/Talks/symposia

Annual/extension lectures, talks and symposia are held regularly wherein eminent scholars are invited to deliver lectures and present their papers This is the easiest means of imparting knowledge in a crucible; a big chunk within a short span. These lectures, the substance of life long study and experiences, are being published regularly. During the period, April-November, 1998, the following lectures were delivered:

(1) "Urdu Poetry in Post Independence Pakistan" by Prof. Aftab Husain Shah, Lahore;

(2) "Indian Woman" by Dr. Sayeda Sayyedain, Member, National Commission for Women;

(3) "Economic Problems of Muslims in Post Independence India" by Prof. Fazlur Rahman Faridi, Aligarh;

(4) "How should we prepare ourselves for the 21st Century" by Mr. Saiyid Hamid, former Vice Chancellor, Aligarh Muslim University.

Reference service

Besides its regular routine-services to book borrowers, the

Library is providing reference facilities widely to scholars round the globe by supplying required information, in the form of trancribed copies and microfilms. During the period April 1998 - November 1998 the Library rendered the following services:

Services rendered by the Library	*No.*
Reference provided on the spot	4207
Reference provided by correspondence	1609
Queries replied on phone	2560
Xerox copies of printed books exposures	4123
Microfilm copies of manuscripts exposures	25
Reference provided about manuscripts	838

Khudabaksh research fellowships

To accelerate the speed of research, 1 National, 2 Visiting, 3 Senior and 7 junior Fellowships have been created on the pattern of the UGC to work on the hidden store of knowledge as speedily as possible. These Fellowships are offered for doing independent research or for research leading to the award of Ph.D./D.Lit. Degrees. Kashmir University, Gulbarga University, Jamia Millia Islamia, Magadh University, Bihar University and Santiniketan have recognised the Library as their Research Centre.

Research and publications

Critical edition and publication of the rarities of the Library have been taken up and a number of rarities have been critically edited and published * The Library's programme of bringing out rare and important printed books/periodicals is continuing. During the period April-November 1998, 22 such publications have been brought out.

Descriptive catalogue of manuscripts

To facilitate availability of the material, the Library has

been descriptively cataloguing its entire collection of manuscripts. Thirty-six volumes of descriptive catalogues of the manuscripts which were out of stock were re-printed during the last few years. This covers only 60% of the manuscripts collection. Efforts are being made to prepare and publish the descriptive catalogues of the remaining manuscripts.

Khudabaksh library journal

The Library's quarterly Research journal, containing research articles is yet another effort to introduce the material to the scholarly world of knowledge. One hundred and thirteen issues of the journal have been brought out so far.

Translation of significant books

Literature plays a significant role in effecting the concept of national integration. The Library is, therefore, working on a scheme to translate outstanding pieces of literature of Hindi and other regional languages into Urdu and of Urdu into Hindi. Award winning books have been taken up first; and the translated versions of the Sahitya Akademi Award winning Kashmiri book "Kante" has been published. Some other significant books/ manuscripts such as Shamsul Bayan (Hindi Dictionary of Shah Alain's period, and the first Hindi dictionary produced at the instance of Aufangzeb) and Aurangzeb Naya Zaviya - ENazar, Pandit Motilal Nehru Ka Udghatan Bhashan, have been published. The Urdu translation of the book on Bi Amma (mother of Ali brothers) is in progress.

Award for outstanding contributions

The Library has also instituted an Award to be given to scholars for outstanding research contributions in the Library's special fields of Arabic/Persian/Urdu/Islamic Studies/Tibb/South Asian Studies/West Asian Studies/

Central Asian Studies/ Comparative Religion/Sufism/ Composite Culture of India. The awards are on the pattern of the ones instituted by the Sahitya Akademi and Jnanpith Award and carries a cash award of Rs.1,00,000/-.

So far three Awards have been conferred. The first Khuda Baksh Award was conferred on Mr. B.N. Pande for his outstanding services in the field of National Integration, the second and third Awards were conferred on Mr. Anwer Jamal Kidwai (posthumous) and Mrs. Subhadra Joshi for their contributions to the Composite Culture of India and National Integration, respectively.

Other activities

The Library chalked out various programmes for commemorating 50 years of India's Independence. The first programme, an exhibition of material on Freedom Movement preserved in the Library was held from 17th August to 26th August 1997 The exhibition got a very good response as a large number of persons from all walks of life visited the exhibition.

An Indo-Pak Mushaira was held on 9th May, 1998 at Patna wherein renowned poets of the sub-continent participated. Besides, a Kavi Sammelan was also held on 28th November 1998.

A National Seminar was also held at New Delhi from 29th August to 31st August 1998 in collaboration with Jamia Haindard. The subject of the Seminar was "Free India : Retrospect and Prospects." In the series of lectures, three lectures were delivered by Mr. Saiyid Hamid, Dr. Saiyeda Saiyedain and Mr. Sardar Ali respectively.

The Library established a full-fledged Computer Centre with Internet and LAN facilities.

The Centre is to be inaugurated by H.E., the Governor of Bihar shortly.

Rampur Raza Library, Rampur

The Library is renowned all over the world and is considered to be a highly valued treasure house of thousands of rare manuscripts, miniature paintings, illustrated manuscripts, specimens of great calligraphers of the Islamic world, historical documents, letters, printed books, newspapers and periodicals.

The library was taken over by the Government of India on I st July 1975, through an Act passed by Parliament declaring it an institution of National importance. It is managed by an Executive Board, presided over by the Governor of Uttar Pradesh.

The Library is a centre for Indo Islamic studies as it is a repository of classical and modern source material in Arabic, Persian, Sanskrit, Tamil, Telugu, Hindi, Urdu, Turkish and English.

Collection

The Library has a valuable collection of 15,041 manuscripts of books, farmans and historical documents, 5,255 printed books, 1068 paintings and 205 palm leaf manuscripts. It consists of authentic, academic work in many classical oriental languages namely Arabic, Persian, Sanskrit, Hindi, Urdu, Tamil, Push to and Turkish.

New acquisitions and binding

During the period under review, 846 new books on various subjects were acquired. The one hundred and seven historically important antiquities and art objects namely paintings, manuscripts, specimens of Islamic calligraphy, terra-cotta statues and 241 rare coins of gold, silver, copper and bullion have been added to the collection.

Among the rare acquisitions mention may be made of one decorated coloured beautiful glass jar, with the portrait of Qajar, King of Iran, one ivory female figure of 18th - 19th Century A.D., one specimen of Islamic calligraphy of Muhammad Hussain AM dated A.H. 1162 (1748-49 AD) original architectural drawings and maps of Rampur. The most striking object is a rare gold coin of Shahjahan struck at Shahjahanabad (Delhi) mint of 32nd regnal year, A.H. 1068 (1657-1658) a date which also occurs on the coins of Aurangazeb.

The binding of books including journals and newspapers totalling 700 were carried out as a regular work of the Library. In addition, the binders also attended to the work of binding the Library's registers, Annual Reports, etc.

Publications

The Library has the distinction of having regular publication programmes of texts of manuscripts and books on history, culture and literature. The following new publications have been published and released including a monograph of Rampur Raza Library in English to mark the celebrations of the 50th Anniversary of Indias Independence and 200 years of Rampur Raza library.

1. Khat-ki-Kahani Taswiron ki-Zabani (Urdu) by Syyed Ahmed Khattat (famous calligrapher)
2. Text of the rare manuscript namely Tarikh - i -Shahia-i-Nishapuria (Persian) (History of Avadh) by Qasu, Ali Nishapuri
3. Maulana Muhammad Ali our Jang-e-Azadi (Urdu) by Dr. Zaheer Ali Siddiqui.

4. Rampur Raza library Monograph, (English) compiled by Dr. W.H. Siddiqui.
5. Tarikh-i-Kitab-Khana-i-Raza (Urdu) (History of Rampur Raza Library) by Hafiz Ahmad Ali

   Shauqu Rampuri with introduction and commentary by Dr. W.H. Siddiqui.

Conservation

The most recent development has been the establishment of a conservation laboratory in February 1995, in collaboration with INTACH, Indian Conservation Institute, Lucknow. During 1998-99, the laboratory has done yeomen service in preserving the damaged manuscripts, old books, specimens of Islamic calligraphy, paintings, rare historical documents and other art objects of Raza Library collection. These badly deteriorated art objects having various problems were treated successfully by using various scientific methods.

Some of the notable works done by the conservation laboratory are in shown below:-

A. 1300 books were disinfected in fumigation chamber.

B. 1337 folios of old manuscripts and 496 pages of old books were chemically treated.

C. 89 delicate golden ornamented Islamic calligraphy specimens with exquisitely fine embellishment in gold and mineral colours and large size Tughras were scientifically conserved.

D. 1088 damaged pages of hand written Persian and Arabic catalogues were repaired.

E. 91 rare weather-beaten historical documents of Sufi Settlement of Makanpur, Dist. Kanpur (U.P.) including sanads, farmans and revenue documents of the Mughal period were chemically restored.

F. 30 art objects were also chemically treated.

Service to readers and scholars

During the period, more than six hundred research scholars from India and abroad visited the Library to consult manuscripts, miniatures, books and journals for their research work. 27,031 photocopies and photographs of printed books were supplied to them on payment basis.

Reference service

Besides its routine services, the Library provides reference facilities to scholars around the globe by supplying required information in the form of transcribed copies and photographs. During 1998-99, nearly 200 enquiries, long term and short term, were received, and relevant information was provided besides photographs/ slides and which microfilms which were supplied on payment.

Cataloguing, classifying of books and periodicals

2500 cards have been prepared which are based on Dewey Decimal System including author, title and subjects. More than 900 new books have been accessioned. 6000 index cards of Arabic manuscripts have also been prepared.

Photo documentation

The system of coloured photo documentation of rare manuscripts and paintings of the collection of the Library has been continued and nearly 5000 coloured photographs have been prepared and arranged in albums, with captions and sizes

Progress report on computerisation

The Rampur Raza Library has a rich collection of nearly 15,000 manuscripts and more than 50,000 printed books besides other historical archives and documents preserved in it. A Pentium computer of 200 MHz. with 2.1 G.B. Hard Disk and software i.e. Fox Pro, Windows 95 and Inpage Urdu was installed in the Library in August 1996. For operating this computer a qualified and trained person, earlier worked in INSDOC, Delhi, was engaged who started with Data base programming.

A comprehensive list of 3395 new Hindi and English printed books was prepared, accessioned and indexed with class numbers in computerized format.

4325 English printed books were verified and computerized. Moreover a list of 326 items of rare manuscripts, paintings and specimens of Islamic calligraphy which were selected for display in the special exhibition on the occasion of the Golden jubilee Celebrations of India's Independence and 200 years of the establishment of the Rampur Raza Library was prepared and printed. The computer is also used for preparing the Annual Report, official letters and maintaining important records, etc.

Cultural and academic activities and exhibitions

Celebrations of the Golden Jubilee of Indian Independence

The grand celebrations were organized from 25th to 28th July 1998 and was inaugurated by His Excellency, Shri Suraj Bhan, Governor of Uttar Pradesh and Chairman of Rampur Raza Library Board. It was followed by an international seminar "History, Culture and Literature of Rohilkhand." Seventy-seven distinguished scholars from India and abroad participated in the Seminar and cultural programmes were organized in the evenings. On 25th July, the famous T.V. artist, Junaid Akhtar gave a ghazal recital of both classical and modem Urdu poetry.

The evening of 28th July was enriched by the traditional Pathan folk songs of Charbait and on the evening of 28th July an exhilarating classical vocal performance was held by the Rampur Sahaswan Gharana artists.

An International Mushaira was organized on the night of 28th July at Rang Mahal Hall. Thirty five poets and poetesses from different parts of India and Pakistan participated in the mushaira. The celebrated Urdu poet Kaifi Azmi presided over the mushaira.

Rampur Raza Library organized a Qawwali night on 15th August 1998 to mark the closing ceremony of Golden Jubilee year of India's Independence.

Special exhibitions

As part of the grand celebrations of the 50th Anniversary of India's Independence and completion of 200 years of Rampur Raza Library, a special exhibition of the blow ups of the rare manuscripts, paintings and collection of antique objects was mounted in Hamid Manzil of the Library from 25th July to 16th August 1998. The exhibition was declared open to the public by Shri Ajay Shanker, I.A.S., Director General, Archaeological Survey of India. It was witnessed by more than 60,000 visitors and scholars from various parts of India.

The display included three hundred blow ups, one hundred and fifty original manuscripts (both plain and illustrated) besides one hundred and fifty rare specimens of Islamic calligraphy. The blow ups of pre-conservation and post conservation of damaged manuscripts, paintings and other art objects which were treated in the Library's conservation laboratory were also put on display in the Darbar Hall of Hamid Manzil.

In addition to the selected items of the collection of the Library a good number of antiquities such as harpoons, axes and swords of Copper Hoard culture, terracotta statues and figures from Mauryan, Sunga-Kushan and Gupta periods, beads and a series of coins including punch marked coins of silver and copper were taken on loan from Shri Surendra Mohan Mishra of Moradabad.

Exhibition in foreign countries

As apart of the celebrations of the 50th Anniversary of India's Independence and bicentenary of the Rampur Raza Library, exhibitions of the blow ups of selected manuscripts and miniatures of the collection were organized at Copenhagen (Denmark), Berlin (Germany), London (England), Brussels (Belgium), Singapore, Kuala Lumpur (Malaysia), Madrid (Spain), Ifrane (Morocco) and Rabat (Morocco) from June to September 1998.

Rampur Raza library award

The Rampur Raza Library instituted three awards namely the Nawab Faizullah Khan award of Rs.51,000, Nawab Raza Ali Khan award of Rs.11,000 and the Chairman's award of Rs.11,000, for encouraging and honouring distinguished scholars and experts in arts, architecture, painting, calligraphy and literature.

His excellency Governor of Uttar Pradesh and Chairman of Rampur Raza Library Board awarded Faizullah Khan Award of Rs.51,000/- to Maulana Muhammad Abdus Salam Khan, who made valuable contributions to Arabic literature and philosophy. The Nawab Raza Ali Khan award of Rs. 11,000/- was given to Shri Sayyed Ahmed, the famous calligraphist of Rampur.

Rampur Raza library fellowship

The Rampur Raza Library awarded six fellowships of Rs.3,000/- per month to those research scholars who are not getting any financial assistance from U.G.C. or any other agency for carrying out their research work besides assisting in the editing of the rare manuscripts of historical and scientific nature. The text of Hindi manuscript 'Ras Prabodh' of Syed Ghulam Nabi Rasleen Bilgrami (1741 AD) in Persian script has been transcribed in Nagari and edited for publication.

Two senior fellowships of Rs.6,000/- and Rs.5,000/- per month respectively were awarded to Professor Mukhtarud-din Arzoo and Master Imtiaz who are editing Arabic and Persian manuscripts for publication and preparing catalogues of paintings of Akbar's album.

Security of Rampur raza library

The Security of Rampur Raza Library was strengthened by appointing one battalion of Central Industrial Security Force (CISF). In addition, iron grills were provided to all the doors and windows of the Library's rooms.

Thanjavur Maharaja serfoji's saraswati mahal library

The Thanjavur Maharaja Serfoji's Saraswati Mahal Library is one among the few medieval libraries that exist in the world. It is a priceless repository of culture and a time defying treasure house of knowledge, built up by the successive dynasties of Nayaks and the Marathas of Thanjavur. The library embodies a rich and rare collection of manuscripts on art, culture and literature.

Conceived and christened the Royal Palace Library, the Nayak kings of Tanjore (1535-1673 AD) nourished it for intellectual enrichment. The development of the library into a monumental institution was due to the Maratha kings of Thanjavur. Maharaja Serfoji (1676-1855 AD) was an intellectual mandarin, a most pre-eminent scholar and a versatile cognoscente. While on pilgrimage to Banaras, he employed many pandits to collect, buy and copy a vast number of works from all the renowned centres of Sanskrit learning in the north and other areas. It is on account of his singular devotion to this cause that the library is called. 'Thanjavur Maharaja Serfoji's Saraswati Mahal Library'.

Manuscript collection

The Library has the richest collection of manuscripts which are truly reflective of the culture of South India. In addition to the central collections, the Library was able to get possession of the Private Libraries of several pandits and patrons living in and around Thanjavur. The manuscripts are available both in palm-leaf and paper form on various subjects in Indian languages like Tamil, Telugu, Marathi and Sanskrit.

The major part of the manuscripts of this library are in Sanskrit and number over 39,300. They are written in different scripts such as Grantha, Devnagari, Nadinagiri, Telugu, etc. The total number of Tamil manuscripts is about 3,500, comprising of titles in literature and medicine. The Library has a collection of 3075 Marathi manuscripts the works of South Indian Maharashtrians of the 171, 18th and 19th centuries and the hierarchy of the saints of Maharashtra belonging to the Ramadasi and Dattatreya Mutts. The Marathi manuscripts are mostly on paper and a few in the palm-leaf form, which are written in Telugu script. There are 802 Telugu manuscripts in this library, which are mostly on palm-leaf and a few in paper form.

Apart from these manuscripts, there are 850 bundles of the Maratha Raj records available in the library. The Raj records were written in the Modi script (fast script for Devnagari) of the Marathi language. These records encompass the information on the political, cultural and social administration of the Maratha kings of Thanjavur.

Book collection

The book collection of the Library, exceeding 51,000 is eclectic. The rare book collections were made by King Serfoji during his lifetime. In his collection there are more than 4500 books in English, French, German, Italian, Greek and Danish.

Other collection

Besides manuscripts and books the Library possesses beautifully decorated Thanjavur style paintings on wood (33 nos.), canvas (2 nos.) and glass (2) about 5,000 folios of illustrated paper paintings such as Gaja Sastra, Aswa Sastra, mythological paintings, botanical specimen paintings, military costumes, Chitra Ramayana, about 500 maps in 20 atlases and prints and drawings.

Museum

A Museum functions in the Library and is open to common visitors on all days except national holidays. Rare manuscripts and books, illustrated manuscripts, paintings, rare atlases, portraits of Thanjavur Maratha kings, Daniel paintings, Fraser prints of Indian sceneries, punishments of China depicted in picture form, physiognomy charts of Charles Le-Brun, bathing ghats of Banaras, etc., are exhibited. During the year, nearly 61,354 people, which included nearly 2759 foreign visitors visited the Museum.

The circadian functional focus

The main functions of the Library are 'preservation, publication, cataloguing and service to readers. Modern conservation techniques such as fumigation, lamination, deacidification are being followed to avoid deterioration caused by insects, acidity and other mechanical damage. Citronella Oil is smeared to give flexibility to palm leaves and to get rid of insects. An indigenously prepared preservative consisting of a powder of mixture of sweet flag, black cumin, cloves, pepper and bark of ,cinnamon with camphor is used. The conservation section conserved 670 paper manuscripts, 776 palmleaf manuscripts, 1800 books and fumigated 460 Modi bundles.

The Library is publishing rare and unpublished manuscripts in book form to disseminate the knowledge contained in the manuscripts. So far, the Library has published 380 books.

The Microfilm unit of this Library is engaged in microfilming Sanskrit manuscripts for the Indira Gandhi National Centre for Arts, New Delhi for preservation and national accessibility. 1943 manuscripts have been microfilmed during the year.

Acquisitions during the year

Acquisition of rare books and manuscripts is through gift. During this year, 80 palm leaf manuscripts, 213 books and 45 paper manuscripts were purchased for this library.

The asiatic society

The Asiatic Society was founded in 1784 to enquire into whatever is performed by 'Man' and produced by 'Nature' within the limits of Asia. The foundation of scientific, research and the development of science in modern India was laid by the Asiatic Society. It has changed its name over the centuries starting from Royal Asiatic Society of Bengal to its present one. The Society's journal became the main research periodical in this country. The publication of the Society became a treasure house of Indian wisdom, its publications include a series called Bibliothica Indica which started publishing critical editions of old treatise in oriental studies including Sanskrit and Persian. Most of the scientific and learned societies and institutions were founded in this country at the initiative of the Asiatic Society. Studies in modem sciences also started from the Society. The Indian Museum which is now considered as one of the biggest institutions of its kind in the country was a creation of the Asiatic Society. Then a series of institutions such as different Surveys, Calcutta University, Calcutta Medical College and even Indian National Science Academy, Indian Science Congress Association, Indian Photographic Association and the like came up one after another under the patronage of the Asiatic Society.

But with the growth of diverse specialised institutions and societies, in the words of Dr. Meghnad Saha, the Society became somewhat like that of its contemporary, the great Banyan tree of the Shibpur Botanical Gardens. Like that tree, it has thrown out of itself several roots which have developed into independent and self-contained institutions having little contact with the mother body. The original Society itself is now reduced to a mere trunk. This will also be apparent from the subsequent activities of the Society. It was brought down to the level of a narrow study in the field of Indology. Dr. Meghnad Saha, therefore, wanted that the Society should infuse into its working a life giving activity. Similarly, Mr. David Ezra suggested that the very special functions of the Society are to provide a common platform for the study of Asia in all its aspects, not to confine its studies to India alone to the exclusion of the remainder of Asia. He suggested that it should provide a meeting place for East and West for Indian and non-Indians to work together, for the specialist to cooperate, for the private individual and the officials to meet, for the dilettante and the expert to exchange views.

These ideas of Dr. Meghnad Saha and Mr. David Ezra were in tune with what Sir William Jones visualised.

The world of today is not the same as it was in 1784.

Technological innovations have taken a quantum leap and notions and ideas have come closer to help individuals, institutions and nations and in the process further the development of thought.

In recent days, therefore, the Society took up the task of transforming itself into a platform for academic interaction among scholars from every discipline, so that knowledge may be widened by exploring in particular the interfaces of different disciplines. With that end in view the Society organized itself with an emphasis in three directions viz., (1) infrastructural development depending on modem technology (2) augmentation and diversification of research, studies and other academic programmes and (3) finding more space so that the treasures of the Society may be stored in a proper scientific way to provide a user friendly environment.

Against this background the Society is now functioning from four different places in the city. Apart from the premises at 1, Park Street, the original building which is called old building constructed in 1808 and a new building constructed sometime in 1964, there are Metcalfe Hall and CMC building. There is another premise at 91, Ballygunge Place which has been donated to the Society by Late Prof. S.D. Chatteijee, a former life member and a Professor of Physics of Jadavpur University.

From these different centres, the Society is now functioning through its various sections, namely Library, Museum, Conservation, Publication and Academic.

The Society functions according to the provisions of the Regulations as well provisions of the Asiatic Society Act 1948. In terms of the Regulations of the Society, administration, direction and management of the affairs of the Society is vested in the Council which is formed on the basis of the Annual Election. But the Council includes besides the elected members four nominees of the Government of India and one nominee of the Government of West Bengal. The Council is assisted by various committees namely Library Committee, Publication Committee and B.I. Committee. Publication Committee and B.I. Committee are formed by the Council itself. The S.F.C. even though it is constituted by the Council includes three representatives of the Government of India and one representative of the Government of West Bengal with the power of the Government to appoint the Chairman of the Committee. The Planning Board, on the other hand, is wholly constituted by the Government of India under Section 8 of the Asiatic Society Act 1948. It is the usual practice that the Chairman of the SFC is usually the Financial Adviser, Ministry of Human Resource Development, Government of India. During the year under report the Government has constituted the Planning Board with Dr. Pratap Chandra Chunder, the former Union Education Minister as its Chairman.

Academic activities

The activities relating to these sections during the period 1998-99 are presented below:

(a) *Research* : The research activities of the Society are conducted through in house research by appointment of Research Professor, Research Associates and Research Fellows, (2) by sponsoring research projects to outside scholars, and (3) by undertaking collaborative research programmes with other institutions, both within and outside the country.

During the year under report the in house research is being carried on by 12 Research ' Professors, 2 Research Associates and 20 Research Fellows who are working in the field of history of the Asiatic Society, Folklore and Culture, Persian languages, Bengali Dictionary, Buddhist Studies, Chinese Studies, Women Studies, History of Science, History of Medicine, Islamic Culture and IndoRussian Relations.

Of the research programmes that are currently going on in the Society, the following are worth mentioning: -

i. Lafont, Sircar and 19th Century Science Movement in India.

ii. History of Indian Medicine as Reflected in the Early Classical Sanskrit Texts.

iii. Trends of Folklore Research in **India; and** Contemporary Trends in Indian Cultural Anthropology.

iv Women in Science.

v. Indian Concept of Nature and Concern for Environment in Medieval Period, etc.

In respect of sponsored research, six such projects are being pursued during the year under report namely :

i. Critical Edition of the Diwan-i-Bahuram Sagg

ii. Tribal Ecology in India - A Study in L Usages and Process of Development.

iii. Studies on the Progress of Biological / Life Science and the concept of Environment in India.

iv. A concise biographical dictionary of the members and associates of the Asiatic Society, Calcutta (1784-1994).

v. Compilation of History of Indian Photography.

vi Agricultural Practices and Crop Calendars: Traditional Lore and Modem Compulsions.

In so far as collaborative research programmes are

concerned the study of Indo-Russian Relations in collaboration with Institute of Oriental Studies, Moscow, is continuing. Two volumes of this collaborative programme are expected to come out within this year. A new collaborative research programme is now in the process of being implemented with the Institute of Oriental Studies, St. Petersburg. This is a part of the cultural agreement between the Government of India and the Government of Russia. In terms of the cultural agreement a protocol is to be signed very soon. Similarly there are other collaborative research programmes with institutions both within the country and abroad which are in the process of negotiation.

The progress of work in the academic section suffered during the year under report because the process of finalisation of IX Plan was delayed. The Planning Board which is entrusted with this responsibility came into existence only in July and it completed its task only in October 1998. The activities as such are expected to be stepped up during the last quarter of the year under report.

Academic courses

The academic courses which the Society was conducting were kept in abeyance till the finalisation of the 9th Five Year Plan of the Asiatic Society. Previously, the Society was running courses on History of Science, Manuscriptology and Museum Appreciation. Two more areas were also approved by the earlier Planning Board in the field of Art~ History and Culture Civilization. These have not started as yet. The Planning Board has since decided that besides the existing programme the Society should initiate such courses on Prakrit, Old Tamil and Indian Paliography. The preliminaries are being worked out and the History of Science course will start during the last quarter of this year.

Short term fellowships, seminars and lectures

The short term fellowship was kept suspended during the year pending finalisation of the Plan of the Asiatic Society. Now since the Plan has been finalised and approved, it is expected that this programme of Short Term Fellowships will be initiated during the last quarter of the year. During the year under report, seminars and lectures were stepped up. Twenty two lectures on different subjects and Five seminars were organised during the three quarters of this year. The subjects of the seminars and that of the lectures are fairly wide

Some of the seminars conducted during the year under report.

- i Indian Art.
- ii. Kherwali language & literature.
- iii. Rev. John Mack - Pioneer of the Study of Chemistry in Bengali language.
- iv. The Contributions of Dr. P.C. Bagchi on IndoSino Tibetology.
- v. Epistomology
- vi. Utility of Ayurveda in the Modern World.

Some of the lectures organized by the Society during the year under report :

- i. New Materials on Raja Rammohan Roy
- ii. Demographic Indicators of Social Change.
- iii. National Spirit of Bengali Folk Songs.
- iv. Architecture: Environment & Rabindranath
- v. Population Environment and Food Security.

Library

The Library of the Society is very rich in its collections particularly to serve the purpose of source materials for research. During the period, 465 books and 900 issues of different journals were acquired by the Society. Besides we have received donations from various individuals particularly from Rangila Haldar wife of Shri Gopal Haldar, a renowned scholar and literateur and Shri Niharendu Dutta Mazumdar, former Minister of Government of West Bengal and a Freedom Fighter and a close associate of Shri Sublias Chandra Bose. The Director of Census, West Bengal also donated District Handbooks of Birbhum, Murshidabad, West Dinajpur, Burdwan, Nadia and Purulia.

During the year the Society has also joined the DELNET (Delhi Library Network) and has also installed internet facilities. Through the library a website is being prepared and negotiations are going on with the National Informatic Centre to use their server for the website of the Asiatic Society so that the world of scholars may be aware of the rich collections of the Asiatic Society and also of its other functions. In the matter of computerisation of the library, the basic ground work is nearly complete with the National Informatic Centre to use their software. This software is also being used by the DELNET. The library of the Metcalfe Hall has also been developed during the year under report for extending reader services. Cataloguing of the journals and books placed at the Metcalfe Hall has also been started and in order to expedite the work an arrangement has been made to undertake the work on a piece rate basis under the supervision of Chief Librarian, Indian Statistical Institute and the former Librarian of the Calcutta University. The usual job of cataloguing of the articles published in the Asiatic Society till date has also been completed. The microfiche and microfilm services have also improved during the year under report.

Museum

Renovation of the Museum has been undertaken and it is

expected that it will be completed within a month. A programme of computerisation of the Museum is also going on simultaneously. The software is under preparation along with the training of the staff of the Museum. The stage is therefore being set for complete computerisation of the Museum. The valuable manuscripts, artifacts and the archival materials have been completely brought under report. We are preparing a catalogue of the archival materials for publication so that the users may use those materials more effectively. The artplates which were recovered recently have been catalogued. Similarly an album of the paintings of the Society is nearly complete.

Conservation

The Asiatic Society has developed a well-equipped conservation unit. But unfortunately the capacity of the conservation laboratory is not sufficient to take care of the problems of the Society in the matter of preservation and conservation of books, journals, manuscripts and archival materials. This is because the Asiatic Society's library is one of the oldest and a large portion of the existing library is full of old books, journals, manuscripts, etc. As such, it requires very careful handling. Attempts are being made to step up the work by contracting out some of the existing work to outside agencies.

Reprography

The Reprography Section of the Society is well equipped with modern equipment. It has microfilm and microfiche equipment and the Society is preparing a microfilm of the old books and journals of valuable manuscripts. It is also planned to prepare microfiche for commercial purposes.

During the year under report the following works have been done.

1. Xerox	
2. Microfilm	1,55,234
a) Project	1,500 Exp.
b) Non-Project	2,105 Exp.
3. Photo coverage	557 Nos.
4. Film Processing	11 Rolls
5. Enlargements	295 prints
6. Chemical compounding	26 Its.

Publication

The Society brought out 15 books and 6 journals and one research transaction. Besides, the Society is publishing Monthly Bulletins each month on a regular basis. Some of the publications include;

i. Modern Bengali Dictionary for foreigners, Vol. 1,

ii. Faith and Reason,

iii. Can Technology Lead to a Prosperous Society,

iv. Kathakali,,

v. Akbarnama

7

Libraries

National library, Calcutta

The National Library, Calcutta was established in 1948 with the enactment of the Imperial Library Act, 1948. It is an institution of national importance which acts as a reference centre for research scholars. It coordinates and determines standards in the field of library services in the country. The library finds a special mention in Article 62 of the 7th Schedule of the Union list of the Constitution of India as an institution of national importance.

Basic functions of the National Library

1. Acquisition and conservation of all significant materials to the exclusion of ephemeras.
2. Collection of printed material concerning the country, no matter where this is published and as a corollary, the acquisition of photographic records of such material that is not available within the country.
3. Acquisition and conservation of manuscripts of national importance.
4. Planned acquisition of reading materials of foreign origin-printed or otherwise.
5. Rendering bibliographic and documentation services, both general and specialised. This implies the responsibility to produce current National

Bibliography and retrospective bibliographies on various aspects of the country.

6. Acting as a referral centre purveying full and accurate knowledge of all sources of bibliographical information and participation in international bibliographical activities.
7. Provision of photocopying and reprographic services.
8. Acting as a centre of international book exchange and loan.

The Library has the following broad elements in its 'Action Plan', which are to be treated as on going schemes.

Collection building and book production statisstics

This scheme was aimed at organising and building up the collection of reading material at the National Library by acquisition through

(i) purchase,
(ii) implementation of the 'Delivery of Books Act'.
(iii) exchange and gift, for the use of readers and research scholars.

Under its cultural exchange programme, the library maintains exchange relations with 211 libraries and organizations/institutions in 86 countries. The exchange comprises of two aspects:

(a) exchange of publications and
(b) exchange of library personnel.

During the year the Library has received 1403 publications and six CD ROM Cassettes under the book exchange programme;

A special drive was undertaken to make the Delivery of Books Act more effective and enhance the collection of publications from Indian publishers. The total number of books received under the Act is 8,669 and it is expected that around 15,000 books would be received by the end of the financial year.

The library added 200 rolls to its collection of microfilms of monographs, newspapers and government publications during the year.

Readers' services programme

This programme aims at strengthening the Reading Room services which include' reference and bibliographic services, offer lending/loan facilities at local, national and international levels and so on. The Reading Rooms remain open from 9 a.m. to 8 p.m. on all working days. On holidays (except national holidays) it remains open from 9.30 a.m. to 6 p.m.

The total number of new members in the reading rooms went up to 5300.

The Library attended to around 1 lakh reference and bibliographic queries during the year. Select bibliographies and reading lists on specific topics were supplied to readers and scholars on demand.

As an on-going programme the Library has supplied, 45 entries of bibliographies published (till Oct., 98) in India to the Indian National Commission for Cooperation with UNESCO, New Delhi, for inclusion in the 'Bibliography Documentation Terminology' published by UNESCO. More than 300 entries will be sent to UNESCO for inclusion in the INDEX TRANSLATIONUM vol. 51 (1998) during the financial year.

Modernisation & conservation

At the time of its establishment as the Imperial Library in 1903, the Library took nearly 40,000 books belonging to the Calcutta Public Library, established in 1836. In addition it received the collection of the Home

Department Library and the Fort William College and gifts from other sources. The preservation and conservation of precious books and other materials remains the prime duty of the National Library.

Three units of Library, namely Reprography, Preservation Laboratory and the Preservation Bindery are involved in the work of conservation. The laboratory unit chemically treats very old publications and uses pesticides to control termites and other insects. The Reprography unit microfilms old monographs, documents, newspapers, rare publications etc. It has also prepared 30 negative and 12 positive rolls. It is expected that by the end of the financial year 101660 xerox prints would be supplied to readers and research scholars. The library has plans to spend Rs.40 lakhs up to February '99 for conservation.

Modernisation programme

The computer centre has done the following work:

i. CALIBNET programme with CALIBLINK is continuing

ii. Steps for participation in the INTERNET Programme are underway.

iii. Steps for procurement of Server, Printers, Nodes and CD Servers are being taken.

iv. Computerised Document Management System: The first phase of scanning, indexing and archiving 4,21,000 pages of rare and brittle documents/books on Compact Discs has been sanctioned and approved by the Department of Culture, the work on which will start soon.

Capital work/building programme

The construction of the multi-storeyed Bhasha Bhawan was started in 1994. The pile foundation and raft in all blocks have been cast and about 7000 sq.mts. of slab cast in Blocks No. 1,2,4,5,6 and 8. Structural parts have been completed in all respects. Repair work of the roof of the main building has been completed.

Library modernisation

Electronic media for recording and preserving books, journals, documents etc. are available in diverse form such as Computer hard discs, CD-ROM and other electronic devices which save space and time and are in extensive demand. Nowadays much of this work is undertaken by contract. The library has initiated steps for such contract based services. Progress made in the automation programme is given below.

1. Continuity with CALIBNET Programme and participation in INTERNET and DELNET
2. Procurement of software and Reference Databases on CD-ROMs.
3. 20,79,000 pages were scanned and indexed on Cds.
4. Local Area Network (LAN) installed in several divisions of the Library.

Schemes for development of SC and ST

For the development of personnel belonging to Scheduled Castes and Scheduled Tribes, a Special Component Plan has been proposed here under

1. The Library proposes to periodically arrange special training courses and workshops for improving the technical efficiency of the SC and ST personnel. Such courses will enable them to qualify and/or compete with others for promotion/appointment.
2. Special drives will be undertaken to depute SC and ST candidates/employees for training conducted by different institutions in the country.
3. It is intended to create a post of Liaison Officer who will keep in touch with institutions in different parts of the country which specializes in research

and development activities relating to the betterment of SC and ST employees. It is expected that they will be able to contribute to the formulation of the activities of the Institute so as to focus more intensely on the problems of these two communities.

4. The Library intends to create a separate section of the 'Santhal Language Collection'. Under a senior technical hand the Library will conduct a survey of publications in other tribal languages to make preparations for building up separate tribal language collections for the benefit and promotion of tribal readers.

Delhi public libbrary

The Delhi Public Library came into existence on 27th October, 1951, as a Pilot Project in collaboration with UNESCO, to introduce the concept of free public library and information services to the populace of Delhi. It has grown into a premier public library system of modem India in the National Capital Territory of Delhi and has become the busiest public library in South East Asia.

The Library has a network consisting of a Central Library at the Headquarter; a Zonal Library at Sarojini Nagar; 3 Branch Libraries; 25 Sub Branch Libraries; 22 Libraries at Re-settlement Colonies of NCT of Delhi; 6 Community Libraries 11 Reading Rooms which inculcate reading habits among the weaker sections of the Society; a network of 102 mobile service points to serve the urban and rural areas in the National Capital Territory of Delhi; a Braille Library with a network of 20 mobile service points and 7 deposit stations for the visually handicapped, both students and adults; 3 sports libraries of the status of Sub-branch located in different stadia in Delhi; special services in 2 Hospitals for the patients and one at Central Jail for the prisoners. In short, the Library provides its services to the rural and urban folk, adults, children, students, the visually handicapped, sportsmen, prisoners and patients.

Total book stock

The Library has a stock of approximately 15,48,109 volumes and has 9044 gramophone records/cassettes in its collection.

Issue of books

The Delhi Public Library issued 16,96,031 books to, the readers. The average number of books issued to the readers per day is 6013. Photocopy services are also provided. Total membership of the library is 66,292.

Purchase of books

The Delhi Public library purchased 32,000 books on various subjects in Hindi, English, Urdu and Punjabi during the period.

Books received under the delivery of books act

8.24 Under the D.B. Act, the DPL received 1,57,154 books in various Indian languages during the period. Monthly lists of new arrivals are prepared in English, Hindi, Tamil and in other languages regularly. DPL has been nominated as the depository library for Asian Development Bank Publications since 1994.

Computerisation of library activities

The computers installed at the Central Library, S.P. Mukherjee Marg and at the Zonal Library Sarojini Nagar are now operational. A machine readable database of periodicals received under the Delivery of Books Act was prepared. Computerised cataloguing had also started on an experimental basis during this period. Hands-on training is being imparted to the staff members to make them computer literate. DPL has already brought out a directory of periodicals published in India. Bibliographies of dictionaries and library science are underway. DPL is also a member of DELNET. During the current year new computers are being installed in the branch libraries.

Lecture series

The library has initiated a lecture series by prominent personalities on books and other topics of interest.

Other activities

The reading room in Gole Market has been converted into a sub-branch level library and R.C. library has been opened at Sawan Park, Ashok Vihar.

Bhoomi Pujan has been performed for Janakpuri Library in collaboration with Sahitya Kala Parishad, an organisation of Government of NCT of Delhi. Display and exhibition of Books and New Arrivals. Foreign visitors from Slovenia, Switzerland, Germany etc. visited the library.

Staff members were deputed to refresher courses conducted by the Centre for Research Planning and Action (CERPA). Besides this library professionals were also deputed to NACLIN'98 Workshop' organized by DELNET, 49th FID conference and IBBY Congress.

Central reference library

The Central Reference Library, (CRL), Calcutta, a subordinate office of the Department of Culture is mainly responsible for the implementation of two schemes, viz.(i) Compilation and Publication of the Indian National Bibliography (both Roman Script and in the respective language scripts). This is a monthly record of current Indian publications in 14 languages including English based on receipts in the National Library, Calcutta, under the provisions of the D.B. Act. 1954 .(ii) Compilation and Publication of Index Indiana (in Roman

Script) an Index to select articles appearing in current Indian periodicals presently in six languages.

Indian national bibliography: monthly fascicules

The Indian National Bibliography is published as a monthly and as cumulated annual volumes. Monthly volumes up to December 1993 have already been published. The Annual Volume 1993 is also expected to be released soon. The backlog of 1994 1995,1996 and 1997 annual volumes are to be published shortly. The work has been entrusted to M/s Educational Consultants India Limited. Work on the monthly issues of Indian National Bibliography has been computerised.

Index Indiana

Index Indiana is a project to index articles appearing in regional language periodicals. At present it covers only six Indian languages namely Bengali, Gujarati, Hindi, Malayalam, Marathi and Tamil. Index Indiana 1989-1991 volume has been published. Manuscript for 1992-97 is getting ready.

Setting up of a computer network in the central reference library

On the basis of the recommendations of an Expert Group in the Department of Culture, efforts have been undertaken to computerise the publication of the Indian National Bibliography and Index Indiana. The work has been entrusted to M/s Educational Consultants India Ltd. The Central Reference Library is also participating in the formation of a National Data Base. It also intends to have Local Area Network with the National Library.

Language bibliographies

Assemese - Manuscript of Assamese bibliography 1971-80 is ready. Compilation of 1981-90 is going on.

Bengali - Manuscripts for the five years cumulated volume pertaining to 1992-96 is ready. Compilation of 1997-98 volume has been taken up.

Hindi - Hindi bibliography 1992-93 and 1994-95 are being printed by Government of U.P. Press, Allahabad.

Malayalam- Compilation of Malayalam Bibliography 1997-98 is under process.

Marathi - Manuscript of Marathi Bibliography 1991-95 is being sent to State Central Library, Bombay for printing.

Oriya - Ten years cumulative volume for 1981-92 has been handed over to the Orissa Sahitya Akademy, Bhubaneshwar.

Tamil - Librarian, Connemera Library, Madras, has been requested to take up the printing of 199296 volume of the Tamil Bibliography.

Telugu - 1992-96 Telugu Bibliography is under compilation.

Urdu - Compilation and editing of Urdu Bibliography 1997-98 is in progress.

Training of personnel

One Assistant Editor and a Sub-Editor were deputed to a workshop on multimedia held at Rabindra Bharathi University, Calcutta from 24th August to 5th September 1998. One Assistant Editor and a Sub Editor participated in IASLIC Conference held at Kerala Agricultural University, Trichur from 20th to 24th December 1998.

Progressive use of hindi for official purposes

An Official Language Implementation Committee has been functioning for the past few years for the progressive implementation of Hindi. More than 90% of the employees have passed Hindi Examination under the Hindi Temaching Scheme.

Visit by the students of library science

Students from different Universities visited the Library and worked on their projects.

Raja rammohan roy library foundation

The Raja Rammohan Roy Library Foundation, a fully financed autonomous organisation. under the Department of Culture was set up in May 1972 as a part of the bi-centenary birth celebrations of Raja Rammohan Roy. The main objective of the Foundation is to promote and support the public library movement in the country by providing adequate library services and by popularising reading habits, particularly in rural areas, with the active cooperation of the State Library Authorities, Union Territories and Voluntary Organisations operating in the field of library services.

The Foundation with its limited resources is operating two types of schemes - Matching and Non-Matching as detailed below:-

Matching schemes

i. Assistance towards building up adequate stocks of books.
ii. Assistance towards storage of books.
iii. Assistance towards seminars, workshops, book exhibitions etc.
iv. Assistance to state, central and district Libraries to acquire TV-cum-VCR sets and cassettes for educational purposes.
v. Assistance to libraries below the district level for increasing accommodation.

Non-Matching schemes

vi. Assistance to state, central and district Libraries towards supply of books through central selection.
vii. Financial assistance to voluntary organisations, working in the field of Public Libraries.
viii. Assistance to Central Sponsored Libraries
ix. Assistance to Children's Libraries and Children's Sections of general Public Libraries.

x. Assistance to Public Libraries towards Centenary celebrations.

xi. Assistance to All India Library Association for seminars, conferences, etc.

xii. Assistance towards collection and compilation of library statistics through official and non-official agencies.

Matching Schemes are operated from the Matching Fund created with State Government's contribution (which varies from Rs.1 lakh to Rs.15 lakhs depending on size, population and past utilisation) and equal share from the Foundation. Non Matching Schemes are operated fully from the Foundation's funds.

During the year under report, the Library spent Rs.850 lakhs on 8,200 libraries under both the Matching and Non-matching Schemes.

Besides being a funding body, the Foundation also functions as a national agency for coordinating, monitoring and developing the Public Library services in the country. The Foundation brings out a quarterly Newsletter which not only publishes the activities of the Foundation but also disseminates important news on library services being rendered in different parts of the country and abroad. It has also a special library on Library and Information Science.

The Foundation celebrated the 225th Birth Anniversary of Raja Rammohan Roy as well as the Silver Jubilee of the Foundation and conducted the following programmes:

a) Production of a documentary on the life of Raja Rammohan Roy, activities of the Foundation and the development of public libraries in the post-independence period.

b) A marble statue of Raja Rammohan Roy, sculpted

by the eminent sculptor Sarbari Roy Choudhury of Vishwa Bharathi was installed by Master Artist, Shri Ganesh Halui on 17th September 1998. The Raja Rammohan Roy Memorial lecture for the year 1998-99 was delivered by eminent Assamese Creative writer, Shri Navakanta Barua and internationally eminent scientist Prof. J.V. Narlikar at Guwahati and Mumbai during April 1998 and December 1998 respectively.

c) As a part of the Silver Jubilee Celebrations, the Foundation organized two seminars on "Scenario of Public Libraries in the 21st Century" at Delhi, and Guwahati. The concluding session of the Silver Jubilee Celebrations was held at Delhi in May 1998 with the organization of the ninth All India Conveners' Conference which was inaugurated by Dr. R.V. Vaidyanatha Ayyar, Secretary (Culture), Ministry of Human Resource Development.

d) R.R.R.L.F. would be introducing Local Area Network, Internet connectivity and resource sharing for better coordination.

e) At the instance of the Department of Culture, the Foundation finalized the draft Model Public Library Bill and forwarded it to the State Governments for their comments.

Central secretariat library

The Central Secretariat library is one of the oldest (1891) libraries of the Government of India. In terms of the size of its collection (8,17,215 volumes), it is estimated to be the second largest Central Government Library after the National library at Calcutta. It was originally known as the "IMPERIAL SECRETARIAT LIBRARY" which was founded in Calcutta. With the shifting of the Capital, the Library was also moved to Delhi and since 1969 it has been housed in a separate wing of the Shastri Bhawan Complex.

The Library is well known for its rich and valuable collection of books on Indian History and Culture, Indian Official Publications such as Annual Administrative Reports, Budget and Plan documents, Civil Lists. Census Reports, Legal documents, Directories and Hand Books, Gazettes, Gazetteers, Committee and Commission Reports, Parliamentary Legal documents including microfiche and microfilms, General Reference Books, such as Encyclopedias, Dictionaries etc. Foreign Official Documents including Microfiche/Micro-film collection of U.S. Government Publications and other out of print material etc.

Membership

The library has a centralised membership for Central Secretariat Library, Tulsi Sadan Library and R.K.Purarn Branch Library and 4,115 members were enrolled/ renewed during the year.

CSL has a co-operative acquisition policy for libraries under the Department of Culture in Delhi i.e. National Archives of India, Archaeological Survey of India, National Museum Library, and National Gallery of Modem Art Library for the purchase of document resources of the library were enhanced during the year by acquiring 6,800 books in English, Hindi and regional languages and Indian and Foreign Official Documents including Microfilm and Microfiche and monographs in English, Hindi & Regional Languages. CSL also received 699 Journals on subscription and gratis basis. CSL acquired/ received 133 CD-ROM titles during the period and special efforts are being made for developing a collection of CD-ROM databases, Microfilms of newspapers and census reports.

Under the collection development programme, the central Secretariat Library has made special provisions for the purchase of reference books/material under the plan budget for the current year.

Services

The Central Secretariat I Library, New Delhi is mainly responsible for providing information for Research and Reference to the Registered Members, Policy Planners, Academicians, Research Scholars from various Universities in India, especially University of Delhi, Jawahar Lal Nehru University, Jamia Milia Islamia University and to the general readers etc.

About 2,00,000 users consulted the resources of CSL complex during the year and more than 91,347 titles were issued to the members. The library resources were supplemented by acquiring books on inter-library loan and more than 128 users were attended in person or on telephone by the library staff.

Reprographic services

The Reprography Unit of the library provided approximately 1,10,000 photocopies during the year and 85,000 pages were electronically duplicated. It is estimated that 50,000 photocopies and more than 45,000 electronically duplicated copies may be brought out during the remaining period of the financial year.

Provision for a microfilm repository room in CSL has been made for preserving the master negatives for archival purposes, as CSL is the nodal agency for Microfilming of Indian Publication Project. Requisite accessories are being acquired to monitor the state of stored microfilms.

Acquisition of Microfiche Reader Printer and accessories for microfilming, for Readers' services are in process.

Computer application

The computer section of CSL took a step forward in Networking and Internet Connectivity for the main library, Tulsi Sadan Library (TSL) and R.K.Puram Branch Library by setting up LAN in the main library and in TSL. To implement this, CSL entrusted the job on turnkey basis to EdCIL for supply of computer systems (Hardware and Software) and setting up the LAN at both the places. The Library acquired two servers and nine nodes. NIC has made available three RF links for Internet connectivity to the library.. Presently, Computers are being used in CSL for various house keeping activities in Acquisition Section, Processing Section, Coordination & Publication Section. Circulation, Serials and Reference Section, Indian Official Documents Section, Area Study Section and Foreign Official Documents Section.

Computer training programs conducted by CSL

- Computer awareness training program
- Guest lecture-cum-training workshop 'Designing and Publication' in coordination with IGNCA
- Training in UNIMARC and MINISIS
- Unix training for CSL and TSL staff
- Advanced CD-Publishing training
- Meetings for hands on work on Networking for resource sharing, standardization of Cataloguing format and Cooperative Acquisition are proposed to be held soon.

Use of computers in Tulsi Sadan library

The work of Book selection, acquisition and processing of Indian language reading materials have been started since 1.1.1998. Using GIST terminals -2000 fully processed records of Hindi, Tamil, Telugu, Punjabi, Sanskrit and Marathi language books are available on line

Other computer related activities:

1. Retrospective Conversion of cataloging data for making on line public access catalogue. About 65,000 records have been converted. Fields for

UNIMARC format have been decided. Remaining data will be converted using UNIMARC format. This will help in contributing data to National Bibliographic Database.

2. Book News-Current list of latest English books acquired in CSL in a quarter.
3. Publication work-seminar publications -preparation of camera ready copies and other ad-hoc publications.
4. Barcode will be introduced for setting up a mechanized circulation system.
5. Document imaging project of Annual Reports to be published in CD-ROM format.
6. Publication of bibliography of rare books in CD-ROM format duly linking images of tide page and contents page.

E-Mail facilities are also available for networking and Resource sharing. CSL is also a member of DELNET (Delhi Library Network) in addition to RENNIC (Research and Education Network of NIC) and ERNET (Education and Research Network).

Publications

For rendering better services to its clientele, the library is in the process of augmenting its activities by bringing out professional publications.The camera-ready copies of the following publications will be prepared in house.

- Proceedings of seminar on "Contribution of Indian litterateurs to the Freedom Movement India (1900-1947)".
- Proceedings of "Seminar on Assessing Information Needs and Services in the Government Decision Making Processes".
- CSL Quarterly Book News.
- Mahabharata Database Project-conversion of slokas into electronic format.

Library extension and development activities:

The library organised a 'meeting on networking, resource sharing and co-operative acquisition and information exchange' at the Central Secretariat Library in January and February 1999.

In addition to the above, CSL staff is deputed for various workshops, training courses, guest lectures and annual conferences of professional bodies in the field of library and information sciences. The library is also extending consultancy and advice to important libraries such as the PMO Library and the Rashtrapati Bhawan Library.

8

Institute of Buddhist and Tibetan Studies

Central institute of higher tibetan studies Sarnath, Varanasi

The Central Institute of Higher Tibetan Studies was established in 1967 by the efforts of Pt. Jawahar Lal Nehru and His Holiness the Dalai Lama. The institution remained associated with the Varanaseya Sanskrit Visvavidyalaya (now Sampurnanand Sanskrit University) till 1975. It was granted autonomy in 1978 under the Department of Culture. Distinguished scholars and higher authorities in the Ministry became members of the Board of Governors. In the beginning, mostly monks (Lamas) were admitted as students in different subjects, and the emphasis was on the study of 'Vinaya'. Gradually the syllabus was revised, and at present lay persons as well as monks and nuns constitute the body of students enrolled at the Institute. In 1988, the Institute was declared a Deemed University, managed by financial support from the Department of Culture.

Aims

The organization was established for attaining certain specific objectives. They are as follows:

i. Preservation of Tibetan Culture and Traditions: This has been of primary concern to His Holiness the Dalai Lama as how best to maintain and preserve Tibetan culture and traditions.

ii. Restoration of Ancient learning and implementation of multi dimensional Tibetan Studies:

It covers the wide range of Buddhist scriptures, metaphysics, spirituality, literature, iconography, astronomy and medical science which are nestled in ancient Indian Shastras.

iii. To offer alternative arrangements for instruction to students hailing from the border areas of Ladakh, Himachal Pradesh, Uttar Pradesh, Sikkim, North Bengal, Assam and Arunachal Pradesh who were left bereft of such vital knowledge and spiritual training under the altered circumstances.

iv. Revival of traditional education under modern university educational system:

It is conceded that the entire monastic education is additional in basic character as there has been lack of modern educational methods and resources in Tibet. The needs of the time and the exodus of the Tibetan people have necessitated reorientation of the ancient methods under the modern system. Under this normative experience' traditional Tibetan subjects are taught in this institute on modem curricular modalities.

Activities & events during 1998-99

Seminars

(i) 'The concept of Adharma in various religions was held in association with Triratna Trust on 1st and 2nd April, 1998.

(ii) 'World Unity in Buddha Triratna' was held in the Institute on 6th & 7th Nov. 1998.

Conferences/Lectures

(i) As a part of the programme to celebrate the 50' anniversary of India's Independence, a conference on 'Gandhi ke Gram Swaraj Siddhant Ki

Pratyaveksha' was held on 8th and 9th August, '98 in the Institute which was attended by many distinguished scholars and social workers of repute.

(ii) A Conference of Vice-Chancellor's/Directors of Non-conventional Universities was held in the institute. Five Vice-chancellors/Directors/ representatives participated in the conference.

(iii) Dr. K.N.Mishra, Professor in Sanskrit, visited Paris University as Visiting professor from 28th April to l4th May, 1998, and participated in an International - Conference on Jainism and Buddhism at Luanda, Sweden. He also visited Vienna to attend an International Conference on 'Vedanta and Creative Realism' and delivered extension lectures in different Universities in Romania.

Meditation camps

Three Meditation camps were organized in the institute campus in collaboration with Vipassana Meditation Centre.

Summer camp for students

A short summer camp was organized by Voluntary Community Social Service of the Institute from 22nd to 24th May, 1998 in which 40 students participated. Discussions and debates on various topics such as Hind Swaraj, Non-violent Action, Role of Students in Upliftment of Nation, Significance of Culture and Tradition etc. took place.

Training camp

A Sanskrit Training Camp was organised from lst to 10th September in the Institute in collaboration with Sanskrit Bhartiya. The camp was inaugurated by Pt. Janardan Pandey and the valedictory session was presided over by Prof. S. Rinpoche.

Two Educational Tours led by teachers of Tibetan Medicine Dr. Lobsang Tenzin (with 8 students) and Dr. Dojee Damdul (with 2 students) started for Tawang in Arunachal Pradesh and Manali in Himachal Pradesh respectively.

Celebrations

Asadh Purnima (Guru Purnima), was celebrated as Dharma Chakra Diwas' on 9th July in the Institute in collaboration with Triratna Trust. Vice-Chancellor of Sampurnanand Sanskrit University Dr. Mandan Mishra graced the occasion as Chief Guest Dr. Kedar Nath Mishra delivered a lecture on 'The Concept of Bhagawan in Buddhist Canonical Literature: and Prof. S. Rinpoche, Director of CIHTS, explained the importance of the day.

News letters

A quarterly News Letter based on the activities of the Institute is being brought out by the Institute.

Workshop

A workshop on New Media Orientation was held in the Institute as scheduled on 8th and 9th October in collaboration with the Orient Foundation and AIU. A number of delegates from all over India participated in the workshop.

Sikkim research institute off Tibetology, Gangtok

The Sikkim Research Institute of Tibetology, Gangtok is an autonomous organization under the Government of Sikkim with the Governor of Sikkim as the President of its Governing Body. It was set up for research and studies in Tibetology. The Institute has done significant work in promoting research in Tibetology and associated subjects like iconography, medicine, astrology and history. It has special research and publication programmes. The Bulletin of Tibetology is the Institute's regular research journal which is published thrice a year. The Institute received an annual grant of Rs.13.34 lakhs from the Government of India during 1998-99.

Library off Tibetan works and archives, Dharmashala

The Library of Tibetan Works and Archives, an autonomous registered institution, was established by H.H., the Dalai Lama in 1971, with a view to preserve and promote the rich heritage of Tibetan civilization and Indo-Tibetan learning. Today, this Institution has acquired world stature as a centre for Tibetology and Indo-Tibetan Studies. The Institution has the following Departments:

(i) Tibetan Books and Manuscripts Library
(ii) Foreign Language Reference Library
(iii) Museum and Archives Departments
(iv) Centre for Tibetan Studies comprising of a School of Indo-Tibetan Buddhist studies, a School of Tibetan languages and literature, a School of Thanka painting and School of Traditional Art of wood-carving all recognized by the Govt. of India.

During the year under review, the Library completed preparation, translation and research and publication of major works on Indo-Tibetan studies. It organized a number of workshops and seminars on archaeology and Indo-Tibetan literature. A number of new research and translation works were published. The Oral History Department of the Library has now holdings of 10000 hours containing recordings on music, dance, folk history, customs and culture of Tibet.

The Govt. of India provided a grant of Rs.18.30 lakhs to the Library during 1998-99. There is a specific scheme to give assistance to organizations and monasteries engaged in propagating Buddhist and Tibetan Culture.

Nava Nalanda Maha Vihara, Nalanda, Bihar

The Nava Nalanda Mahavihara is an Institute for Postgraduate teaching and research in Pali language and literature and Buddhist Studies, functioning under the Department of Culture since 25th February 1994. His Excellency the Governor of Bihar is the Chairman and Secretary, Department of Culture is the Vice-Chairman of the Nava Nalanda Mahavihara Society.

There are eleven members of the society of which three are eminent Buddhist scholars nominated by the Department of Culture.

Seminars, conferences and lectures

i. Impact of Pali and Buddhism in Tagore's Literature on 6-5-98.

ii. Significance of Buddha Purnima on 22-5-98.

iii. Colloquium on Ahimsa in Buddhism & Gandhian Philosophy on 14-8-98.

iv. Independence Day was observed on 15-8-1998 by the teaching, non-teaching staff and students both Indian and Foreign.

v. Professor Dr. Basudeb Burman, Vice-Chancellor, Kalyani University, delivered a lecture on Value Based Education under Ven. Jagadish Kashyap Memorial Lecture on 15.10.98.

vi. Dr. H.S.S. Nissenka, a renowned Buddhist Scholar of Sri Lanka, delivered a thought provoking lecture on 'Buddhist Psychotherapy' on 22.10.98.

9.13 Research activities

i. Professor Dr. Dipak Kumar Barua, Director, presented the following papers/articles.

(a) The Basic Foundation of Theraveda Buddhism (Facets of Indian Culture : Gustav Roth Felicitation Volume, Patna, Bihar Puravid Parishad 1998)

(b) Karmad hyana-Prajnamay Prajnajyoti (Vidarshan Bhavana Prajnasadhak Prajnajyoti Mahasthavira, Calcutta, Vidarshan Siksa Kendra, 1998.

(c) Professor Nalinaksha Dutt: A Centenary Tribute (Indo - Iranica: Journal of the Iran Society, Calcutta, Vol.48, 1997-98.

ii. Dr. Prabhakar Mishra, Lecturer in Philosophy

(a) Attended the 43rd session of the "All India Philosophy Association" at Gurukul Kangri University and presented a paper entitled "Life After Death-An introduction lecture" from 13th to 15th September, 1998 in Haridwar, U.P.

(b) Presented a paper entitled "Ahimsa in Buddhism and Gandhian Philosophy" in the concluding session on the completion of the 50th Year of Independence of India at the Nava Nalanda Mahavihara, at Nalanda on 14-8-98.

(c) Presented a paper entitled "The Religious Ideas of Rabindra Nath Tagore" in the 73rd session of the Indian Philosophical Congress held from 29th-31st October, 1998 at Karnataka University, Dharwad, Karnataka.

Publications

Through its publications the Mahavihara has enriched the stock of Indian Scriptures particularly Buddhist Scriptures. The whole of Buddha's teachings preserved in Pali Tripitaka was published for the first time in the Devanagari Script in 41 volumes. 30 volumes of the commentaries (Atthakathas) are the texts of the Pali Tripitaka which have also been published in Devanagari Script. Nava Nalanda Mahavihara Research Volumes I to IV and Nalanda Past and Present have been published by the Mahavihara.

Library

The Mahavihara has a rich library of specialized nature. At present there are 37,076 books on Buddhist scriptures in Pali, Sanskrit, Chinese, Japanese and Tibetan.

Central institute of Buddhist studies, Ladakh

The Central Institute of Buddhist Studies, Leh-Ladakh, formerly known as School of Buddhist Philosophy was established at the behest of late Pandit Jawahar Lal Nehru in the year, 1959 with active cooperation of Rev. Kushok Bakula Rinpoche. It was registered under the J&K Societies Registration Act-VI 194 (1941). In 1962, the Department of Culture, Government of India, took up the task of financing the School. It was later on raised to the level of a degree and post graduate Institute affiliated to Sampurnanand Sanskrit University, Varanasi. The Institute is managed by a Board of Management.

The main objective of the Institute is to develop the multifaceted personality of the student through inculcation of the wisdom of Buddhist thought, literature and to develop familiarity with modern subjects, collection, conservation, translation, publication of rare manuscripts and research work relevant to Buddhist Studies etc.

To achieve its aim and objectives, the Institute is actively imparting education in all spheres of Buddhist Studies to the young Lamas and other interested students. The basic focus is on Buddhist Philosophy taught in Bhoti Tibetan language. However, keeping in view the need for expanding the horizons of knowledge of the students, subjects such as Hindi, English, General Science, Social Studies, Mathematics, Economics and History are also being taught. Besides, six-year courses are offered to interested students in Amchi, Tibetan Scroll Painting, Sculpture and Wood Carving to preserve the rich cultural heritage of the region. The present strength of students in the Institute is 237. The Institute is running 24 feeder schools in different Monasteries of Ladakh to provide basic elementary education to the young Monks. At present 371 students are studying in 24 Gonpa Schools. The Institute has a branch School at Zanskar in Kargil District in which 130 students are studying from Class 1st to 8th. The Institute has a good library, the only one of its kind in Ladakh with a rich collection of books. The Library is enriched every year with new collections of books. Besides, the Institute has built up a modest Archaeological Museum with a good collection of antiquities and other objects. A number of rare manuscripts have been published by the Institute. These publications are reasonably priced for the benefit of interested scholars and students. The Institute offers four fellowships for research work leading to award of Doctorates in the field of Buddhism as well as in four other sects of Buddhism.

A new Institute complex with separate blocks for teaching, administration, Library, Museum, hostel and residences purposes is coming up in a phased manner over a piece of land measuring 208 Kanals and 17 Marlas. The Border Road Organization was entrusted with the job of construction of boundary wall as well as the approach roads in the new campus which have been completed. The remaining work is under execution through C.P.WD. The first phase of the complex: which includes the hostel block for 100 students, 40 residential quarters, internal roads, electricity and water supply have been completed at a cost of Rs.274.86 lakhs. The complex is to be part-commissioned during the next season.

The Institute is funded hundred percent by the Department of Culture, Ministry of Human Resource Development, Govt. of India. Substantial grants are provided to support various activities and programmes of the Institute. During 1998-99 the Board of Management has approved a budget provision of Rs. 153.03 lakhs under Non Plan and Rs. 138.10 lakhs under Plan for the implementation of various programmes.

The sanctioned strength of the staff of the Institute is given in below.

S. No.	*Faculty*	*Sanctioned Posts*	*Filled Up*	*Vacant*	*Remarks*
1.	Teaching staff	32	25	7	Posts already Adver-tised
2.	Administrative Staff	23	18	5	do
3.	Gonpa School	24	24	–	do
4.	Class IV	22	15	7	do
5.	D.P.S. Zkr.	9	7	2	do
	Total	110	89	21	

9

Akademies and the National School of Drama

Sangeet Natak akademi

The Sangeet Natak Akademi - the National Akademy of Music, Dance and Drama - an autonomous organisation funded by the Ministry of Human Resource Development, is devoted to the furtherance of the performing arts of India. The Akademi seeks to achieve this by arranging performances by renowned veterans as well as by talented artists of the younger generation, through training programmes, award of scholarships, documentation etc. The Akademi also bestows honours annually on outstanding artistes in the field of performing arts.

The management of the Akademi vests in its General Council, supported by the Executive Board, which exercises direction and control over the affairs of the Akademi.

The Akademi runs two teaching institutions -Kathak Kendra (New Delhi) and Jawaharlal Nehru Manipur Dance Akademi (Imphal - for Training in Kathak dance and music and Manipuri dance and allied arts). The Akademi also looks after the management of the Rabindra Rangshala in New Delhi.

Major activities of the academy are :

Documentation and dissemination

(i) During the period about 2730 black and white and colour photographs, 154 colour slides, 05 hours of audio and 53 hours of video recordings were added to the archives of the Akademi.

(ii) The Akademi has brought out a set of 3 compact Discs.

(iii) The Akademi has brought out a 30-minute Video Compilation "An Octave in Harmony" on the culture of North Eastern States.

(iv) The Akademi's video collection was screened on the occasion of "Natya Parv" festival organized by the MY Kala Parishad in the first week of December '98.

During 1998-99, besides the regular recording of musicians and dancers identified by the Advisory Committees, the following projects will be taken up:

a. Recording of Gurubani, the devotional music of the Sikh religious tradition, Jagar of Kumaon region of Uttar Pradesh and Kirtan of Bengal and Onge tribe of Andaman.

b. Video films from the compilation of the archives of the Akademi specially recorded during the Swarna Samaroh is proposed to be taken up. The Video films will be on Betacam. format. It is also proposed to compile a few video films from the archival collection of the Akademi.

Museum

The Museum of the Akademi has a collection of about 1300 musical instruments, masks, jewelry etc. Out of which 250 musical instruments are on view in the Gallery of Musical Instruments housed in Rabindra Bhavan.

Systematic numbering, accessioning, cataloguing and indexing of the collection taken up is under. compilation. The photographs and colour slides of the entire collection of the Museum have been completed.

Library

The Library holdings stand at over 21,000 books duly classified, indexed and catalogued. Efforts to augment the collection of regional language publications on performing arts are in process.

Audio visual libbrary

The entire collection of the audio visual library has been classified, and is open to the public, the facility of which is being increasingly used. Details of the collections are given below

S.No.	Collection	Number
1.	Gramophone Records	9678
2.	Commercial Audio-cassettes	1472
3.	Copies of Cassettes from Akademi Archives	762
4.	Video-Cassettes	85
5.	Compact Discs	145

Training and preservation of traditional performing arts

Under the scheme-Training programme, the Akademi continued training in Nadaswaram, Thavil, Kuchipudi, Yakshagana and Sufiana Kalam etc.

Festival of music & dance

The Akademi in collaboration with ICCR presented the Indian component of music & dance at the time of South Asian Dance and Music Festival held at Kamani Auditorium, New Delhi from 28th-31st July 1998. The festival was inaugurated by the Hon'ble Vice-President of India Shri Krishan Kant on 28 July 1998.

Playwrights workshops

The Akademi has launched a new scheme entitled 'Playwright's Workshops', with a view to providing suitable opportunities to poets and young writers to write new plays in Indian languages.

Promotion & preservation of puppetry

A workshop was conducted to prepare new scripts based on Hitopadesha and Panchtantra.

Organization of music, dance and theatre festivals

A major event focusing exclusively on Odissi dance and Music 'Nrutya Parva' was organized in Bhubaneshwar in collaboration with the Orissa Sangeet Natak Akademi from 23rd-30th November, 1998

During the festival, eminent Gurus and senior practitioners of the art like Kumkum Mohanty, Sonal Mansingh, Ramani Ranjan Jena, Gangadhar Pradhan, Durga Charan Ranbir and the maestro Kelucharan Mohapatra, participated.

Indo-British concert series

The Akademi is collaborating with the British Council to present a series of Indo-British Concerts in the four metropolitan cities namely Chennai, Delhi, Calcutta and Mumbai. This concert series will bring together across India over a dozen young British and Indian musicians who have already launched their professional careers and are on their way to international recognition. Both the Sangeet Natak Akademi and the British Council play important roles in show-casing the work of young musicians. The focus in this joint presentation is to provide an India-wide platform for young Indian and British musicians to display their techniques and artistry and to discover common ground together through workshops and interactive sessions in Delhi, Mumbai, Calcutta and Chennai.

Inter-State cultural exchange programme

The programme envisages exchange of individual artistes and groups between the States and Union Territories of the country. While implementation of the programme rests with the State Governments, the Akademi plays a pivotal role in the exchange by way of advising the Governments concerned, subsidising and coordinating the tours sponsored.

Cultural exchange programme between India and other countries

Bilateral Cultural Exchange Programmes are implemented by the Academi in accordance with the decisions taken by the Department of Culture. This mainly consists of exchange of information and material, books, tapes etc. on the performing arts. During the year the Akademi sent books and cassettes worth Rs. 1.80 lakhs to 33 countries. The Akademi also sponsored Shri Tapas Sen, eminent fight designer and Awardee of the Sangeet Natak Akademi to a seminar held in London on theatre designing.

Establishment of national centres for specialised training in music and dance

The Akademi had identified Kutiyattam and Chhau dances of Seraikella, Mayurbhanj and Purulia as artistic traditions that appear to be threatened. Support is to be extended by strengthening existing training centres and through the setting up of new centres.

Support to Kutiyattam and Chhau dance of Mayurbhanj, Orissa

Under the project;

a) Support to Kutiyattam, the Akademi envisages systematic transmission on the art through training and regular performances.
b) Support to Chhau Dance of Mayurbhanj (Orissa)

The training programme in Mayurbhanj Chhau which was launched on 1st February 1994 after a survey of 26 villages is reviewed periodically. Based on encouraging reports the programme is continuing.

The project has achieved notable success - in its primary objective of sustaining and strengthening the tradition of Chhau dance by creating an ambiance for regular training and practice of the art.

Akademi fellowships and awards

The General Council of the Akademi which met on 19th May 1998 in New Delhi, selected 24 artistes and scholars for the Akademi fellowship and Awards. The Akademi fellowship (1) and Awards (23) carry a purse of Rs. 40,000/- and Rs.25,000/- respectively, a shawl and Tamrapatra. The honours were conferred by the Hon'ble President of India Shri K.R. Narayanan at an investiture ceremony at Rashtrapati Bhavan on 9th December 1998. Among the personalities honoured, Shri Badal Sircar received Fellowship. 12 musicians, 6 practitioners of dance and 5 theatre persons were awarded. The Fellow and Awards winners for 1997 are in Box No.10.02

The investiture ceremony was followed by a five day festival featuring some of the recipients of the Awards from 9th-13th December 1998 at Sri Ram Centre, New Delhi. A special morning session devoted to Carnatic Music was also held on 13th December in Kamani Auditorium, New Delhi.

Theatre festivals

In pursuance of the decision taken by the General Council of the Akademi, 2 major national level festivals are scheduled for the year 1998-99. The multilingual theatre festivals will feature some of the finest productions of eminent theatre directors of the country today. The festival in Bangalore was held from 18th-24th

January 1999 in which plays in Kannada, Tamil, Manipur, English, Hindi and Punjabi by Prasanna, N. Muthuswamy, Lokendra Arababam, Maya Rao, Dinesh Thakur, Usha Ganguli and Neelarn Mansingh Chaudhary, were presented. The festival in Allahabad will be held from 15th-21st February 1999 and will feature plays in Hindi, Bengali, Manipur, Telugu, Dogri and Marathi by such eminent directors like Anuradha Kapoor, D.R. Ankur, Meghnath Bhattacharya, L.Doren, Surabhi Theatre, Balwant Thakur and Sunil Shanbhag.

Grants to cultural institutions

Grants amounting to Rs. 29,04,000 lakhs and Rs. 1,06,000 lakhs were sanctioned to 197 cultural institutions and puppet groups and institutions respectively during the year 1998-99 for training, production, purchase of technical equipment etc.

Centre of Indian Music

A new Centre for Indian Music at Gwalior for advanced research and training will be set up by the Akademi in 1998. The Department of Culture has released a sum of Rs.7.50 lakhs towards this Centre. Activities related to workshops/intensive training etc. would be initiated upon receipt of the formal approval from the Department of Culture.

Museum of Performing Arts

At the suggestion of the Akademi, opening of a Museum of Performing Arts in Delhi has been included in the Celebration of 50th Anniversary of India's Independence by the Department of Culture. This would be a learning/ resource centre reflecting traditions of music, dance, theatre and puppetry of tribal and rural areas, classical traditions and traditional theatre all over the country. An attempt would be made to reflect the tribal classical continuum as obtaining in the performing arts situation of the country. Contemporary work in music, dance and theatre would form a section of the Museum. The Museum will focus on performing traditions, their continuity and changes during the past 100-150 years or so as major developments have taken place in the history of several forms and styles during this period.

Kathak Kendra

The Kathak Kendra is one of the leading institutions for training in Kathak dance. Both in its earlier incarnations as Department of Bharatiya Kala Kendra and later (since 1964) as a unit of the Sangeet Natak Akademi, New Delhi, it has rendered significant services in the field of dance education.

Its main objective is to train proficient dancers committed to pursuing the arts as a profession. Eminent masters of Kathak dance and Hindustani music including Pandit Lacchu Maharaj, Shambhu Maharaj, Sunder Prasad, Kundanlal Gangani, Mohanrao Kallyanpurkar, Kumudini Lakhia, Birju Maharaj, Durga Lal, Hafiz Ali Khan, Mustaq Hussain Khan, Mohinuddin and Aminuddin Dagar, Siddeswari Devi and Naina Devi have taught here. Gifted teachers of the younger generation have also been brought in for training purposes. Many dancers trained at Kathak Kendra have received acclaim both for solo dancing and for their choreographic work.

The Kendra has a repertory wing which strives to enrich the repertoire and technique of Kathak through experimental work. Headed by the eminent Kathak maestro Pandit Birju Maharaj, the repertory wing has presented over 15 major dance-dramas and group compositions employing traditional Kathak idiom. Some of these have been hailed as landmarks in Kathak.

Dance Festivals/Programmes

The following festivals/programmes were held during 1998-99.

Dikshantotsava

'Dikshantotsava' was held at the auditorium of Triveni Kala Sangam, New Delhi from 9th through 15th May, 1998 in which 37 final year students of various courses were featured. The programme presented at this festival is a method of evaluating the achievements of the Kendra's students as solo performers.

Other Programmes

On 1st & 2nd December, 1998 'Konark festival', Bhubaneshwar under the sponsorship of 'Odissi Research Centre', Bhubaneshwar and Orissa Tourism Development Corporation was organised.

Programmes during January 1999 to March 1999 were i) Students performance series (in collaboration with Habitat centre), ii) Workshop on Kathak Music, iii) Avartani (Festival of select items from the production unit repertoire), iv) Ten-days Kathak Dance Workshop and v) Kathak Mahotsava.

Annual Examination

The Kendra conducted the Annual Examinations for the Academic session 1997-98 from 9th-15th May, 1998. Out of 155 students 142 students were declared successful.

Jawaharlal Nehru Manipur Dance Academy, Imphal

A constituent unit of the Sangeet Natak Akademi, the Jawaharlal Nehru Manipur Dance Academy, Imphal is the leading teaching institution for Manipuri dance and allied arts. Established in 1954 at the initiative of the late Prime Minister, Pandit Jawaharlal Nehru, the Akademy offers several comprehensive courses in Manipuri dance, music and allied arts. The courses are designed as a foundation for professional artists. It also has a Production Unit which strives to enrich the Manipuri repertoire through experimental work. The production Unit has produced 25 dance-drama so far. These have been presented in India and other countries.

The Foundation day of the JNMDA was held on 1st April 1998 at the Academi Auditorium. Shri O.N. Shrivastava, the Governor of Manipur and Chairman of the Academy. Shri R.K. Priyogopalsana Singh, (Retd.) Pradhan Guru, JNMDA and Shri Ratan Thiyam, Vice-Chairman, JNMDA, graced the function as Chief guest, Guest of Honour and President respectively. Solo performances by the students of the JNMDA were the highlight of the function.

A One day programme of Ibudhou Chakhaba was held at the shrine of Ibudhou Chakhaba at the Academi complex on 21st May 1998. This is a ritual part of the Lai-Haraoba Festival of the Lord. Gurus, artistes and students participated in the programme.

A 15-member troupe of the Academy led by Shri L. Joychandra Singh, Directbr, JNMDA participated in the Path Mark Multi-Cultural Arts Festival on 30th May, 1998 in New York, which was celebrated as a part of America's largest ethnic celebration. They presented a traditional programme of Manipuri Dance & Music.

Two more programmes - the first one at the Auditorium of the World Bank on 2nd June, 1998 in the presence of World Bank President, Mr. James Wolfanstohn and another at the Auditorium of Wheaton High School, Silver Spring, M.D. on 5th June 1998 were presented. The performances received wide acclaim.

The students of the Academi observed "PATRIOT'S DAY" on 13th August, 1998 at the Academi Auditorium.

Gurus, artistes and officials of the Academi spoke on the significance of the day in the history of Manipur.

A forty one member Cultural Troupe of the Academy visited Nabadwip to participate in the 200th Death Anniversary of Rajarshi Bhagychandra organised by Rajarshi Bhagychandra Death Anniversary Celebration Committee, Nabadwip, West Bengal from 21st-26th September, 1998.

The Academi presented Traditional Manipuri Dance and Music on 1st August '98, sponsored by the Regional Institute of Medical Sciences in honour of medical experts from Delhi.

The Annual Examination of the various courses run by the Jawaharlal Nehru Manipur Dance Academy were held in December 1998. A Convocation ceremony will be held in January 1999. The new Academic session will start from the first week of February 1999.

The JNMDA will present two Dance-Dramas "Keibul Lamjao" and "Wainu Pareng" on the occasion of the 5th National Games to be held in Imphal in February 1999.

Sahitya Akademi

The Sahitya Akademi was founded in March 1954 to promote the cause of Indian Literature and promote national integration through literature by way of publications, translations, seminars, workshops, cultural exchange programmes and literary meets organised all over the country. The Sahitya Akademi recognises eminent writers through Awards in 22 Indian languages for creative writing, 22 translation prizes, fellowships for distinguished contributions to literature, Bhasha Samman meant to promote peripheral languages, the Ananda Coomaraswamy Fellowship for South Asian scholars and Honorary fellowships for foreign scholars who have done significant work in Indian literature. The Akademi publishes books in 22 languages and has three journals - Indian Literature (in English), Samakalena Bharatiya Sahitya (in Hindi) and Samskrita Pratibha (in Sanskrit). Besides, it holds the following programmes in various parts of the country.

Meet the Author (here an eminent author reads from his or her work, Kavisandhi (a distinguished poet reads poetry), Kathasandhi (a distinguished fictionist reads from his work), Asmita (a special platform for women writers), Mulakat (a forum for young writers), Men and Books (talk by scholars, scientists and performing artists about the books that have impressed them most), Through my Window (talk by one writer on another writer, who is no more), LOKA: The Many Voices (Lectures on folklore) Avishkar (performance of literature through performing arts, Antaral (End century lectures by eminent men of letters), and a Festival of Letters annually, apart from literary forum meets, seminars, workshops, video films on eminent writers and documentation work to preserve Indian literature.

Important functions and programmes held during the year:

Kavyardharshati

A unique 3-day All India Poetry Festival was organised at New Delhi to celebrate the Golden jubilee of India's Independence. More than 50 poets, representing 22 Indian languages read their poems. As part of the festival excerpts from Dinkar's epic poem Rashmirathi, was staged by the students of the National School of Drama under the direction of Prasanna. The poetry readings of the first two days was followed by a film show "Freedom Struggle and Indian Poetry" on 7th-9th August at New Delhi

Translation prize giving ceremony

Translation Prizes for 1997 were given to 21 practising translators at a function organised in New Delhi on 13 September. Sri Ashokamitran, noted Tamil writer was the Chief Guest. Three Bhasha Sammans were also distributed during this function. The next day, there was a meeting of the prizewinners who spoke about their experiences as translators and writers.

Days of Moscow in Delhi

A seminar on Pushkin was organised in collaboration with the Government of the National Capital Territory of Delhi on 25 September. The events also included a reading of Pushkin's poetry in English and Hindi. The Akademi also released the selected poems of Pushkin in Hindi. Sabyasachi Bhattacharjee talked on the relevance of Bankimchandra Chatterjee in the 21st century on 13th July. French playwright M. Francois Louis Tilly shared his views on French Literature with eminent Indian Writers of the Capital on 22nd September.

Antaral

Prof. Debi Prasad Chattopadhya, the eminent Indian philosopher, delivered the fourth lecture under this series on 9th June.

Prof. Wagish Shukla delivered a lecture on "Death of Language: an Afterword" on 17th October.

Loka: The many voices

Sri Narayan Bharati, a folklorist was invited to speak on Sindhi folklore at Ajmer.

Sri Prapanchan, noted Tamil novelist, read one of his stories "Amanudan" at Chennai on 27 August.

Sri Rangnath Pathare read out his latest stories on 31 August.

Sri Yashwant Chittal, the eminent Kannada writer read out his short story "Kumatege Banda Kindara Jogi" at Bangalore on 22 September

Sri Allam Rajaiah read out his stories at a gathering in Hyderabad 28th September 1998.

Kavisandhi

Tamil poet Sirpi Balasubramaniam read out some of his Tamil poems at Chennai on 29th May '98.

Sri Alokranjan Dasgupta, the eminent Bengali poet and critic read a few of his poems at Calcutta on 6th May '98.

Sri Vinod Kumar Shukla, a senior Hindi poet, recited 11 of his compositions at New Delhi on 19th August '98.

Sri Vishnu Narayanan Namboodiri, Malayalam poet, recited his poems related to patriotism, spirituality and environment. on 21st August '98.

Sri Adil Mansuri, noted Gujarati poet read out some of his poems to a select gathering at Ahmedabad on 27th August '98.

Prof. Gopi read out his poems at a gathering in Hyderabad on 27th November '98.

Sri Allam Rajaiah read from his poetry on 28th November '98.

Sri Su Samuthiram, the Tamil writer, spoke on his life and works on 29th April '98.

Sri B.V.Baliga, well known Konkani writer spoke on his life and works. The event was organised in collaboration with Karnataka Konkani Sahitya Akademi at Mangalore on 5th October '98.

Sri N.K. Pandya 'Ushanas' eminent Gujarati poet was invited to speak on his life and works. The event was organised in collaboration with Narmad Sahitya Sabha at Mumbai on 1st November '98.

Sri Ali Sardar Jafri spoke on his life and works which was organised in collaboration with the India International Centre on 19th November '98.

Kove Manisekaran spoke on his life and works at Chennai on 12th December '98.

Through my Window

Prof. Perala Bharati Sharma, Telugu writer, gave a lecture on eminent Telugu poet Viwanadha Satyanarayana at Bangalore on 5th June '98.

Sri Navakanta Barua, eminent Assamese poet spoke on the distinguished Assamese writer Hem Barua, on 9th September '98.

Sri Prem Prakash, well known scholar and writer in Sindhi, spoke on the life and works of Sri Shyam Jaisinghani, eminent Sindhi writer, on 7th November '98.

Menand Books

Dr. R.V.Vaidyanatha Ayyar, Secretary, Department of Culture, spoke on the books that have had an impact on his writings and thoughts at New Delhi on 31st July '98.

Mulakat

Three young Hindi poets, Sri Kumar Ambuj, Sri Bodhisatva and Smt. Nilesh Raghuvamshi took part in a Mulakat programme on 23rd September '98.

Seminars and symposiums

Challenges before the Writer at the Turn of the Century at New Delhi, on 6th-7th April '98.

A Symposium on Indian Writing in English and in the other Languages organised in collaboration with Federation of Indian Publishers on 13th August 1998.

Tribal History, Culture and Literature at Baroda on 27th-29th August '98.

Painini and Modern semantics on 5th October '98.

National seminar on Painini and Modern Semantics at Calicut on 10th-12th October '98.

Konkani Language and Literature, Udipi on 19th-20th November '98.

International Seminar on Mirza Ghalib, New Delhi on 13th-15th December '98.

Sane Guruji, Dapoli on 25th-26th December '98.

Workshops

Rajasthani translation Workshop on 20th-27th December '98.

Books published

About 244 books were brought out.

Books releases

English translation of MARTHANDA VARMA at Trivandrum on 5 July '98.

A copy of Medieval Indian Literature Vol. 1 was received by the President K.R. Narayanan at a special function organised at Rashtrapati Bhawan on 17th July '98.

The Bengali translation of Ramakanta Rath's Sri Radha, released at Calcutta on 29th August '98.

Freedom and Fissures, an anthology of Sindhi Partition Poetry in Mumbai on 31st August '98.

Raja Rao: A Katha Classic was released in New Delhi on 9th November '98.

Shrestha Burmee Kahaniyan was released in New Delhi on 13th November '98.

Kassandra Dagh was released in New Delhi on 11 December '98.

Hindi Week was celebrated by the Akademi from 21st-25th September '98. The events included essay competions, quiz contests, general knowledge tests etc. It concluded with a Kavi Goshti.

Some Future Events

Poetry Reading by Yasmine Ladha, Keshav Malik and Sukrita Paul Kumar on 15 January 99. Symposium on the State of Literary Criticism in India 18 January 1999. (in collaboration with India International Centre)

Annual festival of Letters- The Sahitya Akademi '98 exhibition was inaugurated on 22nd February 1999 Annual awards for Literature in 22 languages was given away on 23rd February 1999 with S.L. Bhyrappa as Chief Guest and Changhiz Aitmatov as Guest of Honour. Samvatsar Lectures was delivered by M.T. Vasudevan Nair on 24th and 25th February 1999. A Writers' Meet was organised on 24th February 1999, a National Seminar on 'Novel in Search of Nation' was held from 2 6th to 28th February.

The Akademi has recently started an 'Archives of Indian Literature' meant to preserve manuscripts, photographs, audio and video materials and films on writers and writing in India.

It has also launched four Translation centres in Delhi, Ahmedabad, Bangalore and Shantiniketan respectively to bring out quality translations of old and new classics in the four regions.

The Akademi also has begun projects for translation of Indian classics into foreign languages with the collaboration of various Governments and literary institutions, besides continuing the Indo-Russian and Indo-Latin-American Literary exchange programmes.

The Akademi published more than 300 books this year and its net sales has crossed the Rupee One Crore mark.

Sahitya Akademi publishes books in twenty two languages and has so far published 3,222 titles including 2372 translations. Of them the maximum number of books are in Hindi followed by English. The books include old contemporary classics. Sahitya Akademi award winning books monographs on eminent writers, histories of different literatures anthologies collections of seminar papers bibliographies and memorial volumes. Some of the prestigious publications of Akademi are 'Encyclopedia of Indian Literature' (six volumes), Who's Who of Indian Writers Ancient Indian Literature (three volumes) medieval India Literature (four volumes) Modern Indian literature (three volumes) Rabindranath Tagore (Centenary Volume) Bankim Chandra Chatterjee - Essays in perspective. A History of Indian literature (eight volumes - two published) and selections from Jnandev and Vemana. Sahitya Akademi has been publishing inter-language translations of significant woks for the last forty years besides publishing two bi-monthly journals -Indian Literature' in English and 'Samakaleen Bharatiya Sahitya' in Hindi, exclusively devoted to translations of contemporary writing in Indian languages. Sahitya Akademi publishes one book every thirty hours, has a network of agencies in the country and abroad and has just launched a new project modern classics in Translation in collaboration with the National Book Trust, India.

Lalit Kala akademi

The Lalit Kala Akademi (National Akademi of Fine Arts) was established by the Government of India at New Delhi in 1954, to promote and propagate an understanding of Indian Art, both within the country and abroad. The Akademi has regional Centres at Lucknow, Calcutta, Chennai and Bhubaneswar as well as a small office at Mumbai where it has set up Community Artists'

Studios with workshop facilities in painting, sculpture, print making and ceramics. There is a similar studio centre at Garhi in New Delhi.

Since its inception, the Akademi has been organising National Exhibitions of Contemporary Indian Art during which 10 National Awards, each of Rs.25,000/- are awarded. Special exhibitions are also organized every three years. The Akademi organises Triennale India, an International exhibition of contemporary art at New Delhi.

To propagate Indian art, the Akademi participates in International Biennales and Triennales abroad and also organizes exhibitions of works of art from other countries. To foster contacts with artists abroad, it sponsors exchange of artists with other countries under the various Cultural Exchange Programmes and Agreements of the Government of India.

The Lalit Kala Akademi extends financial assistance to State Akademies and artists through prizes in exhibitions organized by them. The Akademi also brings out publications of art works and multi-colour reproductions and portfolios for sale.

From the Artists Aid Fund, financial assistance is given to ailing artists. The major activities undertaken by the Akademi during the year 1998-99 were:

Exhibitions

i. An exhibition of 'Random Selection of the. Works of Women Artists of India' from the Lalit Kala Akademi's Permanent Collection was organized at the Lalit Kala Akademi galleries from 21st May '98 to 20th June '98.

ii. On the occasion of the culmination of the year long celebrations of 50 years of Indian Independence, an exhibition of selection from the permanent collections of the Akademi was held from 7.8.98 to 20.9.98 in the galleries of the Akademi.

iii. The 41st National exhibition of Art was held from 16.11.98 to 4.12.98 in the galleries of the Akademi. From 6889 works of 1689 artists, 179 works were selected for display by the jury. 10 of the works were given awards and five were given honourable mentions. In addition the jury selected 8 artists as invitees, for display of their work.

Lecture talk/slide show

i. An artist from Korea, Ms. Kim Yongmi gave a talk on her work and held a slide show on 12-5.98 at Garhi Studio.

ii. Ms. Sadia from Canada delivered a lecture and Slide Show on 4.9.98 at Garhi Studio.

iii. An Artist, Ms. Bastienne Karamer delivered a lecture and slide show on Pottery at Garhi Studio.

Workshop

i. Regional Centre, Chennai organized a seven day workshop on Wood Sculpture at Hyderabad from 31st August to 6th September, 1998.

ii. Young Artists Workshop on 'Low Melting Ceramics' was organized by Regional Centre, Chennai at Pondicherry from 26th October to 1st Nov. 1998.

iii. An experimental workshop on 'Advanced Print-Making was organized by Regional Centre' Chennai, at Bangalore from 23rd Nov. to 28th Nov., 1998.

iv. The Rashtriya Lalit Kala Kendra, Calcutta organized a slide show and lecture on contemporary Western Indian Art by Dr.Shivaji Panikar, an eminent art historian at the Kendra Premises on 24th September, 1998.

v. The Rashtriya Lalit Kala Kendra, Lucknow in collaboration with the Himachal Kala Sanskriti Bhasha Akademi organized a Painters Camp at Shimla from 19th to 25th September 1998.

vi. An exhibition of works of the best art students was organized by R.L.K.K., Lucknow in collaboration with North Central Zone Cultural Centre at Allahabad from 3rd November to 9th November, 1998.

vii. The R.L.K.K., Bhubaneshwar organized the Dhokra Workshop at Phulbani from 18.9.98 to 22.9.98.

viii. An Art Appreciation Workshop (Lecture cum slide show) was organized by R.L.K.K., Bhubaneshwar, at Bhadrak on 12.10.98.

ix. The R.L.L.K. Bhubaneshwar, organized a Young Print makers workshop at Khairagarh, M.P. from 20.10.98 to 26.10.98.

Publications

A catalogue of the 41st National Exhibition of Art has been brought out by the Akademi.

National school of drama

The National School of Drama, one of the foremost theatre training institutions in the world, and the only one of it's kind in India was set up by the Sangeet Natak Academy in 1959. In 1975, it became an independent entity, fully financed by the Department of Culture, Ministry of Human Resource Development.

Over the years, the School has made rapid strides on various fronts including a rapid expansion of its activities in all parts of the country. It has produced a galaxy of talents - actors, directors, script writers, designers, technicians, and educationists who work not only in theatre but also in films and television- winning several awards national and international.

Training in the School is based on a thorough comprehensive, carefully planned syllabus which covers every aspect of theatre in which theory is related to practice, and in which all work is ultimately put to test before the public. The syllabus takes into account the methods of great theatre personalities who have shaped contemporary theatre, in all its facets of expressional forms. The systematic study and practical performing experience in Sanskrit Drama, Modern Indian Drama, Traditional Indian theatre forms, Asian drama and western drama gives the students a solid grounding and a wide perspective in the art of theatre. In order to establish linkages between the traditional theatre forms of India and modem expressions, the School invites experts to train the students in these forms and also sends students to regional centres for training in traditional theatre. The School has also attached to its teaching faculty, some of the finest creative talents from within the country and abroad.

The National School of Drama has a faculty of 14 members. To provide a varied and wide ranging syllabus the school regularly invites professors, theatre personalities and experts from India and abroad to supplement the teaching process. The school admits 20 students per year in the first year of the three-year diploma course. The selection is on an all India basis. All students admitted are awarded a scholarship of Rs. 2,000/- for meeting their academic and other expenses.

The School awards apprentice fellowships to its students after completion of their course for widening their field of work and also for gaining more experience in theatre and in allied arts. Under this scheme, the fellowship holders are required to work on a variety of projects such as survey of traditional and folk forms of various regions of the country, to translate plays and conduct intensive theatre workshops in remote, rural areas etc.

As a part of the training programme, the students of the school produced 4 dramas in Hindi. These productions were directed by eminent Directors like Shri Prasanna. Prof. D.R. Ankur, Shri V.B. Karant etc., Similarly, nine productions by outsiders were also arranged by the School.

The School has a Repertory Company, which is the performing wing. It consists of a group of artists and technicians who are mainly alumni of the school. The Repertory Company staged 58 shows during the period.

Theatre-in-Education Company, now renamed as Sanskar Rang Toli was established in 1989 with a view to prepare plays and perform them for ultimately Children and adults at Delhi and neighbouring areas. The major thrust of the company is in going to schools with plays and organising workshops specially designed for specific age groups. In the summer workshop held by the company, 530 students from various schools participated.

Under the extension programmes, the school plans to organise intensive theatre workshops at Delhi and at various other parts of the country for children and young theatre workers with the objective of creating awareness about theatre and its techniques.

Various other activities of the school for the period under review are given below:-

(i) Study Tour of first year students to Ajanta & Ellora Caves during December 1998.

(ii) Workshop of second year students at Ahmedabad. As a part of the workshop, the students produced the play "Gulliton ki Gutthi". Three public performance of the play were given in Gujarat and four in Delhi.

(iii) Staging of 3 shows of the plays named Dekho Dragon Hindustani, Vikramovarshiyam and Veer Abhimanyu by second year students.

(iv) A 13-day full time workshop on Film Appreciation Course for the final year students was organized from 27th December 97 to 8th January '98. Ms. Gayathri Chatterjee from National Film Archives of India, Pune was invited to conduct the course.

10

Grants from the Department

The Department of Culture operates a number of schemes intended to provide monetary assistance to individuals, groups and voluntary organisations engaged in promoting a particular art form and/or to sustain cultural activities in the country. The contribution of the Department of Culture in giving financial assistance to young individuals who wish to pursue the arts as a profession has been immense. Scholarships are awarded to young workers in the field of art and later on followed by Junior and Senior Fellowships. The evaluation of this scheme has shown that many prominent artists in the field of dance, painting and music today have been the young recipients of this scholarship, or at a later stage the fellowships offered by the Department.

During 1998-99, the Department enhanced the number of Fellowships and Scholarships by around 50 per cent. The state-wise distribution of Senior/junior Fellowships and Scholarships sanctioned during 1998-99.

The indicated list of private and voluntary organizations which have been sanctioned grants of Rupees one lakh or more during 1998-99.

1998-99 the Department of Culture provided an outlay of around Rs.29 crores under these schemes.

11

Promotion and Dissemination of Art and Culture

Zonal Cultural Centres

Seven Zonal Cultural Centres (ZCCs) were set up under the VIIth Five Year Plan for the creative development of Indian Culture in various regions. The essential thrust of these Centres has been to create a cultural awareness and to identify, -nurture and promote vanishing folk art traditions in the rural and semi urban areas of the states.

Apart from organising a chain of cultural programmes in major city centres as well as in rural and far-flung areas, the ZCC's have established linkages with State Departments and NGOs for preservation, promotion and propagation of tribal and folk art forms. The ZCCs have also taken up the following three schemes of the Department of Culture during the VIIIth Plan.

(i) National Cultural Exchange Programme i.e. exchange of artists, musicologists, performers and scholars within the country. (ii) Setting up of Shilpgrams to provide promotion and marketing facilities to craftsmen. (iii) Setting up of Documentation Centres to document vanishing and dying art forms.

Three Zonal Cultural Centres spread folk culture among youth by bringing school children from far-flung areas of the country to display folk dance skills in the Republic Day Parade 1999.

The Zonal Cultural Centres presented programmes of folk dances at the concluding function of the Golden Jubilee celebrations of India's Independence on 141 August 1998 at Rajpath, New Delhi and Regional level functions were also organised by the ZCCs at their Headquarters.

Anathamoorthy committee report

The Government of India set up a High Powered Committee on 19th August, 1994, to review the working of the seven Zonal Cultural Centres. This was headed by Prof. U. R. Ananthamoorthy.

The Committee was also supposed to suggest how the Centres can serve the purpose of enriching and highlighting the cultural patterns in their respective areas. The Committee submitted its report to the Govt. in January, 1996.

The committee recommended changes in the structure of ZCCs, reduction in the administrative expenditure and suggestion for better coordination with the noted Akademies. The recommendations of the High Powered Committee were discussed in a meeting of the Chairmen of ZCCs under the chairmanship of the HRM. There were detailed discussions on the recommendations, in the two day Conference of Directors (ZCCs), the Secretaries of Akademies and Secretaries (Culture) of State Governments, held on February 11th- 12th 1998 at the National Museum, under the Chairmanship of Secretary(Culture).

A review meeting was held on 14th May, 1998 with the Secretaries of Akademies/Directors (ZCCs), etc. under the Chairmanship of Secretary(C) to review action taken report on the 2 day Conference of Directors (ZCCs)

Secretaries of Akademies & the State Secretaries. Secretary (C) had also addressed the Chief Secretaries/ Secretaries (Culture) State Govts./UTs etc. Most of the recommendations of the Committee are proposed to be implemented during the year 1999-2000 in the programmes of Zonal Cultural Centres.

Major cultural events

Some of the major cultural events organized by ZCCs during the year under report are as follows:-

EZCC, Calcutta

1. National Drama Festival, at Kalyani and Calcutta
2. Vagyachandra National Festival of Classical Dance, Imphal, Manipur.
3. Dweep Mahotsav, Port Blair
4. Adibasi Baha Parab, Birbhurn
5. Birth Centenary of Kavi Nazrul Islam
6. Celebration of Golden Jubilee Finale of India's Independence, Santiniketan.

NEZCC, Dimapur

1. North East Youth Dance Drama Festival, Agartala
2. Classical & innovative Dance programme, Assam
3. Best of Music from the North-East, Kohima, Nagaland.
4. Patriotic song and dance festival N.A.P. Chumudkedima
5. Best of folk dances of the North-East, Agartala, Tripura
6. Grand Finale of 50th Year of India's Independence, Raj Path, New Delhi.
7. Hozagiri Festival, Tripura
8. Cultural meet 1998, Tawang, Arunachal Pradesh.

WZCC, Udaipur

1. Shilpgram Utsav, Udaipur.
2. 50th Anniversary of India's Independence
3. Umang - Festival of Disabled Children.
4. Traditional Theatre Festival, Panaji, Goa
5. Natyotsav, Jodhpur, Bharuch, Aurangabad & Goa.
6. Balotsav at Bhavnagar
7. Classical Dance Festival at Jaipur, Sawai Madhopur.
8. Folk Festival at Sanskriti Kunj, Gandhinagar.
9. Rashtriya Upanishad - Seminar on Kalaon ki Moolya Dhristi.

SZCC, Thanjavur

1. Musicians in the making, Bragadeeswarar Temple, Thanjavur.
2. Participated in Republic Day Parade 1998.
3. Divisional Classical & Folk Dance Festival, Gulbarga, Karnataka.
4. Dweep Mahotsav, Port Blair.
5. Fete-de-Pondicherry'97 - Festival of Colour & Pageantry, Pondicherry.
6. Ponpurakkal Golden Jubilee Celebrations, Marina, Chennai.
7. Participated in INA Trial Commemoration Day, New Delhi.
8. Release of audio cassettes of Patriotic Songs in Tamil.

NCZCC, Allahabad

1. Folk Artists Camp, Bhopal
2. Uttar Dakshin Sangeet Sangam, New Delhi.
3. 'Saawan'- Cultural Programme, Dilli Hatt, New Delhi.
4. Janjatiya Parva, Allahabad, Bihar and Rajasthan.

5.Lecture-cum-Demonstration, Patna, Bihar

6. National Theatre Festival, Allahabad & Lucknow..
7. Bharat Jyoti, Haryana & U.P.
8. Shilp Mela & Cultural Programme, Allahabad
9. A brush with Ghalib, New Delhi.
10. Chalo Man Ganga Jamuna Teer, Allahabad
11. Leela Parva, Bhopal, Allahabad
12. International Women Day Celebrations, Allahabad

SCZCC, Nagpur

1. Modern Theatre Festival, Gadag.
2. Modern Dance Festival, Nagpur
3. Folk Dance Festival, Nagpur.
4. Fete-De-Pondicherry, Pondicherry, Mahe-Yamen.
5. Pune Festival, Pune
6. Traditional Theatre Festival, Udipi, Kindapur, Bhakkal, Honavar, Kumta, Ankola, Mancheri. Shilpgram Utsav, Udaipur.
7. Shilpgram Utsav, Udaipur
8. Bharat Jyoti Festival, Allahabad & 12 venues.
9. Dweep Mahotsav, Port Blair.

NZCC, Patiala

1. Summer Festival, Shimla, Dharamsala, Noorpur
2. International Cultural Exchange Programme, Telford, U.K.
3. Sham-e-Ghazal, Srinagar
4. Classical Music/Dances, Chandigarh
5. Independence Day Celebrations, Rajpath, Delhi.
6. Folk Singing/Dances state level programmes, Ludhiana.
7. Classical Music & Dance Festival, Jaipur.
8. Kullu Dushera, Kullu, H.P.
9. Kartik Festival, Ballabhgarh.
10. Chandigarh Karnival, Chandigarh.

Republic day folk dance festival & crafts fair '99

The Department of Culture organized the Republic Day Folk Dance Festival 1999 on the occasion of Republic Day. The Festival was inaugurated by the Honourable President of India on January 25th, 1999 at 11.00 a.m. the Talkatora Indoor Stadium. The dances presented were selected by a committee of well known experts. Besides Talkatora Indoor Stadium the shows were also held at Air-Force Auditorium, Subroto Park, Delhi; Delhi Tamil Sangam, R.K. Puram, New Delhi; & Sir Shankar Lal Hall, University of Delhi.

This year the Folk Dance Festival blossomed in 24 colourful dances. An attempt was made to cover as many States as possible, especially the dances from lands afar. From Himachal Pradesh came the colourful devotional Buddhist dance of the Lahul Spiti region known as Chham Chanak, the traditional Ras Dhamali dance of the Waltal tribes from Jammu & Kashmir, the tribal Nicobarese dance from the Andaman & Nicobar Islands, the Mishing Bihu of Assam, the delightful Yak Cham from Sikkim, the Lal Haroba of Manipur, the Rava Dance of West Bengal, the Dalkhai Sambalpuri dance of Orissa, and others were a feast to the eyes- and soothing to the heart.

Besides, the Crafts Fair was inaugurated by the HRM on January 23rd, 1999 at the Talkatora Cricket Ground and the Fair continued upto January 29th, 1999. Special emphasis had been laid on integrating cuisine with the Crafts Fair to present a holistic view of Culture. There were 14 stalls for cuisine and 84 crafts stalls. Cuisine from Chettinad, Kerala, Maharashtra, Gujarat, Rajasthan, Punjab, West Bengal, delicacies of J & K, and various other food items tempted people to visit the Fair. The Craft persons had been selected by the Seven ZCCs, from their participating States. The Crafts Fair offered a rich pot-pourri of delectable handicrafts from all over the country.

The Department contributed to the Republic Day Parade 1999 by organizing three Children's Contingents from WZCC, EZCC, and NEZCC. A camp was organised at Bhartiyarm where 462 children, along with musicians & 660 folk artists & crafts persons from different parts of the country lived together and created a mini-India for about three weeks. A Camp fire was arranged at Bhartiyam on January 26th, 1999 in which Secretary (Culture) congratulated the children for their spectacular show at Rajpath and presented gifts.

The Children's Contingent of North-East Zone Cultural Centre, Dimapur got the first prize.

A Foundation Course was organised by CCRT for the staff of ZCCs, State Akademies and Cultural organisations from 13th-25th July, 1998 in which a total number of 25 officers, out of whom 13 were from ZCCs participated.

A Workshop on 'Documentation: Plans, Problems and Prospects' was organised by S NA from December 21st - 25th 1998. The Workshop was conducted by Akademi under the Directorship of Shri Bhaskar Chandavarkar from 21st to 25th December 1998 at the Conference Hall, Sahitya Akademi, New Delhi. All the Directors (ZCCs) were invited to attend the Workshop. The officers and staff of the documentation unit of the SNA also attended the Workshop. Out of Seven ZCCs, Directors of the EZCC & SZCC made their presentation on the opening day. The others could not attend the Workshop.

The Workshop was inaugurated by Secretary (Culture) and Shri Bhaskar Chandavarkar delivered the keynote address.

Centre for cultural resources and training

The Centre for Cultural Resources and Training (CCRT) is an autonomous organisation under, the Department of Culture. The broad objectives of the Centre is to revitalize the Education System by creating an understanding and awareness among students about the cultural plurality of India and integrating this knowledge with school education.

The main thrust is on linking Education with Culture and making students aware of the importance of Culture in all developmental programmes. The training stresses on the role of Culture in Science and Technology, Housing, Agriculture, Sports etc. An important component of training is creating an awareness amongst students and teachers of their role in solving environmental pollution problems and conservation and preservation of the natural and cultural heritage.

Training

Orientation course

This course has been designed to equip high school teachers throughout India with knowledge and information about the fundamental principles underlying the development of Indian culture. It provides an opportunity to formulate methodologies through which aspects of Indian culture and practical art activities can be made an integral part of the process of learning and teaching and opportunity to interact with teachers of different regions and various disciplines and with scholars and artists, in order to devise ways of making education a fruitful experience. The Centre organized 8 Orientation Courses in which 556 teachers have been trained in the period from April 1998 to November 1998.

Workshops

Workshops are conducted for primary and high school

teachers in various art activities like drama, music, narrative forms etc. to provide practical training and knowledge in arts and crafts. In these workshops, teachers are encouraged to develop programmes in which the art form can be profitably utilised to teach the school curriculum. The role and use of each art form is explained in relation to the significance of art activities in imparting education. Workshops based on a single discipline or theme such as environmental studies enable CCRT to develop a variety of approaches for teachers that can be used in schools in order to provide creative and integrated educational programmes. During the period from April 1998, to November 1998, 1193 teachers and 1055 students were trained in 19 Workshops organized in and outside Delhi.

Seminars

Coinciding with each Orientation Course, CCRT organises Seminars for Principals/Headmasters/ District Education Officers and Senior Administrators for a duration of three to four days. The Seminar aims at providing participants with an understanding of CCRT's aims and objectives, developing methodologies for implementation of CCRT programmes, involving Administrators at the State level in the process of improving school education and creating an awareness of the importance of cultural education for the all round development of the students personality. The Centre organized 4 seminars in the period from April 1998 to November 1998 in which 40 Principals/Headmasters/DEOs/ DSCs participated.

Refresher courses

Selected trained teachers are invited to participate in the Refresher courses in order to recapitulate what they had learnt earlier and share the teaching experience gained during the intervening period. This course is designed to enable CCRT to get feedback from teachers previously trained. Trained teachers are selected on the basis of the work done by them in their respective schools, after receiving training at CCRT and their contribution towards integrating culture with education. One Refresher Course for teachers who were trained in Orientation Courses was organized in which 38 teachers participated. 2 Refresher Courses for teachers who have undergone training in the Course on Puppetry for Education were also organized in the period from April 1998 to November 1998 in which 112 teachers were trained.

Evaluation and feedback

CCRT has been training school teachers from all parts of the country both in the rural and urban areas. A feedback programme has been designed to maintain regular contact with trainees to study their follow-up work in schools and to evaluate the effectiveness of the programmes conducted and educational material provided. The evaluation and suggestions from trainees working in the schools assist CCRT in revitalising and enriching its activities. The number of teachers/educators and students of different states/ UTs trained by CCRT up to January 1999 is in Table IV A, Appendix.

Community and extension services

The Centre organises various educational activities for school students, teachers and children belonging to governmental and non-governmental organisations under its Community and Extension Services programme, which include, Educational tours to Monuments, Museums, Art galleries, Craft Centres/State Emporiums, Zoological Parks/Gardens, camps and Workshops on Learning Crafts using low cost locally available resources, lectures and demonstrations by artists and craft persons in schools, slide-lectures supplementing classroom teaching. Workshops for children in resettlement and basti colonies and Workshops for Handicapped students. During the period from April 1998 to November 1998, 3963 children from various formal and non formal schools have been trained.

Collection of resources

CCRT collects materials on the arts and crafts of the country in the form of audio recordings, slides, photographs, films and written texts enrich the content of the Cultural Kits and provide teacher trainees and other research students with material on the arts of India.

The areas to be documented by CCRT are chosen with a view to create an interest among students in the culture of various regions of the country and develop a sense of appreciation for the diversity and continuity of cultural traditions.

During the period from April 1998 to November 1998 the following forms have been documented on video:

1. Tabla
2. Chikan Work of Lucknow
3. Manipuri dance
4. Sun Temple of Konark
5. Hindustani Classical Vocal Music
6. CCRT Teachers' Award Function

Production

Cultural Kit

In order to fully realise the objectives of the training given to teachers attending the Orientation Course, a Cultural Kit consisting of audio-visual material and the publications of CCRT is provided to the institution from where the teacher has been trained. The kit is issued after evaluating the performance of the teacher in the course.

The institutions which are provided with the Cultural Kit, are duly instructed to send regular half yearly reports on the use of the material of the kit in classroom teaching in their schools and in other institutions and for the community. The kit, at present, comprises of written texts and slide catalogues on the arts of India, two slide albums containing 520 slides on plastic arts and 348 slides on performing arts, one cassette album comprising eight recorded cassettes of nine hours duration on performing arts, publications such as Cultural/ Educational packages, handbooks, posters, etc., and one cassette tape recorder and one 35 mm slide projector to institutions that do not possess these equipment.

During the period from April 1998 to November 1998, 600 cultural kits have been prepared and 406 cultural kits have been distributed to the teachers attending the Orientation Course. The state-wise distribution of Cultural Kits during 1998-99 and cumulative up to March 1998 is in Table IV B, Appendix.

Publications

CCRT aims to disseminate information and create an understanding of Indian Culture amongst teachers and students. Publications for schools and members of the community are prepared such as workbooks, handbooks, monographs on the arts and education, charts, posters, folios, packages etc. on topics related to aspects of Indian culture and ecology and the natural environment.

During the period from April 1998 to November 1998 CCRT has prepared the following educational materials:

— Srotasvini Journal for Aprl-June, 1998 & July-September, 1998
– Product catalogue 1998

- Teacher's Resource Pack
- National Symbols (revised edition)
- Art of Puppetry 2 (revised edition)

Due to increasing demand, CCRT has reprinted the following packages:

- Musical Instruments of India 1 & 2
- Art of Puppetry 1

During the period under report, the research work and compilation of manuscripts of the following publications were completed which will be brought out by March 1999, they are:

- World Natural Heritage Sites 1 & 2
- Annual Report 1997-98 (Bilingual)

Cultural talent search scholarship scheme

The CCRT has been implementing the Cultural Talent Search Scholarship Scheme since 1982. The scheme aims at providing facilities to study performing and other arts to outstanding young children in the 10- 14 age group. Students studying either in recognised schools or belonging to families practicing traditional, performing and other arts are chosen for the award of scholarships in various artistic fields. Special emphasis is laid on rare art forms. 297 students have been selected and offered scholarships in various art forms during the period from April 1998 to November 1998. The state-wise breakup of scholarships awarded under Cultural Talent Search Scholarship Scheme during 1998-99 is in Table IV C, Appendix

CCRT's Teachers' Award

The Centre has also instituted the CCRT Teachers' Award, which is given every year to selected teachers in recognition of the outstanding work done by them in the field of education and culture. This year ten teachers were awarded on 29th June 1998. The award consists of an amount of Rs.10,000/-, an angavastram. and a plaque.

Kalakshetra foundation, Chennai

Kalakshetra, a cultural international repute, was started by Smt. Rukmini Devi Arundale in 1936 as a cultural academy for preservation of traditional values in Indian art, especially in the fields of dance and music. The avowed objective of this institution was to bring about, on the one hand, integration of all art forms and regional variants thereof and to revive the ancient glory of Indian culture and set standards of true art on the other.

Recognising the importance of the institution the Government of India took over the management of Kalakshetra by a Presidential Ordinance issued on 29th September 1993 and declared it an institution of National importance. The order was later replaced by an Act of Parliament namely the Kalakshetra Foundation Act (No.6 of 1994). Since then the Kalakshetra Foundation has been functioning as an autonomous body under the Department of Culture. The management of Kalakshetra Foundation is vested in a Governing Board headed by Shri R. Venkataraman, former President of India.

Activities of Kalakshetra Foundation during the year 1998-99: -

Rukmini Devi College of fine arts

Admissions were made to Diploma Courses and Part time classes for different disciplines after selection and interviews. The number of admissions made are given below:-

	Full Time	*Part Time*	*Total*
Dance	34	21	55
Music	16	41	57
Painting	2	4	6

The total strength of the students in the year 1998-99 is 381 as against 350 last year.

The following programmes were arranged during the period.

The Chitrasena dance troupe from Sri Lanka-Under the Banyan Tree, gave a demonstration of three types of dance prevalent in Sri Lanka (i) Udarata (ii) Patharata and (iii) Subragamu As in the previous years, Citi Bank, Bombay "Remembered Rukmini Devi" by sponsoring four dance programmes from 5.9.98 to 8.9.98. The programmes were very well attended on all the four days.

Scholarships and awards

In addition to seven awards in the fields of Dance, Painting and Music, Scholarships were also awarded by the Kalakshetra Foundation under the various Endowments in force to 16 full time students of Dance and Music and about 12 students of Part time in Dance, Music and Painting. A sum of Rs.54,000/- was distributed under the Kalakshetra Foundation Endowments.

Important visitors

In August 98 Artists from the Royal Academy of Performing Arts, Bhutan visited Kalakshetra Foundation.

Other important news

Kalakshetra Foundation donated a sum of Rs.27,019/- (Rupees Twenty seven thousand and nineteen only) representing a day's salary of all the staff members of the Kalakshetra Foundation to the Prime Minister's National Relief Fund.

At the final examinations held in April, 98 one student each was awarded Post Diploma in

Bharatanatyam, and Music. 19 students were awarded Diploma in Bharatanatyam, 4 students in Music and 5 students in Painting.

Basant Arundale senior secondary school

The School has on its rolls 651 students, consisting of 281 boys and 370 girls. About 108 students are residing at the B.C.C. Hostel and 155 students have opted for the various part time courses at the Rukmini Devi College of Fine Arts.

Smt. Sharadha Balasubramanian assumed charge as Principal on 11th June, 1998. The School has 27 staff members comprising of 12 PGT's, 6 TGT's and 4 SGT's and specialists in Music, Art and Games and a Librarian. There are 14 members in the Non-Teaching cadre. The results of the Board Examinations held in March 1998 continued the tradition of cent percent passes. The Basant Arundale Senior Secondary School celebrated its Silver Jubilee on 4.9.1998. Dr. R. Vaidyanatha Ayyar, Secretary, Department of Culture, Ministry of Human Resource Development was the Chief Guest. The School continued to take part in Inter School Competitions.

Basant cultural centre hostel

A new Hostel Building consisting of 24 rooms with modern facilities and attached bathrooms was completed in May '98. All the senior students of the college are accommodated in this Hostel. A P & T Phone and an Intercom have been provided in the Hostel for easy communication. About 192 students are staying in the Hostel, who belong to the Rukmini Devi College of Fine Arts and other Schools.

Weaving and Kalamkari unit

The Kalamkari Unit continued to impart training in the tie and dye method of patterning textiles and some fabrics were produced. A workshop was conducted by the Craft's Council of India on dyeing of palm leaf and natural fibres with vegetable dyes.

Srimanta SankaradevaKalakshetra, Guwahati

In pursuance of Clause 6 of the Assam Accord, which pertains to providing safeguards for protecting, preserving and promoting the cultural, social linguistic identity and heritage of Assamese people, a multi-purpose cultural complex is being constructed in Guwahati, which has been named after Shri Srimanta Sankaradadeva, a legendary personality of Assam. For the construction of this dream project of the Assamese people - as it is perceived - the Department of Culture released an amount of Rs.12 crores. The complex has been completed and has become operational.

Scheme of financial assistance to professional groups and individuals for specified performing art projects

A very popular scheme, which over the years has encouraged experimental innovative original work in the literary and performing art fields gives financial assistance to individuals or groups. This has given a fillip to artists working in the field and has generated an environment in which creative people can think and work together for promotion of culture. Under the scheme, Financial Assistance is provided to theatre groups, music ensembles and solo artists of all genres of performing art activities on a non-recurring ad hoc basis.

12

Gandhi Smriti and Darshan Samiti

"Gandhi Smriti and Darshan Samiti" was formed in September 1984 with the merger of Gandhi Darshan at Rajghat and Gandhi Smriti at 5, Tees January Marg, and is functioning under the constructive advice and financial support from the Department of Culture, Ministry of Human Resource Development.

Among the basic aims and objectives for which "Gandhi Smriti and Darshan Samiti" were set up are :

(i) Preservation, maintenance and up-keep of Gandhi Smriti and Gandhi Darshan Complex and

(ii) to propagate the life, mission and thoughts of Mahatma Gandhi by organizing various socio-educational and cultural programmes.

Today Gandhi is remembered chiefly for his nonviolent methods of social protest which he first developed in South Africa, and then applied in India to win independence and now has universal application. Gandhi Smriti and Darshan Samiti attaches great importance to the propagation of Gandhian values amongst different segments of society through meaningful programmes.

Regular programmes

The programmes undertaken regularly are (a) Taking Gandhi to Schools (b) Seminars, (c) Arranging Gandhi Memorial Lectures (d) Regular Sarvadharma Prayer everyday at both the campuses,(e) Rendering Gandhi Bhajans and songs on communal harmony (f) Charkha spinning by the employees every morning and free spinning classes for the public on Sundays, and, (g) Khadi sales counters to propagate Khadi at both the campuses.

Shanti Sena training programme

Gandhi's idea of training youth on nonviolence and creating a task force of young men and women to promote communal harmony through Shanti Sena, has now become a regular programme in the Samiti.

Staff orientation programme

Under this programme, periodic lectures by eminent scholars on Gandhi, Indian culture and history are arranged for the Guides' and others involved in the dissemination of information on Gandhi. Such programmes provide them with opportunities to update their knowledge.

Programmes for mass awareness

Among the programmes the Samiti has designed for college and University students are:

(a) Mobile exhibitions on the life and work of Mahatma Gandhi as well as the causes dear to him and other contemporary topics.

(b) Film shows, which projects films on Gandhi and other national heroes.

(c) Discussions, Seminars and Symposia

(d) Short-term condensed orientation programmes for students on the Freedom Movement, the lives of national heroes, national integration, peace force and other constructive programmes.

The name of Mahatma Gandhi, today transcends the boundaries of race, culture, religion, state, country etc.

and stands out as the only viable alternative to the conflict-ridden nuclear bomb scared world of today. Fifty years after he was shot dead, Gandhiji continues to inspire people world over who seek refuge in his message of non-violence in a strife torn world. Continuing with the objective of propagating the message of the Mahatma far and wide, Gandhi Smriti and Darshan Samiti, organized various programmes. Major activities organised are as follows:

Kalp Vriksha - Children's Theatre A short play jointly produced by Gandhi Smriti and Darshan Samiti and IGNCA, was presented by children at Gandhi Darshan, Rajghat on 18th April 1998. The play focuses on basic Gandhian principles of communal harmony, basic education and the significance of constructive programmes, highlighting the message of 'back to nature'.

Young Messengers of Peace and Harmony; A significant programme for children entitled "Gandhi Ek Parichay" was launched by the Samiti to mark the Golden Jubilee Celebrations of Indian Independence, from 14th June to 26th June 1998.

Puppet Show on Folk Tales by Artists from Japan: Bharat Soka Gakkai in collaboration with Gandhi Smriti and Darshan Samiti put up a Puppet show for school children on 5th September 1998. Folk artists from Japan performed the show presenting folk tales from Japan. Around 200 children from different schools of Delhi saw the programme.

Sabarmati Dooryand

A play written by Prof. G. Shankara Pillai and directed by Prof. S. Ramanujam was presented in over 30 stages, during September- October in the 10 educational Sub-districts of Kerala by the Rangaprabhat Children's theatre under the leadership of K. Kochi Narayan Pillai.

Gandhi Campaign on Wheels: The mobile library-cum-pustak bazar is a popular vehicle for taking the message of the Mahatma far and wide. During the period under review, the bus covered Jawaharlal Nehru University, Delhi University, Indian Institute of Technology, Teen Murty, Nehru Place, Jantar Mantar and five schools in Delhi.

Library: There are more than nine thousand books in the in-house library of Gandhi Smriti and Darshan Samiti. Besides books on Gandhi and his thoughts, there are books on the freedom struggle, other leaders of modern India, Environment, Women's studies, literature and a special section for children.

Seminars/Lectures

A seminar on the topic Contemporary American Perspective of Developments in India was organized at Gandhi Darshan, Rajghat on 16th June '98, under the aegis of the International Centre of Gandhian Studies and Research. Dr. Rennison Peter Lalgee from the University of Texas was the key speaker.

Gandhi memorial lecture

As part of its efforts to disseminate Gandhian values, the Samiti has been organising the Gandhi Memorial Lecture every year. These lectures are being delivered by noted parliamentarians, Gandhian constructive workers, politicians, bureaucrats etc. Shri Ashok Vajpeyi, Vice-Chancellor. Mahatma Gandhi Antarrashtriya Hindi Vishwa Vidyalaya delivered the Gandhi Memorial lecture for the year 1998 on "The Gandhian Movement".

The renowned Gandhian constructive worker and social activist, Pt. Omkar Chand, Secretary, Lajpat Rai Bhawan, Chandigarh delivered a lecture on the 50 years of India's efforts to strengthen the foundation of a stable secular democracy as envisioned by Mahatma Gandhi and other freedom fighters on 28th June '98.

Justice V.M. Tarkunde (Retd.) spoke on the "Positive aspects of Gandhiji" in a special lecture under the Gandhian Memorial Lecture series on 10th September 1998 at GSDS.

A discussion on the book titled Gandhi's Autobiography: Moral Lessons authored by Prof. K.D.Gangrade a noted social scientist was held at Gandhi Darshan on 4th July, 1998,

On 1st August 1998 in a special discussion held at Gandhi Smriti, over thirty artists of various age groups shared their vision of the Golden Jubilee of Indian Independence with senior artists like Prof. Niren Sen, former Principal, College of Art and the eminent art historian, Prof. P.N.Mago.

As part of the programmes to mark the Golden Jubilee of India's Independence and the 50th anniversary of Mahatma Gandhi's Martyrdom, Gandhi Smriti and Darshan Samiti organized a 2-day programme on Charkha, Gandhi and the Millennial Challenge on 5th & 6th August in homage to the Mahatma at Gandhi Smriti, 5 Tees January Marg, New Delhi.

Gandhi Smriti and Darshan Samiti, which has been designated as the Nodal Agency by the National Committee for the observance of the 50th Anniversary of the Martyrdom of Mahatma Gandhi. convened a meeting to discuss a nationwide programme entitled Towards a Healthy Environment - A national campaign on 1st August 1998.

A discussion on the theme Women's Empowerment: a Gandhian Approach jointly organized by the Department of Adult Education; Delhi University and Gandhi Darshan, was held at Gandhi Darshan, Rajghat on 2nd Sept. '98.

A Seminar on Rural Development: Gandhian

Approach was organized by Gandhi Smriti and Darshan Samiti in collaboration with the S.N. Sinha Institute of Business Management, Ranchi was held in Gandhi Darshan, Rajghat from 20th to 22nd September.

A seminar titled "The challenges of the New Millennium. and the Role of Education" was jointly organized by Gandhi Smriti and Darshan Samiti and Bharat Soka Gakkai at India International Centre on 25 October 1998.

A two-day national workshop on the Political Development Struggle: Past and Future by Prof. Gene Sharp was organized by International Centre of Gandhian Studies and Research under the aegis of Gandhi Smriti and Darshan Samiti on 18th and 19th September '98.

The Martyrdom 50 Lecture was well attended by luminaries from different educational institutions of Delhi and Gandhian organisations. A two-day seminar on Hind Swaraj for college students of Delhi was held under the aegis of International Centre for Gandhian Studies and Research on 23rd and 24th November 1998. About 70 students from different colleges of Delhi participated in the programme.

A two-day national seminar on The Contributions of Mahatma Gandhi and Swami Shradhanand to the Indian Freedom Struggle and Cultural Heritage, was held at Gurukul Kangri Vishwavidyalaya, Haridwar on 17th and 18th November 1998 .A meeting to discuss the Earth Charter and a Gandhian Response to it was arranged on 21st Nov. '98 at Gandhi Smriti. Dr. Kamla Chowdhury, Chair, SPWD and Prof. N. Radhakrishnan, Director Gandhi Smriti led the discussion.

A discussion on Human Rights-a Gandhian Perspective led by Lou Ann Guvenson, a social and human rights activist from Hawaii was held at Gandhi Smriti on 26th November, 98.

Creative art workshop

A Creative Art Workshop by Sukanya Bharatram of Kasturba Gandhi Memorial, Baktawarpur and Gandhi Smriti was held on 3rd and 4th Oct. 1998. The workshop was conducted by Bulbul Sharma.

Exhibitions

A special exhibition entitled "Gandhi Through the Eyes of three Generations of Artists" was held at Lalit Kala Akademy from 9th to 15th September, 1998. Inaugurated by Shri Krishna Kant, the vice-president of India, the exhibition is a collection of paintings done by artists from different age groups during the 55th anniversary of the "Quit India Movement".

On 2nd Oct. '98, exhibitions were arranged at different venues in Delhi. Details are in given below:-

---

1. Gandhi & Environment at Gandhi Smriti from 27th Sept. 98 to 5th Oct., 98.
2. Bapu Mandap at Red Fort from 2nd Oct. to 5th Oct. 1998,
3. Glimpses of Gandhi at Bapu Samaj Seva Kendra, Community Hall, Panchkuin Road, New Delhi.
4. Exhibition on Gandhiji's Life and Mission at Municipal Corporation Council, Modi Nagar, Ghaziabad, UP.
5. Exhibition on Life and Works of Gandhiji from 2nd Oct. to 5th Oct. 1998 at Balmiki Basti.

India at 50: Through the eyes of Artists, an exhibition comprising. of 45 paintings by amateur artists on 50 years of Indian Independence opened at Gandhi Smriti, 5, Tees January Marg and was inaugurated by Dr. R.V.Vaidyanatha Ayyar, Secretary, Department of Culture on 1st July, '98.

"Gandhi's values of truth and non-violence are eternal and cannot be changed and their relevance cannot be questioned with the passage of time. At the same time artists should be aware of their social responsibilities", Dr. Ayyar said, while inaugurating the special exhibition.

The exhibition remained open at Gandhi Smriti all through the month and was extended up to 30th August for the public and later was sent across the country. An exhibition titled "Martyrdom 50-An Artists Perception" was taken around all over India. Details of venues and dates are given beow:-

Date	*Venue*
10th - 16th November	Maganwadi Sevagrarn Wardha
28th - 30th November	Gandhi Smarak Sangrahalaya, PO -Barrackpore, 14, River side Road, Distt. (N) Parganas-743101
23rd-26th November	Gandhi Memorial Ashrarn PO - Sodepur West Bengal

Tree plantation at Gandhi Darshan

Jaideep Singh Chauhan, an environmentalist from Bhopal after touring ten North Indian States, covering 42,000 km, awakening people to plant trees to save the plants came to Delhi in the last leg of his crusade on 10th July. He planted three saplings of Eucalyptus on the sprawling lawns of Gandhi Darshan.

Renovation of the pavilion "My lifeis my message"

Gandhi Darshan was set up in 1969 on the occasion of the Birth Centenary Celebrations of Mahatma Gandhi for six months. Later it was decided to maintain the place as picture galleries and Gandhi's constructive work Programme centre. Since the place was meant only for six months, no adequate, long term preservation measures were taken. Efforts are being undertaken to restore the pavilion to its past glory. A fresh look is being given to the pavilion besides ensuring that the original theme of the pavilion is not disturbed.

Publications

i. India and Her Neighbours: The Need for Confidence Building (ed) Dr. Savita Singh.
ii. Gandhi's Autobiography: Moral Lesson by Prof. K.D.Gangrade iii. Gandhi and the changing Facets of India: Prof. K.D.Gangrade and Prof. N. Radhakrishnan

A large number of books on Mahatma Gandhi and allied subjects were put on display in the fortnight long Book Fair held at Dilli Haat from 1st August to 14th August, 1998 by the Gandhi Smriti and Darshan Samiti.

Gandhi Smriti and Darshan Samiti also participated in the prestigious Delhi Book Fair organized by the India Trade Promotion Organisation at Pragati Maidan from 9th to 16th August '98.

Book release runction

Two books Gandhi the Super Star line drawings by Upendra Maharathi and Gandhi's Life-An Artist's View by Anil Sengupta were dedicated to the nation by Ravi Kant Chopra, Director in the Home Ministry in a solemn function held at Gandhi Smriti on 28th November 1998.

Important visitors

Mr. Vance Engleman and two of his research associates from Gandhi Ashram, Connecticut visited Gandhi Darshan on 29th September. The purpose of the visit was to establish rapport and facilitate exchange programmes with Gandhian organisations and Gandhi Ashram.

Sarvadharama prarthana at balmiki basti

On 2nd October 1998, the GSDS Prayer Group offered

Sarvadharma Prarthana at Bapu Kutir in the Balmiki Basti. The place is of great historical significance because of its association with Mahatma Gandhi who had made it as his residence in Delhi from 1945 to 1947. It was yet another milestone in his quest for complete identification with those whom he called, 'Harijans the Children of God'.

A play entitled 'Sanmati' written and directed by Shri Ramchand Gandhi, choreographed by Shovana Narayan and presented by Gandhi Smriti and Darshan Samiti was held at India International Centre on 8th Oct. '98. A major initiative called Gandhi Sahityotsav. This was launched to help children and youth rediscover and know Gandhi in the right perspective. Some very rare and precious books on Gandhi and the Gandhian Era were made available to book lovers in the fair.

Another highlight of the Sahityotsav was Gandhi-Apostle of Peace and Non Violence on C.D.Rom distributed by Microware Computer Services. Ms. Jharna Chowdhury from Gandhi Ashram, Noakhali, recipient of the BajaJ Award for 1998 was felicitated at Gandhi Smriti on 11th November '98. She received this prestigious International award for promoting Gandhian values outside India.

Jain Visva Bharati Institute, a deemed University', in collaboration with Gandhi Smriti and Darshan Samiti and a few other national and international organisations organized an international conference on World Peace and Anuvrat from 6th-9th November 98 at Sardarshahar.

Nehru memorial museum and library

The Nehru Memorial Museum and Library maintains:

(i) a personalia Museum which portrays the life and times of Jawaharlal Nehru against the backdrop of the different phases of the Indian freedom movement;

(ii)a Library of printed materials, books, periodicals, newspapers and photographs with special focus on the history of modern India;

(iii)a repository of unpublished records of institutions and private papers of eminent Indians which provide a primary source ofinformation for historical research;

(iv) a Reprography Division for microfilming old documents, records and newspapers;

(v) an Oral History Division for recording the reminiscences of eminent personalities from different walks of life who had contributed to the development of the nation;

(vi) a Research and Publications Division for publishing basic Research documents, seminar proceedings and other output of institutional research projects and for monitoring the work of the Centre for Contemporary Studies which encompasses the Research Fellows of the Nehru Memorial Museum and Library.

The Museum provides through visual materials, a vivid account of the life and works of Jawaharlal Nehru and the history of our freedom struggle. The Museum continued to maintain its popularity by attracting sizeable crowds everyday. During the period under review, 6,23,989 visitors came to the Museum with an average of 3,505 visitors a day. On Sundays and other holidays the daily average went up to 3,986.

The Museum also had the privilege of receiving distinguished visitors and delegations like H.E. Julio Castillo, First Vice President of the Chambers of Deputies of Venezuela; a Parliamentary Delegation led by H.E. Laurent Fabius, Chairman of the French National Assembly and former Prime Minister of France; and members of the Lutyens Trust England.

An exhibition on the life and achievements of Sardar Vallabhai Patel (1875-1950) was organized in the Ball Room of the Museum on 25th May 1998 in collaboration with the Sardar Patel Society. Books, photographs, brochures, cassettes, and other literature on Jawaharlal Nehru and other freedom fighters, worth Rs.25,071/- were sold at the sales counter of the Museum.

The Library which focuses modern Indian history and social sciences continued to grow in holdings as well as in the quality of its services during the period under report. Two thousand three hundred and eighty three (2383) books were added to the stock of books in the Library, total stock of which now stands at 1,99,793. The Library also continued to enrich its resources in microforms. Forty-nine dissertations submitted to foreign universities were purchased in different microforms and 398 microfilm rolls of newspapers, periodicals, press-clippings and private papers, supplied by our Reprography Unit, were added. The number of microfilm rolls in the Library now stands at 12,576. The Library at present, receives 545 journals and 22 newspapers. The documentation list - Select Articles on Modern Indian History and Obituaries from Select Indian Newspapers (both in mimeographed form) continued to be brought out regularly. The photo collection was enriched further with the addition of 751 photographs, taking the total number of photographs to 89,157 During the period under review, 432 scholars were registered in the Library and on an average 61 scholars visited the Library daily.

During the remaining five months of the current financial year, the Library shall strive to purchase new and forthcoming publications in the field of social sciences and modern Indian History. The Library has also ordered some dissertations on microfilm which are likely to be received during this financial year.

Collections in the Manuscripts Division continued to record further additions. Some of these were of Bengal Coal Company (1948-49,1963), V.R. Krishna Iyer (1988-98), Madan Mohan Chopra (1947-98), Govind Vidyarthi (1933-90) Shri Santram B.A. (1935-88), Bijoy Singh Nahar (1937-79), Mahadev Desai (1932-34), Valmiki Choudhary (1937-96), D.P. Mishra (1947-72), N.Giri Prasad (1978-97) and E.S. Reddy.

During the period, 1st November 1998 to 31st March, 1999, it is proposed to acquire manuscripts of J.H. Taleyarkhan, K.A. Damodara Menon and Leela Damodara Menon Jagannath Pahadia, Prem Bhatia, Keshav Prasad Agrawal, Darbara Singh, G.S. Dhillon, and Ram Jivan Sharma 'Jivan'. Further instalments of the papers of N.K. Rustornji, Lal Bahadur Shastri, Jamnalal Bajaj, Justice V.R. Krishna Iyer and Ramkrishna Bajaj are also likely to be acquired.

During the period under review, 85 scholars recommended by various universities/institutions in India and abroad, working on various subjects of modern Indian History, consulted 2,153 files in the Reading-Room of the Manuscripts Section.

The Oral History Division interviewed six new persons for the oral history project during the period under review. Forty five sessions were recorded during this period. This brings the total number of persons and sessions recorded till 31st October 1998 to 1,194 and 4,413 respectively.

The Reprography Division enriched the Library's microform collections and extended various reprographic facilities to the scholars. The Division prepared approximately 1,96,733 frames of 35mm and 16 mm negative microfilm of newspapers, journals and private papers. The Reprography Division also continued with the microfilming of rare books during the period. The production of positive microfilm was 13,530 meters for supply to the Library and other institutions in India and abroad. During the period under reference, the Division prepared 172 microfiches (approximately 13,760 frames). 1,06,236 xerox copies were produced. About 1,143 scholars were attended to meet the demands of various types of reprographic services.

During the remaining period of 1998-99, the Reprography Division will be busy preparing microfilm copies of newspapers, journals and private papers and production of positive microfilm copies of newspapers for reference in the Library. Other reprographic facilities will continue to be extended to scholars and institutions. The Preservation Unit continued to render useful services in respect of repair and rehabilitation of old documents through various scientific techniques.

i. 523 sheets were given lamination treatment;

ii. 11,102 documents were given full pasting (tissue and bond papers)

iii. 37,758 sheets were provided with guards and finally made into 270 volumes with full cloth binding for record and preservation in the Manuscripts Division.

iv. In addition to this, 2,901 sheets were deacidified before giving final treatment to ensure longevity.

Fumigation of records was carried out systematically. The number of books and files fumigated was 5,063. The Unit repaired and bound 262 volumes of newspapers and books. The Unit received 1,71,775 sheets of transcripts. Occasional Papers and other research papers and bound/stapled them into 2,455 volumes. The Unit also pasted 275 photographs into albums for record and reference in the Photo Section of the Library. All these activities will continue during the remaining part of the year.

The Research and Publications Divis.. .n continued with its publishing programmes and also monitored various research projects institution. During the period under report, the Division organized 11 one-day seminars as part of the ongoing academic activities. Six occasional papers under the series "History and Society" were also issued.

Under the auspices of our institution, the following two publications were brought out:

i. Between Two Fires: Towards an Understanding of Jawaharlal Nehru's Foreign Policy, Vo1. II by Iqbal Singh.
ii. Selected Works of Motilal Nehru (1929-31) Vol. II, edited by Ravinder Kumar and Hari Dev Sharma.

In addition the following books are in the pipeline

i. Selected Works of Acharya Narendra Deva (1948-52)
ii. Selected Works of Acharya Narendra, Deva (1952-56)
iii. Towards an Equitable Social Order
iv. Jawaharlal Nehru as Writer and Historian

During the remaining part of the financial year 1998-99 the Division will continue with its ongoing seminar programmes. The Division is likely to bring out at least one publication before March 1999 and eleven more Occasional Papers. In addition, the work on Vol. III and IV of Selected Works of Acharya Narendra Deva will be nearing completion and work on the Hindi volumes of Selected Works of Acharya Narendra Deva will commence.

Gandhi peace prize

On the occasion of the 125th Birth Anniversary of Mahatma Gandhi, the Government of India instituted an

Award known as the Gandhi Peace Prize. The Prize carries a cash award of Rs. One crore, a citation and a plaque. The Jury for the Gandhi Peace Prize, under the Chairmanship of the Prime Minister selected Rama Krishna Mission for the award of 1998. The prize was conferred on the Mission by the Honourable President of India at a special ceremony held on 13th February 1999 at the Raj Bhavan, Calcutta.

Maulana Abul Kalam Azad institute of asian studies

Research thrust

Two researchers from the Institute were sent to Uzbekistan, during the middle of February, 1998 for field studies on Central Asia, and their visit was duly assisted by the Indian Council of Social Science Research and the Ministry of External Affairs, Govt. of India. They interacted with the scholars of the Institute of Oriental Studies, visited various libraries and studied a considerable amount of material written in local language, procured photocopies and returned by the middle of March, 1998.

Seminars

The Institute held a seminar on "Issues in Asian Geopolitics: Borders and Trans-border Flows" in Delhi on 23rd-24th March, 1998. The Foreign Secretary to the Govt. of India, Shri K. Raghunath, delivered the keynote address. The Deputy Chairperson of the Rajya Sabha, Dr. Najma Heptullah was the Chief Guest. This was included as a part of the Golden Jubilee celebrations of Indian Independence.

A one-day workshop on establishing a documentation Centre on Asian Studies, as part of the Institute's library, was held in the Institute on 261 June, 1998. Eminent Librarians and documentation experts were present in the meeting. Some language experts, relevant to this Institute's language programme were also present. The participants discussed the I) modalities of building up such a documentation centre; ii) classification of documents according to their contents and forms; iii) possibilities of networking in the field of documentation; iv) task of preparing a Union Catalogue of documents pertaining to the studies in the Institute and available in Calcutta and Eastern India; v) the cost effectiveness or otherwise of such a documentation centre; and vi) the necessity for building up a collaborative approach for the documentation centre involving other institutions in Calcutta, so that the Planning Commission may be approached to adopt such a programme on the basis of need, participation and viability. The workshop ended with the setting up of an Advisory Committee for the purpose of building up the documentation centre as a part of the library.

The President of the Society of the Institute, H.E. the Governor of West Bengal, Dr. A.R. Kidwai, visited the Institute and inspected the research facilities and the library on 25th June 1998. He interacted with the members of the academic staff and stressed the importance of expanding research in the field of Southeast Asian Studies.

The Institute organized a summer workshop on Critical Asian Studies at Darjeeling for M.Phil/ Ph.D students, from 4th to 11th August, 1998. The subjects covered in the workshop were: Geo-political Notion of Asia, Intellectual History of Asian Studies, Decolonisation in Asia, Economic restructuring in the continent, Development of women's studies in South Asia, Borders and border related problems in the region, Religion and social formations in Asia, and finally, Asian Relations - Retrospect and Prospect. In all, 30 classes were held including students' participatory seminars. The total number of participants were 18, and about 500 pages of reading material was made available to each participant. The faculty consisted of eminent professors of IIMC, Calcutta University, Jadavpur University, Presidency College and the Centre for Studies in Social Sciences, Calcutta, besides members of the staff.

Internal Seminars

The following internal seminars were conducted in the Institute

Date	Presented by	Topic
7.4.98	Anita Sengupta & Suchandana Chatterjee	Report of their field trips to Uzbekistan in February '98
16.6.98	Indrani Chatterjee	Slave Manumissions in Chinese Turkistan in the 1890's
14.7.98	Ranabir Samadar	Leaders & Legacies: Maulana Maniruzzaman Islamabadi & Maulana Akhram Khan
8.9.98	Mohd. Tajuddin	Diplomacy of Bangladesh in the formative Phase
20.10.98	Barun De	Paradigms of nationalism in the thought of Maulana Azad with particular reference to his middle period, 1923-40.
23.10.98	Abanti Adhikari	Economic and Intellectual origins of movements of protest in East Pakistan, 1947-71.
4.11.98	Anita Sengupta	The making of a linguistic identity State and language in Uzbekistan
11.11.98	Suchandana Chatterjee	Trarist colonial approach in Turkistan in the 19th Century.
19.11.98	Ranabir Samaddar	Turkey's role in Critical Asian Studies.

Infrastructural facilities :

i) During the period, 8 computers and nodes including CD Rom facilities were acquired

ii) A Shell Account with E-Mail facilities was opened with VSNL.

iii) LAN (Local Area Network) was set up linking all the computers in the Institute.

Library

i) The available resources were utilized to enrich the collection of Books, Journals and Periodicals.

ii) Computerisation of library holding catalogues etc. were completed. Users node was provided.

iii) Documentation Centre was opened.

The Department has formulated a scheme for providing grant in aid to voluntary organizations/societies for the development and maintenance of National Memorials.

13

Promotional Bodies

One of the important activities the , Department of Culture is associated with relates to organization of Centenary Celebrations of important personalities/ events. For this purpose the Department of Culture either constitutes National Committees (which are headed by the Prime Minister/ Minister of Human Resource Development) for rendering advice regarding the programmes for organizing the celebrations at the National level or gives grants to non-governmental organizations, whichever is considered appropriate, for supporting the programmes which the non-governmental organizations propose to organize.

The Government of India had constituted National Committees for:

(a) organizing Birth Centenaries of Mirza Ghalib (27.12.1997- 27.12.1998) Gulzari Lal Nanda (4.7.1998-4.7.1999); Sant Kabir (June 1998 to June 1999); and Birth of Khalsa Panth (13.4.1999-13.4.2000);

(b) organizing 1251 Birth Anniversary of Sri Aurobindo (15.7.1997-15.7.1998);

(c) observing the 50th Anniversary of the Martyrdom of Mahatma Gandhi (30.1.1998-30.1.1999)

As a part of the Centenary of Enlightenment of Bhagwan Ramana, a commemorative stamp was released by the Hon'ble President of India in a function organized on

14th April 1998. The function was attended among others by Shri R. Venkataraman, former President of India, Minister of Parliamentary Affairs and a number of devotees of Bhagwan Ramana.

As a part of the Birth Centenary Celebrations of Dr. Zakir Hussain, a commemorative stamp of Dr. Zakir Hussain was released by the Vice President of India in a function organized on 3rd May, 1998 in the Vice President's House. The function was attended, among others, by Shri Surjit Singh Barnala, Hon'ble Minister of Chemicals and Fertilizers, Shri Khursheed Alam Khan, Governor, Karnataka and Shri Salman Khursheed.

A function to mark the conclusion of the 125th Birth Anniversary Celebrations of Sri Aurobindo was organized on 24th November 1998. Dr. Murli Manohar Joshi, Hon'ble Minister of Human Resource Development released a set of commemorative coins on Sri Aurobindo. The commemorative coins were of the denomination of Rs.100, Rs.50, Rs.10 and Rs.2. This was preceded by a 3-day Seminar, where there was active discussion on Philosophy and Yoga, as propounded by Sri Aurobindo.

A function to release a set of commemorative coins in honour of Deshbandhu Chittaranjan Das on his 128th birth Anniversary was held on December 27, 1998 at Raj Bhavan, Calcutta. His Excellency, the Governor of West Bengal released the commemorative coins.

To make people aware of the contribution of important personalities in different fields, special onetime grants are offered for Celebration of Centenaries of such personalities who have served the nation and contributed to social reforms, culture, education and have been prominent in nation building. Details of the scheme are given below:-

Scheme	*Celebration of Centenaries of important personalities*
Objective	To highlight salient aspects of the life and times of important personalities in order to infuse in the public, particularly the young, the spirit of these great leaders.
Applicable to	Registered Voluntary Organisations and State and National Bodies for achieving the objectives of the scheme
	(i) Grants not exceeding Rupees One Lakh to Voluntary Organisation for appropriate programmes. (ii) Not exceeding Rs. 40 thousand in case of anniversary celebrations of Jubilee years i.e. 125th, 150th, and 175th and so on (iii) Grants will not exceed 75% of total expenditure of (i) or (ii) above. The balance 25% of the expenditure is to be borne by the organisation.

A number of non-governmental organizations were released grants for organizing programmes to celebrate birth centenaries/ anniversaries of important personalities/ events during the current financial year. Details are in Box No.14.02. An amount of Rs.150 lakhs was released to the State Government of Rajasthan for the development of a memorial in memory of Maharana Pratap as a part of observing his 400th death anniversary.

International Cultural Relations

Cultural agreements and culture

Since 1947, India has entered into Cultural Agreements leading to formulation of Cultural Exchange Programmes with a number of countries. Currently we have Cultural Agreements with 107 countries and Cultural Exchange Programmes with 73 countries. While a Cultural Agreement is basically a statement of intent to cooperate in the fields and disciplines specified in the document, a

Cultural Exchange Programme incorporates specific provisions for exchanges for a period of 2-3 years relating to a number of activities concerning culture, education,. sports, youth affairs, mass-media etc.

During the current year, Cultural Exchange Programmes were renewed with Bangladesh, Ethiopia, Iraq, Italy, Portugal and Russia. A high-level delegation from Pakistan visited India from 12th to 13th November, 1998 to discuss friendly exchanges in various cultural fields. The issues were discussed with the Pakistan delegation at the Secretary level. The Indian Delegation to the talks was led by Dr. R.V.Vaidyanatha Ayyar, Secretary (Culture) and the Pakistan Delegation was led by Syed Roshan Zamir, Secretary (Culture) Government of Pakistan.

A six-member delegation led by Mr. A. Andrew de Silva, Secretary, Ministry of Education and Higher Education, Govt. of Sri Lanka visited India from 14.12.1998 to participate in the Fourth Session of India-Sri Lanka Sub-Commission on Cultural, Social & Educational Matters. The Meeting of the Sub-Commission provided an opportunity to discuss and negotiate a fresh Cultural Exchange Programme for 1999-2001 with Sri Lanka. In addition to the CEP, the Sub-Commission was expected to report to the Joint Commission Meeting which was held in New Delhi on 18-19 December, 1998.

A three-member delegation led by Union Minister for Human Resource Development, Dr. Murli Manohar Joshi visited Hungary from 25-10-98 to 28-10-98. During this visit an Indo-Hungarian Cultural Exchange Programme for the years 1999-2001 was signed. The delegation also participated in the celebrations of the 50th Anniversary of the establishment of diplomatic relations between India and Hungary. During his visit the Honourable Minister also inaugurated a joint symposium.

Presentation of books, art objects and essay competitions

The Department of Culture continued to provide funds to ICCR for presentation of books and art objects to foreign Governments, Organisations, libraries and individuals and for organising essay competitions abroad through the Indian Missions.

Indo-foreign friendship societies

The Department of Culture has been extending financial assistance to these societies/associations on the recommendation of the concerned Indian missions abroad. The grants are given for development of cultural relations with foreign countries and projecting India's cultural image in those countries. Grants in aid were given to about 100 such societies functioning in various countries. The budgetary allocation for the Scheme during the year 1998-99 was Rs.27.80 lakhs.

The Government of India has constructed an Indian Students' Hostel in the campus of the Cite Universitaire, Paris and donated it to the University in 1960. The management of the hostel, known as Maison de I'Inde, has however, been retained by India. The Government of India meets the deficit in the running of the hostel each year.

Indira Gandhi national centre for the arts

The Indira Gandhi National Centre for the Arts (IGNCA) was formed as an autonomous Trust vide Government of India Resolution dated the 191h March, 1987. It is visualised as a Centre encompassing study and experience of all the arts-each form with its own integrity, yet within a dimension of mutual inter-dependence. The IGNCA seeks to underpin through its programmes of collection of resource material and fundamental research in the field of the arts and humanities, the inter-relationship with the disciplines of science, physical and material metaphysics as also anthropology and sociology.

The Centre is implementing the project of strengthening the national facility for inter-active multi-media documentation of cultural resources with UNDP assistance. The Centre has established a multi-media lab in collaboration with Xerox Corporation, USA to launch a Project on Gitagovinda with the objective of producing Systems Software for computer compatible CD's.

National culture fund

The Parliamentary Standing Committee on Human Resource Development, in its 101h report, had recommended the setting up of a National Culture Fund (referred to as NCF hereinafter) to enlist public cooperation and support to realise the Directive Principles enshrined in Article 51 (A) of the Constitution, which provides that, it shall be the duty of every citizen to preserve the rich heritage of our composite culture.

Accordingly the Department of Culture has set up the NCF in terms of the Charitable Endowments Act 1890. The NCF constitutes an important innovation that accepts institutions and individuals as equal partners of the Government in the management of the cultural scenario in the country. It enables institutions and the public at large to contribute to culture related endeavours, mobilise extra budgetary resources for culture and help overcome the resource crunch in relation to culture related endeavours.

The income from the NCF will be utilised for :-

1) Preservation and conservation
2) Training and development of a cadre of specialist and cultural administrators.
3) Innovations and experiments in arts

4) Documentation of cultural forms and expressions that are either fading or are facing extinction.
5) Undertaking research
6) Creation of Galleries and Museums and strengthening existing ones
7) International cultural cooperation

NCF has been successful in mobilising extra budgetary resources and the amount so far collected are in given below:-

i)	Indian National Trust for Art and Cultural Heritage	Rs. 1,54,750
ii)	National Mineral Development Corp. Ltd., Hyderabad	Rs. 25,000
iii)	Oberoi Group of Hotels	Rs. 5,00,000
iv)	Shaniwarwada Project	Rs. 17,70,000
v)	Agha Khan Trust	$ 10,000

Steps taken to get the NCF going are:-

a) The NCF was formally launched by the Minister of Human Resource development on 29.3.97.
b) A Council, has been constituted for management and administration of the Fund, in terms of para 7 of the notification dated 28.11.96.
c) An Executive Committee has been set up for the administration of the day to day working of the Fund, as envisaged in Para II of the notification.
d) NCF has been allotted space and is functioning from Janpath Bhawan.
e) NCF has been put on the internet with a website.
f) NCF has been eligible for 100% deduction under section 10 and section 8OG(2) of the Income Tax.
g) NCF has been registered under the FCRA for receiving foreign contributions from abroad.

NCF lays emphasis on involving people in culture related endeavors through their contributions, both intellectual and material. In this context a number of interactive sessions have been held with industrialists, CII, FICCI and some experts in the field of culture.

The Agha Khan Trust has given a commitment to take up the project for revitalisation of water channels and restoration of gardens of the Humayun Tomb complex in Delhi. The estimated cost of Rs.1.5 crores. The Agha Khan Trust has already contributed $10,000 and the Oberoi Group of Hotels Rs.5 lakhs.

As envisaged in the establishment of the NCF, consultative processes have been initiated with Captains of industry. In one such endeavor industrialists in the Pune region have taken up a project to revitalise the environs of the historic Shaniwarwada, the erstwhile seat of power of the Peshwas of Maharashtra. While the project is being finalised under the leadership of Shri B.G.Deshmukh, former Cabinet Secretary and the Director of Tata Sons, contributions amounting to Rs. 17.70 lakhs have been received. More contributions are expected to flow in. The estimated cost of the Project is Rs. 1.50 crores.

The Prince of Wales Museum of Western India, Mumbai have proposed that NCF may undertake the renovation work on the terms and conditions as are applicable for the Shaniwarwada Project. Donations of about Rs. 2 crores are expected.

The challenge before NCF in this year was to gain the confidence of the Industry and public regarding the credibility of the nascent organization while functioning on a shoestring budget with skeletal staff support of a consultant, aid-cum-messenger and assistant appointed on contract basis. The strategy adopted was to start a few projects on a modest scale suggested by local communities or corporate entities, raise funds and implement them in collaboration with sponsors and as implementation proceeds raise the public visibility of NCF In the past six months, the strategy has gradually shown encouraging results as indicated in the Shaniwarwada and the Humayun Tomb project.

Golden jubilee of Indian Independence

The Government of India had decided to celebrate the landmark event of fifty years of India's Independence in a befitting manner and constituted 3 High-Powered Committees namely,

i) National Committee under the Chairmanship of the Prime Minister

ii) Cabinet Committee under the Chairmanship of the Home Minister

iii) Implementation Committee under the Chairmanship of the Minister of Human Resource Development

To service the Committees as well as to conceive, coordinate, monitor and implement the various programmes connected with the celebrations, a Secretariat with an officer of the rank of Additional Secretary to the Government of India as head was created.

The celebrations began on 15th August 1997 and continued for one year, up to 15th August 1998. During the year 1998-99, the following events were organised:

Formal closing function of commemoration of 50th Anniversary of India's Independence in the Central Hall of Parliament on 15th August 1998.

This function was held in the Central Hall of Parliament at 11.30 a.m. on 15th August 1998. Excerpts of the recorded speeches of Mahatma Gandhi, Jawaharlal Nehru and Subbash Chandra Bose were relayed. The eminent musician Pt. Jasraj with his troupe sang " Vande

Mataram" and Smt.Anuradha Paudwal rendered the song "Saare Jahan Se Achcha". The Ministry of Science & Technology presented an audio-visual show depicting the achievements of the nation during the last 50 years in various fields. It presented in capsule, a picture of commitment and dedication of our masses, especially in the rural areas, entrepreneurs in small scale and big industries, the scientific community and workers in social sectors. The President of India Shri K.R. Narayanan addressed the nation during the function. The function ended with the playing of the National Anthem.

The function was attended by the Members of the Council of Ministers, Members of Parliament, Members of diplomatic corps and other dignitaries. The President of India, the Vice-President of India, the Prime Minister, Speaker of the Lok Sabha, Minister of Home Affairs and the Minister of Human Resource Development graced the podium. The whole function was telecast live on Doordarshan.

Drums of Freedom-march to millennium - an open air programme for the public at Rajpath onthe night of 15th august 1998

With a view to creating a sense of belonging amongst the people and inculcating a spirit of patriotism in them, a function for the public was organised at Rajpath on the night of 15th, August 1998. The event was conceptualized by the India-50 Secretariat and was organised by the Government of NCT of Delhi. The function was symbolic of the joy of freedom and signalled our determination to march ahead to the new millennium. It was rightly named 'Drums of freedom - March to Millennium.'

The function formally started at 9.00 a.m. on 15th August 1998 with a March by sports-persons and youth of outstanding merit from various parts of the country.

The March started from the National Stadium and culminated at Vijay Chowk, where a giant stage was constructed for cultural performances. The Minister of Human Resource Development and the Chief Minister of NCT of Delhi addressed the gathering. Choir groups rendered patriotic songs in different languages. A well choreographed display of drums from various parts of the country was the main attraction. Artistes from Thailand, South Korea, Sri Lanka and Singapore presented folk dances and cultural programmes. All the important government buildings on either side of Rajpath were illuminated. Inspite of the inclement weather, people thronged the venue with enthusiasm. The entire programme was telecasted live by Doordarshan.

National programmes at the regional level were organised by the different Zonal Cultural Centres on behalf of the Department of Culture at different venues spread out all over the country, details of which are given below:-

	Date function	*Venue of Cultural Centre*	*Name of Zonal*
(a)	7th August	Santiniketan	East Zone
(b)	8th August	Kohima	North East Zone
(c)	9th August	Udaipur	West Zone
(d)	10th August	Patiala	North Zone
(e)	11th August	Chennai	South Zone
(f)	12th August	Allahabad	North-Central Zone
(g)	13th August	Nagpur	South-Central Zone

The Hon'ble Minister of Human Resource Development hosted a dinner on 4th August 1998 for the Heads of foreign Missions residing in India. On the occasion, the Minister presented momentoes commemorating fifty years of India's Independence to the dignitaries who attended the dinner and thanked the foreign Governments who participated as well as rendered valuable help in organising the Golden Jubilee Celebrations in grand and befitting manner.

The Hon'ble Minister of Human Resource Development hosted a dinner on 9th August 1998 for eminent Indians in connection with the closing functions of the Golden Jubilee Celebrations. Celebrations of the Golden Jubilee of Indian Independence by different organizations of the Department of Culture.

Exhibitions organized by the National Museum as a part of the Golden Jubilee Celebrations of India's Independence.

(i)	Karuna 28th February '98	7th February '98 to
(ii)	Columbia: World Heritage Sites	10th March '98 to 19th April '98
(iii)	Art Treasures from Kotah 19th April '98	25th March '98 to
(iv)	An exhibition of Ceramics by Raphael Bordallo Pinheiro	7th April '98 to 14th April '98
(v)	Gods, Kings and Tigers: Art of Kotah. This exhibition had also travelled to Harvard Museum as well as to Zurich	April to June '97
(vi)	Treasures of Indian Art: Germany's contribution to India's cultural heritage. This is the concluding event of the Golden Jubilee Celebrations.	14th August 98 to 30th Sep. 98

As a part of the programme for Celebrating the Golden Jubilee of India's Independence, the National Museum,

New Delhi in collaboration with the Indian Council for Cultural Relations and the Embassy of the Federal Republic of Germany organised a special exhibition entitled "Treasures of Indian Art : Germany's Tribute to India's Cultural Heritage" which was inaugurated by the Hon'ble President of India on 14th Aug., 1998.

Coinciding with this exhibition, the National Museum also organized a series of events such as Lectures by eminent art scholars, Seminars, Workshops and Music, Dance and Theatre performances by eminent artists. Apart from this, activities involving children and teachers by networking with different schools was organized over the six-week span of the exhibition through the Centre for Cultural Resource and Training.

Exhibitions which were mounted at the National Gallery of Modern Art as a part of the celebrations are listed below: -

(i) Shantiniketan - The Making of a Contextual Modernism - 16-8-97

(ii) 50 years of Art in Mumbai (NGMA, Mumbai) - September 1997

(iii) Delhi Shilpi Chakra Group - The Early Years - 4-12-97

(iv) Symbolism and Geometry in Indian Art- February 1998

Exhibitions sent abroad

(i) Indian contemporary art in South Africa at Johannesburg — May to July '97

(ii) Tryst with Destiny - Art in Modem India at Singapore — Oct. '97 to Jan. 98.

(iii) The Yellow Diety, Budapest, Hungary

A unique exhibition developed by NCSM, India - a Tradition in Science, Technology and Culture was opened at Dhaka on 16th June 1998 as a part of the celebrations. The exhibition portrayed the 4500-year history of development of science and technology in India and has attracted a large number of visitors. The exhibition continued for one and half months. A mobile science exhibition "We are One" also travelled throughout Bangladesh during this period.

The Salarjung Museum organized a two-day National Seminar on Concepts of new Museology & Challenges of 21st Çentury on 16'h and 17th August, 98.

The Anthropological Survey of India celebrated the event in an elegant and befitting manner. Two programmes of the Survey were approved by the Government of India for this occasion. An Exhibition entitled Continuity of knowledge: Traditional Wisdom, Crafts and Craftsmanship was organized at all the Regional/ Sub-regional Centres and at the Camp Office of the Survey. The exhibition organized at Port Blair (A & N Islands) was visited by the Hon'ble President of India ,Shri K.R. Narayanan. The Survey has decided to bring out a special publication on the People of India. A few scholars of the Survey have been engaged to finalize the same. The other publication, namely Social Institutions and Cultural Values of Indian Artisans, will be a collection of essays contributed by eminent scholars while the volume on Bio-cultural linkages among the populations of SAARC countries will be prepared by the Survey's researchers on the basis of secondary source material. Work on all these publications continued and is expected to be completed soon.

IGRMS organized a series of events for the preservation of local knowledge systems and deepening awareness about and strengthening the vitality of community traditions and knowledge systems in Kerala and Tamilnadu, by organising a national workshop and exhibition on Tribal Medicine, in collaboration with the Kerla Institute for Research Training and Development Studies of Scheduled Castes and Scheduled Tribes (KIRTADS) at Calicut, with the participation of nearly 100 Tribal Medicine men from all over India. The workshop was attended by representatives from the Ministry of Welfare and from the Department of Indian System of Medicine, Government of India. The workshop was intensely participatory with Tribal Medicine men directly offering suggestions for documentation, popularization, development preservation and compensation of the Tribal Medicinal System. The participating tribal medicine men got together with legal experts, tribal rights spokesmen and representatives of different departments, looking after tribal interests, to evolve suggestions on research and training in Tribal Medicine, and for protecting the Intellectual Property Rights (IPR) of tribal communities. On the basis of the resolution passed by the workshop a committee was set up to compile the available regional, national and international instructions and legislation on IPR for medicine, based on organic forms, extracted by folk and tribal people.

The Museum also organized freedom celebrations in the North-East in collaboration with the State Government of Tripura with programmes in three remote centres of Tripura among different tribal groups with workshops, cultural events and exhibitions focussing on the local literary traditions scripted as well as unscripted, on visual and performing arts and crafts and skills and technologies specially in the area of water management.

In Tamilnadu, the celebrations began with a three-day programme at Devakottal with the participation of about 1000 members of the Chettiar Community from remote villages of what is known as Nagrathar Nadu. A three day seminar on banking, trading educational, cultural, spiritual, and art and craft traditions of the Nagarathars (Chettiars) was accompanied by a workshop on Ethnic. Cuisine and Kollam with the participation of 250 Nagrathar women. Through this programme an attempt was made to look into the possibility of revitalisation of the monastic modes of education, based on Sastras, Agamas, Kala and Sahitya, structured in ten disciplines. This was followed by the Tamil Cultural festival entitled Mannin Maraboo. The programme began with a seminar on the folk logistic remote and prop roots, visual and performing art traditions, literary, ritualistic as well as oral traditions in Tamilnadu. One more workshop was organized on indigenous metallurgy and metal casting traditions in Tamilnadu, designated Ulogavival, in an attempt to explore the possibility of rediscovering the ancient manufacturing process of wootz steel for studying measures for technology upgradation of surviving iron smelters and for protecting their livelihood and intellectual property right.

Three other workshops were organized with performance, presentation interpretation and documentation, entitled Adavu on drums and dramatic and ritualistic dance forms, Bombalatam on string and shadow puppets and Thottil on the prayer, invocation, music and ritual, accompanying the various Tamil rites of passage from birth to death. Along with this, an exhibition-cum-workshop called Izhaigal, was organized on the best Kolam, selected from workshops at Devakottai and Chennai as well as on the costumes and accessories used in performing arts.

The freedom 50 celebrations culminated with a synoptic exhibition titled Sankshep on the various exhibitions, workshops, expeditions, cultural events organized by the museum at Bhopal and in different parts of the country in celebration of the autonomy and variety of community knowledge systems and traditions.

The final celebrations were dedicated to the very strong but neglected element of folk contribution to freedom lore. Two groups of freedom fighters, balladeers, reciters, musicians and scroll painters were invited from Bengal and Andhra Pradesh, to render Swaraj Geet, culled from the repertoire of songs about folk heroes and about burning contemporary issues, created by itinerant musicians, actively engaged in the freedom struggle through direct narrations from participants. This was performed in different venues in Bhopal city, among children as well as among citizens and was accompanied by documentation of rare archival material, about the extremist movement from the Calcutta Police Archives.

An Archival Museum has been established in the premises of the National Archives of India to make people aware of the documentary heritage which the Archives preserves for the present generation and for posterity. The Museum was formally declared open by Shri K.R. Narayanan, Hon'ble President of India on 6th July, 1998 in the presence of eminent personalities like Shri R. Venkataraman, former President of India, Dr. Karan Singh, Shri G.V.G. Krishnamoorthy, Election Commissioner, and representatives from diplomatic missions and freedom fighters.

A visual display entitled In Their Memory highlighting the role of unknown and unsung freedom fighters was organized and opened to the public from 17th August, 1998. It also portrayed the popular literature and poems which were banned by the British Raj. Photographs collected from old Intelligence records, the sacred soil from the cremation site of martyrs Bhagat

Singh, Rajguru, and Sukhdev collected by the mother of martyr Sukhdev; Golden Scroll of the speech "Tryst with Destiny" and memorabilia relating to our freedom movement were some of the significant items of the display.

The Khuda Baksh Oriental Public Library chalked out various programmes for celebrating the occasion. The first programme, an exhibition of material on Freedom Movement preserved in the Library was held from 17th August to 26th August 1997. The exhibition got a very good response as a large number of persons from all walks of life visited the exhibition. An Indo-Pak Mushaira was held on 9th May, 1998 at Patna wherein renowned poets of the subcontinent participated. Besides, a Kavi Sammelan was also held on 28th November 98.

A National Seminar was also held at New Delhi from 29th August to 31st August 98 in collaboration with Jamia Hamdard. The subject of the Seminar was "Free India: : Retrospect and Prospects." In the series of lectures, three lectures were delivered by Mr. Saiyid Hamid, Dr. Saiyeda Saiyedain and Mr. Sardar Ali respectively.

The following new publications have been published and released including a monograph of Rampur Raza Library in English to mark the celebrations of the 50th Anniversary of India's Independence and 200 years of Rampur Raza Library.

1. Khat-Ki-Kahani Taswiron Ki-Zabani (Urdu by Syed Ahmed Khattat (famous calligrapher)
2. Text of the rare manuscript namely Tarikh-I-Shahia-I-Nishapuria (Persian) (History of Avadh) by Qasu, Ali Nishapuri
3. Maulana Muhammad Ali our Jang-e-Azadi (Urdu) by Dr. Zaheer Ali Siddiqui.

4. Rampur Raza Library Monograph. (English) compiled by Dr. W.H. Siddiqui.
5. Tarikh-I-Kitab-Khana-I-Raza (Urdu) (History of Rampur Raza Library) by Hafiz Ahmad Ali Shauq Rampuri with introduction and commentary by Dr. W.H. Siddiqui.

The grand celebrations were organized from 25th to 28th July 1998 and was inaugurated by His Excellency, Shri Suraj Bhan, Governor of Uttar Pradesh and Chairman of Rampur Raza Library Board. It was followed by an international seminar "History, Culture and Literature of Rohilkhand." Seventy-seven distinguished scholars from India and abroad participated in the Seminar and cultural programmes were organized in the evenings. On July 25th , the famous T.V. artist Junaid Akhtar gave a Ghazal recital of both classical and modern Urdu poetry.

The evening of 26th July was enriched by the traditional Pathan folk songs of Charbait and on the evening of 27th July an exhilarating classical vocal performance was held by the Rampur Sahaswan Gharana artists.

An International Mushaira was organized on the night of 28th July at Rang Mahal Hall. Thirty-five poets and poetesses from different parts of India and Pakistan participated in the Mushaira. The celebrated Urdu poet Kaifi Azmi presided over the Mushaira

As part of the grand celebrations of the 50th Anniversary of India's Independence and completion of 200 years of Rampur Raza Library, a special exhibition of the blowups of rare manuscripts, paintings and collection of antique objects was mounted in Hamid Manzil of the Library from 25th July to 16th August 1998. The exhibition was declared open to the public by Shri Ajay Shanker, I.A.S. Director General, Archaeological Survey of India. It was witnessed by more than sixty thousand visitors and scholars from various parts of India.

Exhibitions of the blow ups of selected manuscripts and miniatures of the collection were organized at Copenhagen (Denmark), Berlin (Germany), London (England), Brussels (Belgium), Singapore, Kuala Lumpur (Malaysia), Madrid (Spain), Ifrane (Morocco) Rabat (Morocco) from June to September 1998. Rampur Raza Library organized a Qawwali night on 15th August 1998 to mark the closing ceremony of Golden Jubilee year of India's Independence.

A Museum of Performing Arts has been opened in Delhi. This would be a learning/resource centre reflecting traditions of music, dance, theatre and puppetry of tribal and rural areas, classical traditions and traditional theatre all over the country An attempt would be made to reflect the tribal classical continuum as obtaining in the performing arts situation of the country. Contemporary work in music, dance and theatre would form a section of the Museum. The Museum will focus on performing traditions, their continuity and changes during the past 100-150 years or so as major developments have taken place in the history of several forms and styles during this period.

A unique 3-day All India Poetry Festival was organised at New Delhi by the Sahitya Akademi. More than 50 poets, representing 22 Indian languages read their poems. As part of the festival excerpts from Dinkar's epic poem Rashmirathi, was staged by the students of the National School of Drama under the direction of Prasanna. The poetry readings of the first two days was followed by a film show "Freedom Struggle and Indian Poetry" on 7th-9th August at New Delhi.

An exhibition of selections from the permanent collection of the Lalit Kala Akademi was held from 7.8.98 to 20.9.998 in the galleries of the Akademi.

Zonal Cultural Centres presented programmes of folk dances at the concluding function of the Golden Jubilee celebrations of India's Independence on 14th August 1998 at Rajpath, New Delhi and Regional level functions were also organised by the ZCCs at their Headquarters.

A significant programme for children entitled "Gandhi Ek Parichay" was launched by the Gandhi Smriti and Darshan Samiti to mark the Golden Jubilee Celebrations of Indian Independence, from 14th June to 26th June 1998. As part of the programmes to mark the Golden jubilee of India's Independence and the 50th anniversary of Mahatma Gandhi's Martyrdom, the Samiti organized a 2-day programme on Charkha, Gandhi and the Millennial Challenge on 5th & 6th August in homage to the Mahatma at Gandhi Smriti, 5 Tees January Marg, New Delhi.

An exhibition entitled "India at 50 : Through the eyes of Artists" comprising of 45 paintings by amateur artists on 50 years of Indian Independence opened at Gandhi Smriti, 5, Tees January Marg and was inaugurated by Dr. R.V.Vaidyanatha Ayyar, Secretary, Department of Culture on 1st July, '98. The exhibition remained open at Gandhi Smriti all through the month and was extended up to 30th August for the public and later was sent across the country.

The Maulana Abul Kalam Azad Institute held a seminar on "Issues in Asian Geopolitics : Borders and Trans-border Flows" in Delhi on 23rd-24th March, 1998. The Foreign Secretary to the Government of India, Shri K. Raghunath, delivered the keynote address. The Deputy

Chairperson of the Rajya Sabha, Dr. Najma Heptullah was the Chief Guest. This was included as a part of the Golden jubilee celebrations of Indian Independence.

Training

Training in various aspects of art and culture forms an integral part of the activities of the Department of Culture. The training programmes run by the various institutes/organizations under the Department of Culture cater to all categories of persons. At the one end of the spectrum there are general courses of art appreciation, History of Art and Culture, Summer Vacation Courses etc. run by CCRT, NGMA, National Museum Institute etc., for the general public teachers and school children. On the other end various institutes offer specialist Diploma, Graduate, Post-Graduate Courses in Archives Management, Archaeology and Museology, Buddhist/Tibetan Studies, Drama etc. aimed at fresh graduates, researchers and persons actively engaged in these fields. Various institutions offer in-service training programmes for practising art managers, keepers, conservators etc.

Initiatives in the north eastern states

The States in the North Eastern Region are often considered to be in a disadvantageous position owing to their geographical isolation and poor infrastructure. Department of Culture has been taking many initiatives to highlight and popularise the rich and diverse art and culture of the North Eastern States, including Sikkim. Also an attempt is made to provide equal opportunities to the artists and art and cultural related organisations to avail the assistance being provided by the Department through its various schemes. Often the Department relaxes the conditions and eligibility criteria to enable the North Eastern States to get their due share.

Various activities 'and programmes of the

Department of Culture in the North Eastern Region are as follows:

North eastern zonal cultural centre, Dimapur

North Eastern Zonal Cultural Centre (NEZCC) was set up under the VIIth Five Year Plan at Dimapur, Nagaland. The Centre aims for the creative development of North Eastern Culture and its spread to other regions through the networking with similar cultural centres in other regions. The essential thrust of the Centre has been to create a cultural awareness and to identify, nurture and promote vanishing folk art traditions in the rural and semi urban areas of the States.

The NEZCC have also established linkages with State Departments and NGOs for preservation, promotion and propagation of tribal and folk art forms. The NEZCC, in collaboration with other ZCCs presented programmes of folk dances at the concluding function of the Golden Jubilee celebrations of India's Independence on 14th August 1998 at Rajpath, New Delhi and a Regional level function was also organised at Dimapur. In addition, the NEZCC has organised the following major festivals during 1998-99:

1. North East Youth Dance Drama Festival, Agartala
2. Classical & Innovative dance programme, Assam
3. Best of Music from the North-East, Kohima, Nagaland
4. Patriotic song and dance festival N.A.P. Chumudkedima
5. Best of folk dances of the North-East, Agartala, Tripura
6. Hozagiri Festival, Tripura
7. Cultural meet 1998, Tawang, Arunachal Pradesh.

As part of the Republic Day Parade, 1998-99, a camp was

organised where 462 children along with musicians, folk artists and crafts persons participated. NEZCC also sent one Children's contingent for this Camp. The Children's contingent of the North East got the first prize.

Jawaharlal Nehru Manipuru dance academy, Imphal

A constituent unit of the Sangeet Natak Akademi, the Jawaharalal Nehru Manipur Dance Academy, Imphal is the leading teaching institution for Manipuri dance and allied arts. The Academy was established in 1954 and offers several comprehensive courses in Manipuri dance, music and allied arts. The courses are designed as a foundation for professional artists. It also has a Production Unit which strives to enrich the Manipuri repertoire through experimental works. The production unit has produced 25 dance dramas so far. These have been presented in India and other countries.

The Major activities of the Academy during 1998-99 are as follows:

The Foundation day of the JNMDA was held on 1st April 1998 at the Academy Auditorium. Solo performances by the students of the JNMDA were the highlight of the function. A One-day programme of lbudhou Chakhaba was held at the shrine of lbudhou Chakhaba at the Academy complex on 21st May 1998. This is a ritual part of the Lai-Haraoba Festival of the Lord. Gurus, artists and students participated in the programme.

A 15-member troupe of the Academy led by Shri L.Joychandra Singh, Director, JNMDA participated in the path mark Multi-cultural Arts Festival on 30th May, 1998 in New York, which was celebrated as a part of America's largest ethnic celebration. They presented a traditional programme of Manipuri Dance & Music. A forty-one member cultural troupe of the Academy visited

Nabadwip to participate in the 200th

Death Anniversary of Rajarshi Bhagyachandra organised by Rajashri Bhagyachandra Death Anniversary Celebration Committee, Nabadwip, West Bengal from 21st - 26th September, 1998.

The Academy presented Traditional Manipuri Dance and Music on 1st August '98, sponsored by the Regional Institute of Medical Sciences in honour of medical experts from Delhi. The JNMDA presented two Dance-Dramas "Keibul Lamjao" and "Wainu Pareng" on the occasion of the 5th National Games held in Imphal in February 1999.

Srimanta Shankaradeva cultural complex

Under the Assam Accord, the Government of India was committed to meet the expenditure relating to the construction of Cultural Complex at Guwahati. The complex has since been completed at a cost of Rs. 18.85 crores. It was inaugurated by the President of India in November, 1998. Government proposes to release the balance Rs. 6.85 crores for the project during this year. Out of this Rs. 4.85 crores is being provided from the non-lapsable fund created for the North East Region.

Sikkim research institute of Tibetology, Gangtok

The Sikkim Research Institute of Tibetology, Gangtok is an autonomous organization under the Government of Sikkim with the Governor of Sikkim as the President of its Governing Body. It was set up for research and studies in Tibetology. The Institute has done significant work in promoting research in Tibetology and associated subjects like iconography, medicine, astrology and history. It has special research and publication programmes. The Bulletin of Tibetology is the Institute's regular research journal which is published thrice a year.

The Institute received an annual grant of Rs. 13.34 lakhs from the Government of India during 1998-99.

Other activities

Indira Gandhi Rashtriya Manav Sanghralaya, Bhopal, organizes events for the preservation of local knowledge systems and deepening awareness about and strengthening the vitality of community traditions and knowledge systems in different States. The Museum organized freedom celebrations in the North East in collaboration with the State Government of Tripura with programmes in three remote centres of Tripura among different tribal groups with workshops, cultural events and exhibitions focusing on the local literary traditions, scripted as well as unscripted, on visual and performing arts and crafts and skills and technologies specially in the area of water management.

Archaeological Survey of India maintains around 72 monuments under Guwahati Circle. State-wise list of centrally protected monuments in the North East.

S.No.	*State*	*No. of Monuments*
1.	Arunachal Pradesh	5
2.	Assam	49
3.	Manipur	1
4.	Meghalaya	6
5.	Nagaland	4
6.	Sikkim	3
7.	Tripura	5

The important structural repairs, chemical conservation and environmental development were taken up for a number of monuments under the Guwahati Circle.

Under the Schemes of Department of Culture for Award of Fellowships and Scholarships, 6 Senior fellowships, 20 Junior fellowships and 25 scholarships have been awarded in the fields of music, dance, visual arts, theatre and folk, traditional and indigenous arts to the applicants from the North Eastern States during 1998-99.

Out of the Eight cultural organisations which received building grants of Rs.1 lakh and above, 2 organisations from Manipur were sanctioned Rs. 20 lakhs during 1998-99. Similarly, 8 organisations in Manipur received Rs. 18 lakhs as salary grants under the scheme operated by the Department.